Exemplary Science in Grades PreK-4

Standards-Based Success Stories

Robert E. Yager
and
Sandra K. Enger, Editors

NSTApress

NATIONAL SCIENCE TEACHERS ASSOCIATION

Arlington, Virginia

NATIONAL SCIENCE TEACHERS ASSOCIATION

Claire Reinburg, Director
Judy Cusick, Senior Editor
J. Andrew Cocke, Associate Editor
Betty Smith, Associate Editor
Robin Allan, Book Acquisitions Coordinator

ART AND DESIGN, Will Thomas, Jr., Director

PRINTING AND PRODUCTION, Catherine Lorrain, Director
   Nguyet Tran, Assistant Production Manager
   Jack Parker, Electronic Prepress Technician

NATIONAL SCIENCE TEACHERS ASSOCIATION
Gerald F. Wheeler, Executive Director
David Beacom, Publisher

Library of Congress Cataloging-in-Publication Data
Yager, Robert Eugene, 1930-
Exemplary science in grades PreK-4 : standards-based success stories / edited by Robert E. Yager and Sandra K. Enger.
    p. cm.
 Includes bibliographical references and index.
 ISBN-13: 978-0-87355-261-5 (alk. paper)
 ISBN-10: 0-87355-261-X (alk. paper)
 1. Science--Study and teaching (Early childhood) I. Enger, Sandra K. II. Title.
 LB1139.5.S35Y34 2006
 372.3'5--dc22
                                2006023089

Contents

Implementing the Changes in PreK–4 School Programs Envisioned in the National Science Education Standards:
Where Are We Ten Years Later?

Robert E. Yager, Editor
University of Iowa

How This Book Came About

Ten years have elapsed since the 1996 publication of the National Science Education Standards (NSES) (NRC 1996). The critical issues in science education now are these: How far have we progressed in putting the vision of the NSES into practice? What remains to be done? What new visions are worthy of new trials?

The four monographs in the NSTA Exemplary Science monograph series seek to answer these questions. The monographs are *Exemplary Science: Best Practices in Professional Development; Exemplary Science in Grades 9–12; Exemplary Science in Grades 5–8;* and *Exemplary Science in Grades PreK–4* (the book you are reading).

The series was conceived in 2001 by an advisory board of science educators, many of whom had participated in the development of the National Science Education Standards. The advisory board members (who are all active and involved NSTA members; see pp. xi–xii for their names) decided to seek exemplars of the NSES *More Emphasis* conditions as a way to evaluate progress toward the visions of the NSES. The *More Emphasis* conditions provide summaries of the NSES recommendations in science teaching, professional development, assessment, science content, and science education programs and systems. (See Appendix 1 for the six *Less Emphasis/More Emphasis* lists.) The board sent information about the projected series to the NSTA leadership team and to all the NSTA affiliates, chapters, and associated groups. A call for papers on exemplary programs also appeared in all NSTA publications. In addition, more than a thousand letters inviting nominations were sent to leaders identified in the *2001–2002 NSTA Handbook,* and personal letters were sent to leaders of all science education organizations.

After preliminary responses were received, the advisory board identified teachers and programs that it felt should be encouraged to prepare formal drafts for further review and evaluation.

The goal was to identify 15 of the best situations in each of the four areas—professional development and grades 9–12, 5–8, and PreK–4—where facets of the teaching, professional development, assessment, and content standards were being met in an exemplary manner.

The most important aspect of the selection process was the evidence the authors of each article could provide about how their programs affected student learning. This aspect proved the most elusive. Most of us "know" when something is going well, but we are not well equipped to provide real evidence for this knowing. Many exciting program descriptions were not among the final titles—simply because little or no evidence other than personal testimony was available in the materials forwarded. The NSTA advisory board chose the 14 elementary school models that make up this monograph as the best examples of programs that fulfill the *More Emphasis* conditions; each has had a clear, positive impact on student science learning.

The History of the National Science Education Standards

Before discussing the contents of this book at greater length, I would like to offer a brief history of how the National Science Education Standards came to be.

Most educators credit the National Council of Teachers of Mathematics (NCTM) with initiating the many efforts to produce national standards for programs in U.S. schools. In 1986 (10 years before the publication of the National Science Education Standards), the board of directors of NCTM established a Commission on Standards for School Mathematics with the aim of improving the quality of school mathematics. A draft of these standards was developed during the summer of 1987, revised during the summer of 1988 after much discussion among NCTM members, and finally published as the *Curriculum and Evaluation Standards for School Mathematics* in 1989.

The NCTM standards did much for mathematics education by providing a consensus for what mathematics should be. The National Science Foundation (NSF) and other funding groups had not been involved in developing the math standards, but these groups quickly funded research and training to move schools and teachers in the direction of those standards. Having such a "national" statement regarding needed reforms resulted in funding from private and government foundations to produce school standards in other disciplines, including science.

NSF encouraged the science education community to develop standards modeled after the NCTM document (1989). Interestingly, both the American Association for the Advancement of Science (AAAS) and the National Science Teachers Association (NSTA) expressed interest in preparing science standards. Both organizations indicated that they had made a significant start on such national standards—AAAS with its Project 2061 and NSTA with its Scope, Sequence, and Coordination project. Both of these national projects had support from NSF, private foundations, and industries. The compromise on this "competition" between AAAS and NSTA leaders led to the recommendation that the National Research Council (NRC) of the National Academy of Science be funded to develop the National Science Education Standards. With NSF funding provided in 1992, both NSTA and AAAS helped select the science leaders who would prepare the NSES. Several early drafts were circulated among hundreds of people with invitations to comment, suggest, debate, and assist with a consensus document. A full-time director of consensus provided leadership and assistance as final drafts were assembled. Eventually, it took $7 million and four years of debate to produce the 262-page NSES publication in 1996.

There was never any intention that the Standards would indicate minimum competencies that would be required of all. Instead, the focus was on visions of how teaching, assessment, and content should be changed. Early on, programs and systems were added as follow-ups to teaching, assessment, and content.

The NSES and the Elementary School Classroom

The NSES suggest changes across the board for elementary levels K–4. Teachers of these grade levels are often poorly prepared in the quantity and quality of collegiate work they have completed in science. In fact, the typical elementary school teacher is quite frank in reporting that he or she never liked science in high school, experienced little in his or her own elementary school program when a student, and completed only minimal science courses as part of the elementary education major in college.

Further, science has never been emphasized as a core part of the elementary school curriculum—certainly not as one of the basics like reading and mathematics. Too many administrators, parents, community leaders, and politicians are content to focus on the skills related to reading and mathematics with the belief and assertion that these skills are needed before doing science. Of course their view of science is that it is information that has amassed concerning natural world objects and events and that the important ideas of these can and should be given to students via textbooks, worksheets, and teacher directions. Also, in that view, assessment focuses upon student ability to recall, report, and recite on what has been covered.

The National Standards advocate the use of real-world contexts in which the skills of science are needed—as opposed to deciding for the students what they will need and giving them the information to develop those "needed" skills without helping them first establish the relevant context.

Elementary students start with skills and curiosity about the objects and events in the natural world in which they find themselves. The sadness is that this natural interest and curiosity declines the longer students study science in a traditional way—with teachers giving directions and determining what will be studied and how.

Elementary teachers know their students and how eager they are to learn. However, these teachers' reservations about their own abilities in traditional science make them less likely to spend even minimal time on science. Often science is an afternoon class, and often it is scheduled before recess. Too often, too, the science class focuses on vocabulary in the belief that students need a special vocabulary before they can do science. A focus on vocabulary, unfortunately, does little to encourage students to pursue their own interests and questions and leads students to believe that science is strange, with complicated terms that are never used except in science classes. Although they learn the definitions to get good grades and impress their teachers and their parents, they rarely see any other use for their efforts and the things they are directed to do by teachers.

Elementary teachers need more confidence. They need experience with the real meaning of science as a human endeavor. They need to realize that they can and do know science; it just is not the science from most of the courses in their own K–16 experiences. Elementary teachers are often the most successful in staff development programs, especially when they find the fun of doing science. They also can learn readily that their own students can help determine the content, help identify sources of information, can work cooperatively with other students, and can use their science learning in their daily living and in improving their own schools and communities.

The 14 exemplary programs in this book will be seen, I hope, as models for other teachers—not just to copy, but as templates for ways of approaching science and encouraging their students to do more of what they like. The best students become experts; they learn by doing rather than by remembering or duplicating what texts and teachers tell them.

The Standards have probably done more to change science at the elementary school level than at the other grade levels. It has been hard to change high school programs, most likely because of the great focus on college preparation and the discipline-bound curriculum that frequently has little connection or relevance across grade levels.

Elementary teachers often become enthused about teaching science when they understand the visions outlined in the NSES. When both teachers and students are inspired, curious, and involved, science becomes central to the lives of students and others in the community and can give the subject relevance in the real world.

References

Harms, N. C., and R. E. Yager, eds. 1981. *What research says to the science teacher, Vol. 3.* Arlington, VA: National Science Teachers Association.

National Council of Teachers of Mathematics (NCTM). 1989. *Curriculum and evaluation standards for school mathematics.* Reston, VA: Author.

National Research Council (NRC). 1996. *National Science Education Standards.* Washington, DC: National Academy Press.

National Science Teachers Association (NSTA). 2003. *NSTA handbook.* Arlington, VA: Author.

Weiss, I. R., E. R. Banilower, R. A. Crawford, and C. M. Overstreet. 2003. *Local systemic change through teacher enhancement, year eight cross-site report.* Chapel Hill, NC: Horizon Research.

Wiggins, G., and J. McTighe. 1998. *Understanding by design.* Alexandria, VA: Association for Supervision and Curriculum Development (ASCD).

Acknowledgments

Members of the National Advisory Board for the Exemplary Science Series

Hans O. Andersen
Indiana University-Bloomington
3240 Wright Education Building
Indiana University
Bloomington, IN 47405-1006

Charles R. Barman
Indiana University School of Education
504 Pheasant Run
Zionsville, IN 46077

Bonnie Brunkhorst
California State University-San Bernardino
6288 Alegre Court
Riverside, CA 92506

Rodger Bybee
Executive Director
BSCS
5415 Mark Dabling Blvd.
Colorado Springs, CO 80918

Audrey Champagne
State University of New York
Educational Theory & Practice
ED 122, 1400 Washington Ave.
Albany, NY 12222

Fred Johnson
8890 Bridlewood Lane
Cordova, TN 38016

Roger Johnson
University of Minnesota
Dept of Curriculum & Instruction
60 Peik Hill
Minneapolis, MN 55455

Mozell Lang
Pontiac Northern High School
1051 Arlene St.
Pontiac, MI 48340

LeRoy R. Lee
Executive Director
Wisconsin Science Network
4420 Gray Road
De Forest, WI 53532-2506

Shelley A. Lee
Science Consultant
Dept. of Public Instruction
804 Brook St.
De Forest, WI 53532-3210

Gerry Madrazo
The University of North Carolina at
Chapel Hill
Cb #3345
Chapel Hill, NC 27599-3345

Dick Merrill
Science Curriculum Specialist, Retired
Mount Diablo Unified School District
Concord, CA

Nick Micozzi
Plymouth Public Schools
253 S. Meadow Road
Plymouth, MA 02360

Edward P. Ortleb
Science Consultant
5663 Pernod Ave.
St Louis, MO 63139

Jack Rhoton
Professor of Science Education
East Tennessee State University
601 West Valley View Circle
Kingsport, TN 37664

Gerald Skoog
Texas Tech University
15th and Boston
College of Education
Lubbock, TX 79409-1071

Emma Walton
2014 Crataegus Circle
Anchorage, AK 99508

Sandra West
Southwest Texas University
P.O. Box 1441
Canyon Lake, TX 78130

Karen Worth
Senior Scientist
Education Development Center
55 Chapel St.
Newton, MA 02458

Assistant Editor at the University of Iowa
Mary Ann Mullinnix

About the Editors

Robert E. Yager—an active contributor to the development of the National Science Education Standards—has devoted his life to teaching, writing, and advocating on behalf of science education worldwide. Having started his career as a high school science teacher, he has been a professor of science education at the University of Iowa since 1956. He has also served as president of seven national organizations, including NSTA, and been involved in teacher education in Japan, Korea, Taiwan, and Europe. Among his many publications are several NSTA books, including *Focus on Excellence* and *What Research Says to the Science Teacher.* Yager earned a bachelor's degree in biology from the University of Northern Iowa and master's and doctoral degrees in plant physiology from the University of Iowa.

Sandra K. Enger has been an exemplary teacher of biology in Arkansas. She became initially involved in the NSTA Scope, Sequence, and Coordination project in which she assisted many teachers from all levels in developing new and more inclusive assessment efforts. Currently she is an associate professor of science education at the University of Alabama—Huntsville. She has edited a volume on *Assessing Student Understanding in Science* (Corwin Press). Enger earned bachelor's and master's degrees in biology from Winona State University and a doctoral degree in science education from the University of Iowa.

Putting the Question First:

Adapting Science Curricula in the Kindergarten Classroom

Kathy Hollinger
Arlington Heights Elementary School

Valarie L. Akerson
Indiana University

Setting

rlington Heights Elementary School is located on the north side of Bloomington, Indiana, one of the 11 elementary schools in the Monroe County Community School Corporation. About 300 students attend Arlington in grades K–6, and approximately one-third of them qualify for free or reduced-price lunch. The teaching staff comprises classroom teachers, an inclusion teacher, and certified teachers in music, physical education, and art. As the only kindergarten teacher in the school, I teach two classes of half-day kindergarten each day. The school is a Title I school and has a reading recovery program and Title I services for second graders. Because Indiana University is located in Bloomington, Arlington Heights Elementary can engage in several programs that involve preservice teachers and inservice teachers in professional development activities. I was a participant in the Learning Science by Inquiry professional development program sponsored by Indiana University, a component of the school-university partnership.

Changing My Teaching to an Inquiry Focus

I have never thought that I was a very good science teacher. My teaching preferences were language arts and literacy lessons. But I always thought that science was interesting to children and that it could be a way to hook them into learning and into meaningful reading and writing. Through participation in activities in the Learning Science by Inquiry program and interaction with colleagues who were also seeking to improve their science teaching, I found that I no longer felt comfortable with merely following the science curriculum mandated by our school corporation. The curriculum was not presented in a way that considered the experiences, interests, prior knowledge, and strengths of individual students. It was not focused on inquiry but rather on having students follow prescriptive activities.

I found myself selecting and adapting the curriculum so that the focus shifted to students' understanding and using their scientific knowledge and inquiry processes. I found this new focus to be in alignment with the National Science Education Standards (NSES) (NRC 1996) *More Emphasis* teaching standards recommendations of selecting and adapting curricula as opposed to rigidly following the curriculum. Instead of just giving the students information, I let them talk with me and with each other, and I expected them to share what they knew about science. This approach was in keeping with the recommendation of providing opportunities for scientific discussion and debate rather than just asking for a recitation of acquired knowledge. I perceived that guiding the students in scientific inquiry and providing opportunities for discussion supported their developing knowledge and understanding of the world around them. The *More Emphasis* content and inquiry standards gave me a focus on helping my students develop their understanding of scientific concepts and abilities of inquiry rather than just acquiring facts and information. This helped my students learn to use evidence for developing or revising explanations as opposed to just getting an answer. I wanted my students to come away from my class with a better understanding of scientific concepts, and I also wanted them to build their abilities and strategies in doing inquiry. I wanted them to know about science and the way scientists do science. Instead of watching me as a teacher demonstrating "science," I wanted the children to participate in activities in which they investigated and analyzed science as a subject matter content area and as a way of knowing about the world.

I began to emphasize the NSES content standards in my instruction. My focus became physical science because it was evident to me that I could have students more readily design inquiry investigations by using physical science concepts. The illustration I am using in this chapter will focus on Content Standard B: "As a result of the activities in grades K–4, all students should develop an understanding of position and motion of objects" (NRC 1996, p. 123). I also wanted to focus on helping my students understand that science is a human endeavor and thus also emphasize Content Standard G: "As a result of activities in grades K–4, all students should develop understanding of science as a human endeavor" (NRC 1996, p. 141). Because my strongest desire is to help my students understand and be able to do scientific inquiries, I also focused on Content Standard A, in which I want my students to be able to

- ask questions about objects and events in the environment,
- plan and conduct a simple investigation,
- employ simple equipment and tools to gather data,

- use data to construct a reasonable explanation,
- communicate investigations and explanations, and
- understand how scientists do their work (NRC 1996, pp. 122–123).

Inquiry Science in My Classroom: An Example of Pushes and Pulls

I have taught kindergarten for 31 years. The two half-day sections of kindergarten—one morning and one afternoon—I teach every day have approximately 18 students each. There is a wide range among the children developmentally, with some having attended preschool and having been exposed to reading and numbers before enrolling in kindergarten and others having no prior experience with letters and numbers. I have a structured group-lesson time each day and a time for children to further explore at small-group activity centers. I try to teach all lessons and subject matter in a child-focused way. It is not unusual for me to adjust my instruction and time for lessons to allow students to explore ideas in depth.

Before I participated in the professional development program to emphasize standards-based instruction, the science I taught had been very much textbook based. I figured the textbook developers knew a lot about teaching science. Because I did not, I believed that I should follow what they recommended. Plus, my textbook used many hands-on activities that were very active and engaging. I realized, however, that I could meet the needs of my students much better and help them attain knowledge of content standards through standards-based instruction. I began to review the textbook before instructing and to revise and rewrite the lessons so they focused on inquiry and allowed students to answer their own questions that were related to the recommended topics. Table 1 shows the features of my instruction contrasted with my former instructional format.

Table 1. Comparison of Pre and Post Standards-Based Instructional Approaches

Pre Standards-Based Instruction	Post Standards-Based Instruction
I used hands-on activities straight from the text.	I adapt the text to focus on inquiry.
I taught from the text; I had no plan to identify students' prior ideas.	I begin with asking students for their prior knowledge; investigations are based on student knowledge and what they want to find out.
The text presented activities first, then questions.	I raise questions first, with the students, and then we plan an activity based on questions.
We conducted investigations as prescribed by the text.	Students plan the investigation with my support.

To illustrate my instruction of kindergarten science, I will describe how I adapt instruction and adjust activities in our textbooks to focus on inquiry. I have taught from our text series for several years, using the text as a guideline for many different activities. The textbook has a hands-on activity to teach students about "how things move" and emphasizes pushes and pulls. In the textbook series children are asked to tell how things move and then to do an investigation in which they are told to move a toy car on the floor, on waxed paper, and on a towel. They describe the differences in the way the surfaces influenced the motion and why they thought cars moved faster on one surface than the others. This is exactly the approach I took to the activity, and, while it was active and hands on, there was no inquiry focus. I was not sure whether the students realized why we were doing the investigation or whether they just thought they got to play with cars that day. In the ensuing two years, I have adapted the textbook activity to help the students investigate their ideas, through an inquiry that they design, of how surfaces influence the motion of toy cars. Table 2 illustrates the adaptations I made in the lesson to ensure that I was attending to students' ideas and to teaching through and about scientific inquiry.

Table 2. Changes in Specific Activity—Pushes and Pulls

Lesson Prior to Adaptation	Lesson After Adaptation
I had no activation of prior knowledge; the activity was presented from the textbook.	I held a discussion of "How do things move? What influences things as they move?" prior to instruction, and recorded student views on chart paper.
I instructed students to carry out the investigation as prescribed in the textbook.	I asked students "How can we explore the influence different surfaces have on how toy cars move?" and then asked students to design investigation as a group. I recorded their designs on chart paper.
We tested the surfaces as prescribed by the textbook: floor, waxed paper, and a towel.	I had the students choose different surfaces on which to test their cars: carpet, tile, linoleum, and asphalt.
The lesson debrief was straight from the book: Why did cars move faster on one surface than the others?	The lesson debriefing was more open-ended and focused on their design: What did you find out about pushes on the ramps? How did the different surfaces affect the motion of the cars? Which surface is faster or slower? What more do you want to know about how surfaces affect how toy cars move? I encouraged students to investigate more about surfaces in other activities, including at-home investigations.
Because I was following the textbook, I put no emphasis on how this activity is like what scientists do because the text did not.	I asked students to describe how they thought this activity is like what scientists do. How would scientists know which surface is better for cars to move on?

In teaching my revised lesson to my kindergartners I began by engaging them in a discussion of what they think makes things move. I recorded their responses on chart paper as we were discussing the topic. The students described the necessity of either pushing something or pulling something to make it move. Thus, they generated the idea that things required a force to move and, unless they were alive, could not move on their own. I was excited to see their ideas emerge, rather than have them listen to me tell them that things need to be pushed or pulled to be moved.

We then began a discussion about what influence different surfaces might have on the motion of items moving across them. This discussion ended up being very long—first I realized that students did not necessarily have a good understanding about *surface*. My students did initially recognize that things move differently in different media, such as air, on the ground, and in water, but did not generate ideas about different surfaces they could move across. I then asked them to consider the different kinds of

Kathy Hollinger encourages her students to use their own ideas.

surfaces that "they walk on," and they began to give examples of things such as the carpet, the tile (two different types in the school), asphalt, wood, and grass. I realized that, if I had not asked them about their ideas, I would have assumed they understood what I was talking about, but maybe they never really did understand what I meant by *surface* in previous years. After I was certain they understood what *surface* meant, I asked them to think about how they could figure out which was the surface on which things would move the best. I asked them to think about how different surfaces would influence or affect the motion of items. The students thought about different things they could try moving, such as balls, animals, and toy cars. I eventually got them focused on selecting toy cars so we could test the same items.

Once we had selected the item to test, I asked them to think about how to test the toy cars. They discussed hard pushes and soft pushes and decided to test both, so we could see if there were any differences. They also thought about rolling the cars down ramps to see how they would move without any pushes. They discussed the importance of starting all the cars from the same point. I asked them how they would know which surface the cars moved farther on, and they realized they needed to measure the distance the cars went. I asked them to decide on which surfaces they wanted to test the cars. They decided to test them on the linoleum tile in the hall outside our classroom, on the carpet inside our classroom, and outside on the asphalt. I had about five students test each surface four different ways: soft push, hard push, soft push on ramps, and hard push on ramps. We tested all the surfaces, marking the distances the cars went on each of the surfaces.

After testing all the surfaces, we reconvened in the classroom to debrief the activity. I asked them to think about which surface the cars moved on the farthest, the fastest, the shortest, and the slowest. I recorded their responses in full sentences on chart paper. I asked them to think about how they knew the answers they gave, directing them toward the evidence of their responses. If they had trouble in thinking about the evidence, we looked at the markings on the ground we had made with tape that indicated the distances the cars had moved under various conditions. This reference to evidence helped them to justify their statements, and I hoped it would help them understand that scientists also use evidence when they do investigations.

I asked my students then to infer why they thought the cars moved differently on different surfaces, and they responded with "the smoother the surface, the better the cars moved." So they realized that, while the cars moved on all surfaces, the smoother surfaces made it easier for the cars to move.

I did not mention *friction* as a force that influenced the cars' motion, but allowed them to use their own vocabulary (smooth and bumpy).

Because I really wanted to focus my students on knowing that the kind of inquiry they designed and engaged in was like what scientists do, I asked them, "How is what we were doing like what scientists do?" and "Do you think scientists have to do investigations to find out answers to their questions?" The students stated that scientists definitely did investigations when they wanted to find answers to their questions and that scientists need to "get evidence like we did" when they wanted to draw conclusions.

The students recognized that scientists design different investigations depending on what they want to find out and that they did not use just one "scientific method" for answering their questions. They generated the idea that scientists were not sure about their results, "just like them," but would be pretty sure because they had evidence. They also recognized that scientists may disagree about the meaning of the evidence but still would make their claims based on evidence.

I found the lesson very exhilarating, and the students and I were so engaged that I did not realize we had conducted a two-hour science investigation—in a two-and-a-half-hour day. This was a big difference from the first years I taught the lesson, when our investigation was very scripted and took about 30 minutes. During that time I did not really assess the students, nor did I know whether they understood why they were testing the cars on different surfaces.

Assessment

Our text series recommends that we provide the students with a worksheet entitled "Different Surfaces." There are three sets of two pictures of children moving on different surfaces, and students are asked to circle the picture in the pairs on which the children are moving more easily. For example, in the first pair there is a picture of a child riding a tricycle in the grass and another of a child riding a tricycle on the pavement. Students should circle the picture of the child riding on the pavement as the surface on which they can move more easily. In my experience, my students could easily do this before the activity. I decided to devise an assessment task that would tell me what the students actually did gain from the investigation. I wanted to know what knowledge they generated from the investigation they had designed about the different surfaces on which the cars moved.

I began to use the charts on which I recorded student responses to my questions. For instance, before this investigation I had asked students how they thought things moved. I recorded their responses on the chart paper. Following the investigation I asked students what they learned from the investigation and on what surface the cars moved most easily. By comparing student responses on the charts I could tell, in general, what my students gained and learned from the investigation. I wanted, however, a more individual measure of learning as well. Thus, two weeks after the investigation, I decided to ask my teaching assistant to talk with each student about what he or she had learned from the investigation. She recorded their responses on separate papers. I asked for students first to recall the investigation and then describe what they learned. The specific questions I asked are in Appendix A. These brief interviews, which took about 10 minutes, gave me the information I wanted about what each student gained from the activity.

All students recalled the activity, and all described that the cars moved the farthest and fastest because cars "move the fastest on smooth surfaces." For example, one student said, "It slows down on the asphalt because it is bumpy. But because tile is flat and smooth, when you push hard, the car is going to go fast!" This response, typical of my students' responses, shows that the students recognize that smooth surfaces allow cars to roll faster and that there is a difference between a hard push and a soft push. They remembered the investigation and the results two weeks later. I think they gained so much because they designed the investigation and carried it out and because they were asked to draw their own conclusions from the evidence.

Because I wanted students to understand how their investigations were like scientists' investigations, I asked them to draw comparisons of what they did to what scientists do. Students had a little more difficulty with this question, with one student responding with "I don't know—that's hard!" However, half of my students were able to draw reasonable comparisons, meaning that (a) I could assess their knowledge of this idea and thus know what they understood, and (b) I could use this knowledge in planning future lessons to emphasize the nature of science in my inquiry lessons. Students who responded with comparison statements generally stated that, "We were like scientists because we used evidence," "We figured out what surface they go faster and slower on," and "We figured it out for ourselves." These students had gained and demonstrated knowledge that scientists use evidence and figure out the answers to their questions through investigations. I am hoping to help more of my students understand that as I continue to teach science and emphasize how scientists do their work. Now that I assess their understandings of the nature of science, I can adjust my instruction to help them have even better understandings. Table 3 shows a comparison of changes in my assessment strategies.

Table 3. Adaptations of Assessment Strategies

Assessment Prior to Adaptation	Assessment Following Adaptation
Use of worksheet from text series.	Use of chart paper recordings of class discussions pre- and postinvestigation. Ask students to tell what they know about the investigation two weeks following their participation to check understanding and retention of new information.

Summary

My students are always very excited when it is time for science. I think it is because they get to engage in activities that they design to answer questions that either I, or they, raise. Although my previous students enjoyed the hands-on aspects of science, my current students are enjoying it even more because they have input into the design of the investigations and into the interpretation of the meaning of the data they collect.

The main changes in my instruction have been to adapt activities in the textbook series to raise the question first and then allow my students to design investigations, with my help, to allow them to answer the question. I then use a more open-ended assessment to find out what students gained from their investigation. The assessments include charted recordings of class discussions pre- and postinvestigation and individual student responses to questions about what they learned from their investigations. I like to ask these questions several weeks after the investigations so I can see whether my students still recall the investigations and whether they retained the knowledge they gained.

From my assessments, I can see that my students are growing in their science content understanding and that some students are making the connection between what they are doing and what scientists do in their work. I also see that I need to continue to emphasize explicitly the connections between their investigations and scientific investigations so that even more students will make that connection.

References

Badders, W., V. Fu, L. Bethel, D. Peck, C. Sumners, C. Valentino, and R. M. Mullane. 1999. Pushes and pulls. *Discovery works*. Parsippany, NJ: Silver Burdett Ginn.

National Research Council (NRC). 1996. *National Science Education Standards*. Washington, DC: National Academy Press.

Appendix A

Postinstruction Questions Asked of Students

1. Do you remember your investigation with the toy cars on different surfaces? What did you do?
2. What surfaces did you find that the toy cards moved the farthest on? The fastest?
3. Why do you think the toy cars moved farther and fastest on that surface?
4. What differences did you see when you used the ramps?
5. How is what you did in this investigation like what scientists do in their investigations?

Building On the Natural Wonder Inherent in Us All

Becky Fish
Gladbrook-Reinbeck School District

Setting

The Gladbrook-Reinbeck School District is located in Iowa, a state of just over three million people. The rich farmland that surrounds our district produces corn, beans, cattle, swine, and proud hardworking people. Naturally, many of the businesses in our area are farm related. The parents of the children in our district are farmers, laborers and blue-collar workers, and college-educated professionals. Our district has two sites, one in Gladbrook and the other in Reinbeck. The Gladbrook facility houses an elementary and a middle school. In Reinbeck, there are two buildings to serve the Gladbrook and Reinbeck students: another elementary school and the high school. Our school district provides an education for 800 students in the entire K–12 program.

There are plenty of rich educational opportunities for teachers in this area. Our Area Education Association (intermediate service units between the Iowa Department of Education and the more than 300 local school districts in our state), the University of Northern Iowa, and the University of Iowa are all within 90 miles of Gladbrook. The leaders in these institutions keep us up-to-date with educational practices that are research based and developmentally appropriate.

My classroom is located at the Gladbrook site. Gladbrook is a rural community of about 1,000 people. I teach kindergarten. The kindergartners in our district meet in an all-day, every-day program. With the help of our county conservationist, we've planted a little prairie just outside the west windows of our kindergarten room. There is a large grassy, tree-filled playground to the north of our room. Both areas allow us to explore, question, experiment, and learn.

Emphasizing the NSES in My Kindergarten Classroom

I'm in the process of becoming the teacher I want to be by incorporating the visions embodied in the National Science Education Standards (NSES) into my science teaching. I'm sharing my story to encourage other regular education elementary teachers to gain the courage to step out of their common routines, learn more about constructivist teaching, and begin to include inquiry-based teaching in their curriculums.

Because of my participation in recent science and math workshops and extensive conversations with my teaching peers who have been working to develop the same kinds of constructivist programs, I've embraced several National Science Education Standards. I'm now purposefully providing many occasions for my students to create and follow through with their own inquiries, consciously working to develop chosen concepts over an extended period of time, encouraging collaboration, leading discussions that help my young students discuss some real science social issues, and helping them record and organize their observations and draw conclusions. I know that I'm nurturing our future scientists, and learning in general, by giving my students many opportunities to be involved in the inquiry process.

Keeping the Wonder Alive: Our Gladbrook Prairie

The tall grass prairie area that the elementary students and teachers planted outside the kindergarten room has become a major teaching aid. I'm learning that the area is not only fertile ground for the native grasses and flowers of our midwestern section of the country but also a rich educational resource for our students, stimulating them to learn more about the process of inquiry. Through inquiry my students practice lifelong learning skills.

The Gladbrook prairie area.

Through an "aha" experience in our little prairie, I learned that in the fall our prairie is filled with dozens of giant black-and-yellow garden spiders building webs and making egg sacs. I still remember the first time I discovered them—they were everywhere. My heart began to pound, and, let me tell you, I jumped back to get out of their way. After I stood there for awhile, noticing their color, the way they moved, and their environment, I felt a need to learn more about them. I'd become a learner once more. Slowly, I walked closer so I could get a better look. I had questions. What kind of spiders were they? What were they so busy doing? My senses and emotions were engaged. I felt the urge to hurry inside to share my wonderful discovery with my teaching buddies.

In reflecting on this encounter with the beautiful garden spiders, I realized that an engaging classroom inquiry experience would feel a lot like this. There would be joy and challenge, exploration, discovery, observation, questioning, sharing, and making a plan to learn more. I knew what I wanted to do for my kindergartners. I was eager to create learning opportunities for my students that would replicate my experience in the prairie. Lessons in which my students would be encouraged to think about topics that are connected to their world. Experiences that would put them in control of their own learning. The kind of encounters for which details become important and memorable. Learning they could apply to their lives right now. I began to build an inquiry-based classroom.

How Do I Put It All Together?

That's a good question. I'm still learning. I've found that the destination is always the same, even though the path I take to reach that destination is different every year. These are the goals I work toward. I want to mold confident young scientists who

- have encountered real science experiences,
- are comfortable with the science process,
- have had the chance to be in charge of their own learning,
- have had countless opportunities to engage in higher-level thinking, and
- have developed scientific knowledge by meeting our district's standards and benchmarks.

The direction I take to help my students reach these goals depends on the prior knowledge, skills, and the interests of the children I am working with. Because of that, I always find myself taking a zigzag, instead of a straight, path to reach those important end goals.

If the path to reach this destination is different every year and the children do a big share of the planning, you might wonder, "How does a teacher prepare?" There are some constants to my job as a teacher of inquiry. They are to

1. gather background information with regard to the Standard/benchmark about to be addressed.
2. set out the stimuli to capture interest and engage the senses.
3. be equipped with good questions myself that will allow me to help my students
   - identify the questions that are important to them,
   - discover processes that will help them answer their questions,
   - persist through their struggles,
   - connect experiences together to make meaning, and
   - follow through to use the information they have gained.
4. consider materials needed and
   - provide a clipboard and paper, and science journal to gather data,
   - provide easy access to classroom accumulation of different science materials, and
   - provide time for students to brainstorm lists of needed materials.
5. step back and observe students interactions to determine when group discussions would be beneficial to students. The purpose of discussion could be to
   - form, collect, and record questions;
   - teach, model, and discuss process skills used;
   - make plans for next steps;
   - notice connections with other investigations, understandings, and concepts;

- talk over what has been learned—details, the big picture;
- discuss ways we will communicate to others what we've discovered; and
- evaluate the learning experience (did our tests answer our questions?).

6. Plan for the challenge of assessment (evidence that students can use the information and skills in new situations). Details come later in the chapter.

Excerpts From Kindergarten Inquiry Experiences

Here are a few examples of what my students have accomplished with inquiry.

The Life Cycle of the Butterfly

The first experience I will share, "The Life Cycle of the Butterfly," is common in early childhood programs. I found that the topic offered me an opportunity to develop a true inquiry experience and supported real social debate as encouraged by the NSES. I had led my children through this unit many times before with hands-on strategies. But, because I realized the value of the inquiry process, I decided to raise the bar for myself and go beyond the hands-on approach. I would try to create a classroom environment in which my youngsters could not only learn scienctific facts but also begin to think like scientists and take more responsibility for their own learning.

I had the scientific background knowledge of the topic *butterflies,* so my next step was to think about the stimulus. Sometimes I plant the invitation to learn, but this time I was sure that someone would bring in a caterpillar or butterfly to share. So, my next step was to just wait. I wasn't the one to set the date to begin instruction; the children now acquired that job. As predicted, the larva of the monarch butterfly arrived in room 110. We were ready to begin.

Instead of using the beautiful caterpillar as an impetus to share my knowledge with the children as I used to do, I stayed in the background, listened to their conversations, and took notes. I heard some accurate facts, some incorrect understandings, and some questions. I was very much aware of their interest and had gained a good understanding of their level of knowledge. My students had opened the door. I was ready to lead the way.

Equipped with questions and a basic plan of where I hoped to go with this first group meeting, I organized a large-group discussion. "I heard you talking about the caterpillar. It sounds like you are interested in that little caterpillar. Are you? Would you like to spend some time finding out more about him? Tell me what you're wondering about." The children and I talked about the things they thought they knew and the questions they had about caterpillars, chrysalises, and butterflies. Their understandings and questions were recorded on chart paper to refer back to.

They asked, "Where did the caterpillar come from? I wonder what caterpillars eat. How long does it take to change to a butterfly? Should we keep the butterfly or let him go? I wonder what will happen next? What should we feed the butterfly? How many wings does a butterfly have? How does a butterfly eat?" By themselves, they listed all of the objectives I had included in my lesson plans. Instead of giving the children an oratory on the life cycle and structure of the butterfly, and maybe an additional few minutes sharing my own personal opinion on the release of the butterfly, I asked them to think of ways they could learn more to answer their own questions.

In the past—the plain old hands-on way—I would have immediately corrected their misunderstandings and moved on with the lesson plan. But one of my new goals was to help them think and reason. So, without pointing out exactly what was right or wrong with their thinking, I told them that we could work together to plan ways they could prove or disprove the information they had. It's very important to help my students understand that it is good when they are able to change their minds about a previous understanding. I tell them that if the evidence proves otherwise and if there are many who value that new evidence, it might be wise to consider the new facts and change your mind. That's what scientists do.

The interactions in our initial discussion helped us identify, narrow, and record our questions. Our interactions also began to instill in my young students a sense of what it's like to be a scientist.

The unit continued for three to four weeks with the children leading the way. The anticipation was great. The children learned about habitats that were friendly to the butterflies. The prairie allowed them to identify the plant where the monarch liked to lay its eggs. They learned about the body structure and coloring of the larva that crawled out of those eggs. They watched as the larva made its chrysalis, and they waited for the butterfly to emerge. A fews days of debate ended in the release of our butterflies. All the time we were asking questions, observing, predicting, collecting data, communicating, drawing conclusions, asking more questions, and considering new ways to answer those questions. With inquiry the children learned more than facts about butterflies. They also had the opportunity to learn how it feels to be a scientist.

Composting

In the following inquiry experiences, composting helped the children to develop more NSES. They collected, recorded, organized, and reflected on relevant data. The kindergartners had the opportunity to see an investigation through the fall, winter, and spring before all of their questions were answered.

Friends Investigating Pumpkins

In the fall, after our many inquiries about pumpkins, my students noticed that our pumpkins were beginning to rot. They wondered what that "yucky" stuff was inside the pumpkins. And what was that awful smell? Here was another chance for me to use their curiosity to develop logical habits of mind.

Change was the big concept for the year. Now was the perfect time, when the pumpkins were dramatically displaying their life cycle, to ask my young scientists if they could think of ways the life of the pumpkin plant was like the life of the butterfly. Could they connect the two learning experiences? Most of the students looked puzzled. They responded with, "They both were alive." "I loved the butterflies, and I love the pumpkins." Both of those answers were fine, but I wanted them to think deeper. I couldn't get them to the next step, so I began to hum a song the children had learned in September that emphasizes cycles. They recognized the song, "Love Goes Round In

A Circle," recorded by The Bat Chorus. In a short amount of time they did make the connection I was hoping for. They recognized that the life cycle of the pumpkin went around in a circle—seed, vine, flowers, pumpkins, seed, vine, and so on—just as the life cycle of the butterfly did—egg, larva, chrysalis, butterfly, and so on. Both living things, the plant and the animal, went through predictable changes. The children illustrated the life cycle of the pumpkin on our white board and then recorded their new understanding in their science journals. My students were becoming more aware of change and the cycles of things. I also found that, when I offered more opportunities for them to think more deeply and made an extra effort to identify connections to prior learning, their successful responses increased. I was often surprised and pleased by the examples of cycles and change they detected in their everyday lives.

Before we put the pumpkins in the compost bin, several children decided that they wanted to watch them rot. They put a big chunk of a pumpkin in a plastic bag so that we couldn't smell it and left a similar-sized piece right out in the open air. The rest of the pumpkins went outside in the compost bin. They watched with interest—and disgust—to see what happened to the chunks inside and to the pumpkins outside. We of course compared the changes that were occurring in the pumpkins and made journal entries often. When the piece of pumpkin exposed to the warm air of the classroom began to get juicy, the children and I wanted to get it out of the room. I asked them if they'd ever thought about how they could stop the pumpkin from decomposing. They talked about it, but couldn't come up with anything that would help them find the answer to that question. I wanted to jump right in and offer some ideas to consider but resisted and simply suggested that we just keep thinking about it.

The children wondered why the pumpkins in the compost bin didn't decompose as quickly as the ones in our room. My next question was, "Is there anything different about the pumpkins outside and the pumpkins inside?" That led us to talk about the differences in environment, which included temperature. There were so many great opportunities for reasoning. And so it continued, until the children eventually concluded that things decompose more quickly where the temperature is warm and more slowly where the temperature is cold.

A January Visit to Our Compost Bin

The watchful eyes of the children kept track of those pumpkins through the snowy winter and into the warm spring. They entered data from each visit to the compost bin into their pumpkin journals. Over time, the entries revealed more accurate reporting, more detail, and more understanding of decomposition.

Guess what these children found when they came back to school in September? You're right. They witnessed the full life cycle of the pumpkins. Long vines, with yellow flowers, and

The Gladbrook students visit the compost bin.

small pumpkins, were growing from that compost bin. More observing. More questions. Happy kids! Happy teacher!

"Balance"

I've found that it is possible to work science inquiry into my existing curriculum. I have a special unit that the children and I love. We call it "Our Circus Extravaganza." It provides many opportunities to develop physical, emotional, social, and academic growth. Language, math, social studies, and the arts found priority spots in my lesson plans. But I began to wonder how I could incorporate science into this already invigorating unit.

Several years ago I was introduced to some great science kits. I'd acquired a FOSS "Balance and Motion" kit and used it in the prescribed way. The children had great experiences and found success. But, again, I wanted to take those preplanned experiences to the next level to make it a richer encounter with inquiry. Balance would fit perfectly into this circus theme. The content and teaching of the NSES could be addressed. I would be connecting science to other school subjects, and, while learning more about balance, I would be providing challenging, age-appropriate opportunities for all of my students to do science.

I used Jack Prelutsky's book *Circus* (1989), which has wonderful illustrations and explanations of various circus acts. Several pages pertain to balance: clowns balancing plates on sticks, acrobats balancing on one another's shoulders, and seals balancing balls on their noses. When sharing the book with the children, I stopped on those pages and said "Wow," and we talked about the amazing tricks that were pictured there. I asked if anyone in our class was good at balancing things. Some said, "Not me"; others said, "Yes, I can balance." My next questions were, "Would you like to try to balance some objects? Would like to learn more about balance?" Everyone said, "YES!"

The children needed a definition of the word *balance*. They decided that, for a good balancing trick, they couldn't hold on to the object they were balancing and that the object they were trying to balance could wobble a little, but it could not fall down. One child pointed out, and we all agreed that, for an object to be truly balanced, the bigger object needed to be on top of something smaller—pretty good thinking.

We built background knowledge with more books and a video. Some of the children became teachers by describing circus acts they had seen. We brainstormed materials we would gather for our exploration. This was the time I offered the children the materials from the science kit, "Balance and Motion." I didn't give any instructions on how to use the items. We were almost ready to begin to explore the phenomenon of balance.

I needed to stop and reflect on the goals to be accomplished in these balance investigations. What were the essentials of this experience? In addition to another chance for students to become more familiar with the joy of doing science, I wanted to provide experiences with which they could begin to think about what the center of gravity is. The investigations were also an opportunity for me to introduce the value of persistence, present the fact that our experiments with balance needed to be assessed, and begin to explain the advantage gained when scientists work together to find answers to their questions. Most young learners don't know how to get to their next stage of learning. They need a teacher to lead them and find natural ways to introduce these processes, skills, and values.

Time to let the learning continue. When we began experimenting with balance, the children were full of energy, laughing, groaning, moving, and talking. Some were finding success, and some were struggling. After ample time for exploration, we had a group meeting. My questions and comments to them were, "What should we do when our experiments don't work out the way we want them to? Who could we go to, to learn more? You know, scientists learn from each other. Did you notice anything that was the same with every trick where the object was really balanced?" The students buddied up to share our successes and struggles with classmates and then made plans to explore again.

With many opportunities to develop a balancing trick, eventually everyone was ready to share their tricks with their classmates. We circled up, tricks in hand. Each child had a chance to be the ringmaster and introduce an act, and each child had a chance to be in the center ring to amaze their classmates with his or her balancing trick.

It is important for students to be included in the assessment of their own thinking and experimenting.

After every performance, and using the children's definition of balance, I took the opportunity to help each child evaluate his or her trick. I asked, "Did it really balance? Do you know why or why not? Is there anything about your trick that you would like to change to make it balance better? What would that be? Why?"

That year no one chose to do a balancing act in our production of "The Greatest Circus Extravaganza in Gladbrook, Iowa," but everyone did have one more opportunity to be in charge of his or her own learning, think like a scientist, and through their explorations learn more about the phenomenon of balance. They were learning how to learn. Isn't that what an education is truly all about?

Assessing the Ingredients of Science

Assessment is interwoven with instruction. It is ongoing and diagnostic. Teachers must keep track of which students understand the basic ideas, which students can perform the identified skills, and which students are struggling. The results of daily assessments help modify the content, process, depth, and pace of tomorrow's instruction. Teachers must also step back to assess the environment the students are working in. There may be interventions necessary to create the safe, stimulating setting necessary for optimum learning. At this grade level, most of the assessments can be done informally and need not take a teacher a great deal of time to complete.

I've gathered a checklist of objectives that are directly observable and that relate to both subject matter and science process skills. I keep the checklist on my science clipboard, identify the exact skill or understanding that I'm assessing, and, as I informally assess the children, I can jot down the date and a few words to describe the specific instance by the skill or understanding that was successfully demonstrated. I don't often get the time to assess every child during a science lesson. I've found, however, that with this checklist it's quick and easy for me to document the growth of many of my students either during the learning experience or after reflecting on the lesson later in the day.

ASSESSMENTS OF INQUIRY
What it means "to do" science and understand concepts in the
kindergarten classroom.

NAME_____

Generate questions?
Make associations?
Interpret findings?
Willing to change mind in light of findings?
Show evidence of understanding the concept?
Systematic with the procedure?
Notice anything significant in the investigation?
Generate a new idea/possible solution?
Use trial and error?
Use scientific vocabulary?
Drawing/writing complete enough to be recognized by someone else?
Engaged and persistent with the task?
Respectful of others in the group?
Share the work?
Manage materials well?

Teacher Comments:

Examples of Student Assessments

There are daily opportunities for meaningful, authentic assessments. Some of the assessments follow that I use to help myself plan appropriate content, processes, and products so that my students can continue growing.

1. Observations—One of the best times to learn about the development of processes, skills and understandings is when the children are engaged in an investigation. In this example, the lesson, "Fall Visit to the Prairie" had a twofold purpose. The children wanted to examine the seeds of the different prairie plants. I wanted to be able to step back and observe the interactions and abilities of the children. It was early in the kindergarten year, so the ability of my students to stay on task was limited and their skill development was still immature. Accomplishing both goals would be difficult for me without help. The third-grade teacher and I frequently have our kids buddy up. This was a time my youngsters needed some one-on-one assistance, so I asked my teacher friend if her class would like to join us. Her students were familiar with the prairie and also enjoyed the responsibilities given them. The "big buddy" was to stay with his or her "little buddy," help the little buddy stay focused on the task, and help the little buddy pick just one seed head from a variety of plants to put in a collection sack. The teachers and children reviewed what scientists do and the goals of their investigation. Then, with their collection sacks in one hand and their friend's hand in the other, the buddies headed out to the prairie to explore and learn.

I carried my science clipboard to the prairie, ready to make brief notes concerning ability to stay on task, share the work, exchange ideas, and ask questions. The dynamics of each group of children differed. By stepping back to watch both individuals and the group as a whole, I could assess their progress toward our long-term inquiry goals and then determine what my next steps should be. It would take more than one visit to the prairie for me to gather all of the information I wanted. The children found the prairie irresistible and did not hesitate to comply with my request to return soon.

2. Discussions—Sometimes I hear children cite examples of scientific understandings outside of science class. I cherish those comments the most because they tell me that the child is applying what he or she learned from classroom inquiry activities to everyday experiences in the real world.

Let me share one such experience with you. The children and I had spent several weeks working with a motion unit. On our way to lunch, Brady noticed that the floor slants down a bit just as we enter the lunch-

Kindergartners and third graders buddy up.

room. He turned to me and said, "Hey, Mrs. Fish, this is an inclined plane. It would be fun to bring our cars down here to see how far they will roll." My return comment was, "This is a steep inclined plane. You are thinking like a scientist, Brady. I agree. It would be fun to bring our cars to the lunchroom. We will have to talk about it and see if the class is interested. If they are, we can make plans to do just that." I knew that he was engaged in higher-level thinking because he was applying his new science understanding to his everyday life. When we got back to the classroom, I recorded Brady's observation, comment, and understanding on his inquiry assessment sheet.

3. Journaling—In the curriculum section, I shared a little about our composting project. In that narrative I mentioned that we often made journal entries. Here are two pieces of journaling work I collected from those composting investigations. Both journal entries are evidence of growth in science skills and understandings. They also show development in each student's ability to use reading and writing skills in meaningful situations.

Five-year-old Morgan completed her entry in November. She titled and dated her work. The investigation involved the solid pumpkin shell that was placed in a plastic bag in October. The children wanted to watch it decompose. As time passed, it had changed from a solid to a liquid. The drawing in Morgan's journal entry showed me that she recognized and understood that a change had occurred. Her work was complete and was a good representation of the decomposed pumpkin in the plastic bag. She used temporary spelling to record what she observed about the liquid in the plastic bag. I knew who had completed this particular data report because she remembered to put her name on her work. I noticed that she consulted the word bank to spell pumpkin and November.

What was next for Morgan? Morgan was gaining confidence as a scientist and as a writer. I complimented her on the accuracy of her drawing and the word she chose to describe what was in the bag. I encouraged her to keep using the science word bank and her ability to hear the sounds in words to write a complete sentence. It only took a few minutes at the end of the day to note Morgan's growth on her inquiry assessment sheet.

The work that Tyler produced in January was evidence that he is growing in many areas. His observation skills are acute. On our January visit to the compost bin he observed that a spider had left a little white egg sac on one of the top boards of the bin. Tyler noticed the snow in the bin and the sunny day. He included each of those observations in his drawing and writing. He wrote a compound sentence, complete with an end mark, and included the title and date in his entry. Tyler forgot his name, but sometimes that happens. He will try to remember next time. It was quick and easy to use the inquiry assessment sheet to credit Tyler with his accomplishments.

What was next for Tyler? He was still very much a five-year-old. He was very social and, even though his skills were advanced, would not want to be off working alone on a project. Still, I wanted to take advantage of his interest and give him more opportunities to develop a taste for the joy of discovery. I asked him what he wanted to investigate next. He chose to go out to the prairie to dig in the snow and try to find the few pieces of pumpkin shell we'd placed on the ground outside our kindergarten window. Anticipating the usual snowy winter, the children had placed a big rock beside the pumpkin shells so that they would be easy to find. With a friend at his side and wondering if those pieces of pumpkin had decomposed, Tyler headed outside. It was another chance for both of them to be in charge of their own learning. Their understanding of decomposition would grow, and, maybe most important, they would increase their awareness of what it means to be a scientist.

Assessment is a central ingredient of science, so it also should be central with science teaching and learning. Students and teachers need to understand that science is not science without evidence and interpretations that are assessed, validated, and accepted by others. By thoughtfully using the assessment data collected, a teacher can modify lesson plans to meet the current needs of her students.

Building on the Natural Wonder

Over the years many good things have happened in my classroom, but I've been able to see great things happen since inquiry and constructivist teaching have become fundamental components of my kindergarten curriculum. Challenge, real learning, joy, added independence, and freedom have found a home in my room. Letting my students know exactly what they should know, understand, and be able to do has increased their success. It's essential that the investigations the children—and I—design are fun and engaging. If real learning is to result, the inquiry must also be purposeful. When the environment, teachers, and students work together toward a specific, identified purpose, learning is more likely to get to long-term memory. Wonder, ample opportunities for the children to plan ways to find the answers to their questions for themselves, and shared objectives have supported my efforts to make learning meaningful and consequently long-lasting.

Keep the wonder alive. Invite inquiry into your classroom.

References

Lobel, A., and J. Prelutsky. 1989. *Circus.* New York: Simon & Schuster.

National Research Council (NRC). 1997. *Introducing the National Science Education Standards.* Washington, DC: National Academy of Sciences.

National Science Foundation (NSF). *Inquiry: Thoughts, views, and strategies for the K-5 classroom,* Vol. 2 of Foundations. A monograph for professionals in science, mathematics, and technology education. Available at *www.nsf.gov/pubs/2000/nsf99148/start.htm*

Science Workshop:

Kids Doing What Kids Do Best

Daniel Heuser
Mary Scroggs Elementary School

Setting

The science workshop program is a teaching format being implemented in a number of classrooms in my former district. These classrooms are in a primary K–3 school of approximately 500 students in a public school district of a Chicago suburb. The district enrollment is approximately 4,000 students, and the majority of the students in the district and school come from white, upper-middle-class families. About 15 % of the students at the school, however, qualify for free or reduced-price lunch, and some are also English language learners.

More Emphasis Review

The science workshop meets a number of teaching, assessment, and content elements recommended by the National Science Education Standards (NSES) (NRC 1996). Teaching Standards addressed by the science workshop program include understanding and responding to individual students' interests, strengths, experiences, and needs; focusing on student understanding and use of scientific knowledge, and inquiry processes; guiding students in active and extended inquiry; and providing opportunities for scientific discussion and debate among students. Assessment Standards addressed include assessing scientific understanding and reasoning.

The science workshop concentrates on the following content Standards: understanding scientific concepts and developing abilities of inquiry, investigations over extended periods of time, process skills in context, applying the results of experiments to scientific arguments and explanations, and public communication of student ideas and work to classmates.

Teacher, Students, and Classroom

Although a number of teachers in my former district use the science workshop format elements as they teach science, I will focus on the science workshops in my own classroom. I have been teaching for 15 years, and, for 11 of these years, I have been developing a workshop approach to teaching mathematics and science. I teach this approach to graduate students and inservice teachers, and I have written a book and several articles on the subject (Heuser 2000; 2002; 2005a). I taught a combined first- and second-grade class and the first- and second-grade students were taught together for most subjects, including science. The class enrollment was typically 25 students, about half first graders and half second graders. The demographics of these children reflected the school profile.

Program Description

Hands-on inquiry, as taught through the science workshop, is an instructional model that brings to life several of the *More Emphasis* reforms. Often, inquiry skills are taught separately in the earlier grades and then they are gradually brought together so that full inquiry can be done in the later grades. The science workshop model is based on a very different idea. This model builds on the five years of hands-on inquiry young children do between birth and the first day of school. Since young children have considerable experience and expertise in hands-on inquiry, inquiry does not have to be introduced as something new. Instead, children's informal inquiry abilities can be refined by taking questions important to children and then using those questions to support classroom inquiries. In this way, a much more complex type of inquiry can begin in the primary grades.

A Model for Inquiry

The workshop is an instructional format used at first to teach reading and writing and later adapted to teach mathematics and science. Within the workshop format, teachers can use a variety of activity types, such as problem solving, games, and inquiry.

Units are planned by first identifying the student outcomes wanted. These outcomes are often taken directly from the National Science Education Standards, and adapted to meet district and state requirements. Some of the outcomes for a unit on rocks and soil are shown in Table 1.

Table 1. Partial Listing of Student Outcomes for a Unit on Rocks and Soil

Outcome Category	NSES Suggested Student Outcomes
Doing Scientific Inquiry	Develop abilities necessary to do scientific inquiry. Ask a question about objects, organisms, and events in the environment. Plan and conduct a simple investigation. Use simple equipment and tools to gather data and extend the senses. Use data to develop a reasonable explanation. Communicate investigations and explanations.
Understanding Scientific Inquiry	Understand that scientists make the results of their investigations public. Recognize that scientists describe investigations in ways so that others can repeat the investigations.
Understanding Properties of Earth Materials	Earth materials are solid rocks and soils, water, and the gases of the atmosphere. Various materials have different physical and chemical properties that make them useful in different ways, such as building materials, fuel sources, growing plants used for food. Earth materials provide numerous resources that humans use.

With a list of outcomes in hand, the teacher then decides which type of learning activity would best teach each outcome. Students might play games, for example, or do library research. Typically, however, the majority of outcomes can be learned through inquiry. After all, inquiry is not only a primary goal of science education, but also a major way that students learn science content.

Once the outcomes best learned through inquiry are identified, the teacher plans a sequence of workshops using the science workshop inquiry model as set out in Table 2. The model has three phases: exploration, investigation, and reflection.

Table 2. Science Workshop Inquiry Model

Phase	Workshop focused upon:
Exploration	Hands-on experiences intended to produce interest and knowledge of desired science ideas. From exploration, students generate questions.
Investigation	One or several investigations based upon student questions. These investigations include students sharing and discussing their results.
Reflection	Reflective activities to unify investigations around important unit ideas. Usually this includes extending and comparing knowledge through reading, writing, and discussion.

Source: Heuser, D. 2002. *Reworking the workshop: Math and science reform in the primary grades.* Portsmouth, NH: Heinemann.

As an illustration of this model, I will describe an inquiry sequence from a unit on rocks and soil that I taught to my first and second graders. A specific goal of this inquiry was to have children understand that rocks have physical and chemical properties that affect how they break and erode.

Exploration

I began this inquiry sequence with two workshops in the exploration phase. The main purpose of the exploration phase is to help children generate questions they will use later in their investigations. Hands-on exploration stimulates previous knowledge and the curiosity that will lead to questions.

Workshop 1. The objective of the first workshop was to create excitement and activate students' prior knowledge of rocks. We read a picture book about a boy who collects rocks, and then we set off on a rock hunt on the school grounds. The students' job was to collect interesting rocks for display and use in our own classroom rock museum. Back in the classroom, students shared, described, and sketched the rocks they had found. The homework that night was to find a rock at home to bring in to school for a temporary exhibit in our collection.

Workshop 2. After students' awareness of rocks heightened in the first workshop, the purpose of the second workshop was to elicit from them testable questions that would lead to the inquiry outcomes. The second workshop began with children showing their rocks to their classmates. Several children brought in rocks collected on vacations or sent by relatives in faraway places, so that we would have a more varied collection than what we had found the day before. I contributed a number of specimens from my own collection.

When it came time for me to share my rock, I showed the children a piece of sandstone. Sandstone is an aggregate of many grains of sand, and I illustrated how breakable it is by scratching it with my fingernail. As the children saw pieces of sand fall from my rock, they began to finger their own rocks and soon we were into an animated discussion about wearing down rocks.

An important part of this exploration phase is to help focus children's questions around the desired outcomes, and this is done by setting a *guiding question*. "My fingernail can really wear down this sandstone, but fingernails aren't working on all of our rocks," I noted. Then I asked the guiding question: "What are some ways that you can wear down rocks?"

To encourage children to think about this question, I had them explore a number of objects: different varieties of rocks and other objects such as keys and pieces of wood and brick. "See what you can find out about wearing down rocks," I said, and the exploration began. Soon students were rubbing rocks and other objects together.

It was then time for me to confer with the children, and I asked each group what they had noticed. This led to a variety of responses. Children commented on the rocks' varying degrees of hardness, which objects broke, and other properties of the materials they tested. During conferences children start to ask questions such as "How long will it take to wear away this basalt with a key?" or "Which of these rocks is the hardest?" I repeated these questions aloud to the group and encouraged them to think of their own questions. Meanwhile, I wrote down each comment and question on my clipboard. These anecdotal notes are an important part of ongoing assessment.

Reflection in the form of discussion, writing, or drawing is an important part of each workshop. For this day's workshop I began the reflection by listing the questions that I had collected in my conferences. I also took some of the comments such as "This key can break down this whole rock to dust," and I turned them into questions such as "Can a key break down a whole rock to dust?" I then encouraged students to brainstorm more questions. We discussed which questions were testable and which we would have to answer by looking in books or on the internet. Soon we had a list of questions as shown in Table 3. We briefly discussed which questions were testable and moved the untestable questions, such as question 5, to a "books, internet, or experts" list that we would tackle later in the inquiry.

Table 3. Examples of Student Questions

What are some ways that you can wear down rock?
Can a key wear away a whole rock to dust?
Will hot water wear away a rock?
Will acid wear away a rock?
Do volcanoes wear away rocks?
If I put a bunch of rocks in a cup and shake them, will they get smaller?

We finished the workshop with students choosing several questions they wanted to investigate. They recorded these questions in their learning logs.

The exploration the children performed in these two workshops helped me understand and respond to individual student's interests, strengths, experiences, and needs, as recommended in the Standards. These questions became the focus of the second phase of this model—investigation.

Investigation

Once students articulate their curiosities, the next step is to have them plan and conduct their own investigations to answer the questions they generate and to present the results. These investigations involve students in active and oftentimes extended inquiry, as promoted in the NSES. Children can work by themselves or as part of a team. Because our rock study occurred fairly early in the year, I provided the first graders extra support by pairing them with second graders who had chosen the same questions.

Workshop 3. The third workshop was devoted to having these student pairs work out their investigation plans. This plan was recorded in a poster form, with each poster showing the question, a labeled picture of the materials needed for the investigation, and a written plan with procedures. I used these posters to gather materials for each group's investigation. They also served as an assessment of children's abilities to plan a fair test investigation.

My most important role as the teacher during the planning stage was to ask questions that would stimulate the children to refine their plans. In one conference, for example, a partnership was curious about how long it would take to wear away a rock with a key, so I asked, "How will you know how long it took? Is there a tool that could help you know exactly how long?" trying to lead them to pick some way to measure the time. This was a meaningful way to enact an emphasis found in the NSES: contextualizing the process skills. After looking at the size of their rock, I also asked, "Are you going to wear down the whole rock? What if you get tired or we run out of time?" The idea was to push each student's thinking to the limits of his or her capabilities without imposing adult ideas that might not have made sense to a child. Eventually that student pair decided to see how much rock could be scraped off of the rock in 10 minutes. Soon each team had completed its plan.

Workshop 4. In the fourth workshop, children conducted their investigations. Typically there is a lot of rubbing, shaking, pouring, and weighing during investigation workshops, so I recruited several parents for oversight. Some of these investigations are rather brief, such as the 10 minutes that the rock scrapers took. Most of the investigations, however, are more long-term. One group, for example, was leaving a piece of sandstone under an aquarium pump "waterfall" for a week to see the effect falling water had on a "soft stone." This fourth workshop ended up being a week long as we waited for the vinegar, waterfall, and other elements to react or interact with the rocks. As the investigations finished, the pairs recorded their observations on their investigation posters.

Workshop 5. During the fifth workshop, students presented the results of their investigations to their classmates. During these presentations the goals were to discuss the results, have children articulate and defend their ideas, and help make connections among the different investigations.

The waterfall group, for example, reported that its rock was 7 grams lighter than it was at the beginning of the week. Another group who had conducted a similar investigation claimed its rock had lost 12 grams. This seemed to rattle the first group. "That's because you got to use the small piece of sandstone!" "No," replied the other pair, "yours was the same size as ours at the beginning. We just had it right under the waterfall. Yours was a little off to the side. Ours got more of the water's power." The NSES stress the importance of providing these opportunities for scientific discussion and debate among students.

Students then responded in writing to two prompts: "What did you learn from your investigation?" and "What do you disagree with or have questions about from our presentations?" This writing is one way I focus on student understanding and use of scientific knowledge and on the inquiry processes. Responses varied among children. For example, one child responded to the second prompt, "I was surprised that the vinegar broke down the limestone that much. If I left it in there for a year, would the rock disappear?"

Reflection

The final phase of this model of inquiry is reflection. Its purpose is to unify investigations around important unit ideas. Both individual and community understandings are developed in the reflection phase.

Time for reflection is needed so that students can learn from their investigations: Hands-on investigations do not by themselves lead children to the important outcomes (Ridgeway and Padilla 1998). Reflection helps students learn science as they synthesize the results of their investigations with knowledge gained in other unit activities and with what they know from outside school. Reflection focuses on helping children agree to some whole-class as well as individual conclusions.

There is great value in helping the class as a whole try to reach some common beliefs about their investigations. The process of negotiating these shared beliefs calls on children to articulate and defend their own ideas and to incorporate or reject the ideas of others. The NSES promote opportunities for this kind of scientific discussion among students.

It is also important to go beyond whole-class conclusions to allow each child to reach his or her own set of ideas. In a class of 25 students, it is very likely that 25 separate concepts will be built. Because children are different, with different interests, strengths, experiences, and needs, it is to be expected that their understandings vary in sophistication and emphases. Indeed, it would be detrimental if each child were expected to arrive at the "one correct answer." As stated in the NSES, "Learning environments that concentrate on conveying to students what scientists already know do not promote inquiry" (NRC 1996). Instead, the goal of this model of inquiry is to help each child reach understandings consistent with his or her potential.

Workshop 6. The main activity in this workshop was a class discussion. I selected several prompts that would help children begin to unify their different experiences around the unit outcomes. For example, one of the prompts was, "What would you say to a friend who says that rocks are too hard to ever break down?" This prompt was chosen to help children form conclusions about the susceptibility of rocks to weathering.

As the facilitator I kept the discussion orderly, encouraged participation by all students, and furthered the discussion by asking questions and challenging assertions. For example, the children seemed to be hung up on the idea that rock can be worn down only by hard objects. I asked for clarification: "Everyone is saying hard things wear down rock. Is it *just* hard things? Remember in Harlyn's investigation when the vinegar broke little pieces off the limestone? Vinegar isn't hard like a key. How can we say this so it makes more sense?" After much debate the children agreed to this statement, which I recorded on chart paper: "Rocks can be worn down by so many things. Some are hard like keys, others are not hard, like water." Near the end of the workshop we had three chart papers filled with conclusions that we all could agree upon.

The final activity in this workshop was writing in learning logs. This is where each child can form and state his or her own understandings of the outcomes. As I did in the discussion workshop, I gave several prompts: "Tell what you know about how rocks can be broken down," and "If you were to do your investigation all over again, what would you do differently and why?"

Children often draw from the ideas in the discussion to write their responses, as well as incorporate their own ideas. This process helps them use the results of their investigations to form scientific arguments and explanations, an idea supported in the Standards. In addition their responses provide another assessment for me to use to shape instruction. For example, one child wrote that because hot water did not appear to break down rock in the investigations, then "I guess volcanoes don't change rocks that much." I made a note to address this during the next workshop.

Workshop 7. In the seventh, and last, workshop in this inquiry sequence, students were comparing and extending their knowledge by doing library research and having more discussions. To begin this workshop I assigned each partnership a series of questions related to their investigations. For example, the hot-water group was given questions about volcanoes—some from the "books, internet, or experts" list and others that I selected. I wrote these questions on paper, and each pair began looking through nonfiction books for the answers. This was another learning activity which required a lot of adult support, so I asked several parents and our library director to assist. This library research usually takes place over several days, often during our reading time. Nonfiction reading is a goal in both language arts and science.

We concluded this workshop by having the students briefly present their questions and answers. After each pair had presented, we discussed how the new information connected to our investigations. For example, the pair studying volcanoes found that lava is liquid rock that is heated to several thousand degrees. "If that's true," I ask, "then why didn't your rock melt when you put it into hot water?" Questions like this help children compare evidence collected in their investigations to published scientific explanations. "Well, my water wasn't that hot," volunteers one of the presenters. "You're right," I reply. "Your water was only about 200 degrees, not thousands. Another thing to consider is the type of rock. Volcanic rock is a different type than the limestone that you used. Do you think that that could make a difference also?" The presentations and discussions continued until all groups had shared.

The last step of this workshop—and of this inquiry sequence—once again called for the children to respond in writing to prompts. This time the prompts aimed at encouraging them to form links between their explanations and those accepted by the scientific community. This prompt was, "Both people and nature can break down rocks. How does this wearing down of rock help or hurt people?"

Two student responses follow:

> Two ways that people can break down rocks are pollution from factories, and a hammer and chisel. Pollution like acid rain is bad. It hurts by ruining our buildings and environment. A hammer and chisel is good because an artist uses them to make statues.

> Well, one way to break down rock is to throw it into water and wait about a year or so. A second way is an earthquake—all these rocks fall on top of each other and they can break into little pieces and make a lot of dust. People could get hurt by rocks falling on them or by breathing in the dust.

Note how the sophistication and emphases of responses varies. This is consistent with the NSES emphases on understanding and responding to individual student's interests, strengths, experiences, and needs, and focusing on student understanding and use of scientific knowledge.

Embedded Assessment

There is no separate assessment phase in the science workshop inquiry model. According to the assessment addendum to the NSES (NRC 2001), "To be effective as assessment that improves teaching and learning, the information generated from the activity must be used to inform the teacher and/or students in helping to decide what to do next. In such a view, assessment becomes virtually a continuous classroom focus, quite indistinguishable from teaching and curriculum."

Several assessments embedded in the instruction were mentioned in this sample inquiry. The anecdotal notes collected during my conferences while students explored in the second workshop, for example, helped me identify misconceptions and common curiosities about the wearing of rocks. Another assessment was the use of the inquiry posters, from which I could determine the quality of each group's plan. With data on which groups had a plan that was unclear or contained elements that might lead them away from our inquiry outcomes, I could then confer with these children to address these problems. Learning log responses could be assessed using a rubric similar to that found in Heuser (2005b). Other useful assessments were the student presentations and the negotiation. Assessments of a more summative nature are presented in the next section.

Program Data

Because the science workshop has been implemented in a relatively small number of classrooms, no large-scale data have been gathered on its effectiveness. The evidence that has been collected, however, is compelling. These qualitative data focus on both students' understanding of science content and of the inquiry process. The NSES state that assessment of both scientific understanding and reasoning are important. Some of these data have been presented in earlier work (Heuser 2002), but the description of the process has been expanded upon in this chapter. Unfortunately, not all of the qualitative assessment data for the wearing-of-rock inquiry sequence were saved. More complete data were saved from other inquiry sequences, however, and these are described in the section that follows.

Plant Life Cycle Interview

One year my first and second graders conducted inquiries on plants to learn about plant life cycles. I wanted to focus on the concepts of organisms in their environment and life cycles, so students devised ways to test in which solution pea plants would grow best. We set up three "watering" regimens for three groups of plants—water, coffee, and diet cola. Students observed the plants over several weeks in order to see what "watering" regimen best supported plant growth, but at the same time they had the opportunity to watch some of the plants go through their life cycle. Green plants yielded pale white flowers; flowers faded and gave rise to seed pods; and the pods—once matured and dried—were broken open to reveal pea seeds nearly identical to those that we planted to grow the original plants. (More details of this inquiry are described in Heuser 2002.)

As a teacher, I wanted to know how effective this inquiry was in reaching the goals. The excitement the children showed as they observed the plants was obvious, but what did they really *learn* about life cycles? To find out, I devised an interview that I used with each child at the beginning and at the end of our unit. This involved meeting with each child individually and asking questions about an imaginary plant (the juju plant) that I built by sticking a plastic flower and a clay "fruit" onto a house plant. The interview is shown in the following textbox.

Plant Life Cycle Task Interview

This is a pretend plant. I call it the juju plant.

(Point to fruit) This is its fruit. It's called a juju fruit. If I cut it open with a knife, what do you think would be in there? Anything else? Anything else? *(seed)*

(If he or she said "seed"): Let's say that you are right, and there is a seed in here. If we took that seed out and planted it in the ground, what kind of plant would grow? *(juju plant)*

(Point to flower). This is the flower of the juju plant. If I picked this flower (pull flower off) and every time a new flower grew I picked it off right away, would the plant get any new juju fruits, or not? Why or why not? *(No, because the fruit grows from the flower.)*

Source: Heuser, D. 2000. Reworking the workshop for math and science. *Educational Leadership* 58 (10): 34–37.

The pretest and posttest interview results for both first and second graders are shown in Table 4. Students showed varying degrees of understanding of plant life cycles at the beginning of the unit, but all students came to understand two important life cycle concepts: that fruits contain seeds, and those seeds grow into like plants. The third concept (fruit forms from flowers) was a weak point before the unit, and most, but not all students, came to that understanding by unit's end. The difficulty of this concept—and the success of this inquiry—is shown by comparing these data from my first and second graders with that of U.S. fourth graders who had a similar question on the Third International Mathematics and Science Study (TIMSS). My students' success at identifying where seeds developed was twice that of U.S. fourth graders taking the TIMSS (International Association for the Evaluation of Educational Achievement 1995).

Table 4. Plant Life Cycle Interview

Understand that...	First Graders		Second Graders	
	Pretest	Posttest	Pretest	Posttest
Fruits contain seeds.	7 (58%)	12 (100%)	7 (70%)	10 (100%)
Seeds grow into like plants.	11 (92%)	12 (100%)	7 (70%)	10 (100%)
Fruit forms from flowers.	3 (25%)	10 (83%)	2 (20%)	7 (70%)

Source: Heuser, D. 2002. *Reworking the workshop: Math and science reform in the primary grades.* Portsmouth, NH: Heinemann.

Inquiry Data on Planning "Fair" Tests

Another goal of the pea plant inquiry was to refine students' working knowledge of the inquiry process. Following this inquiry, I had pairs of students—first graders paired with second graders—plan their own investigations of plants and their environments. As a group we brainstormed a small number of questions, such as: Is old coffee better than new coffee for plants? Is a big or little pot better? Will a plant grow if it is in a dark closet? Then the pairs were to pick one of the questions (or develop their own) and design an investigation that would answer their question. Their investigation plan was to be shown on a poster that included the question, a written procedure, and a drawing showing the materials that they needed and how they would be set up.

My purpose in doing this was to test the assertion in the NSES that kindergarten to fourth grade students can "entertain the idea of a 'fair' test (a test in which only one variable at a time is changed)" (NRC 1996). To evaluate the student pairs' success at designing a fair-test investigation, I adapted a set of rubrics from Marzano (2000).

The rubrics and results are shown in Table 5. Of the 12 student pairs, 5 showed their plans in detail. Another 5 pairs lacked some important details; quite often these students did not indicate specific measurements to be used, such as showing that a plant should get lemonade but not showing how much. Two of the pairs proposed a fair test scheme but complicated it by adding other elements. An example of this was the idea to give one plant water and another tea but to keep them both in the closet. This data shows that most of these young students could collaboratively design their own fair test to answer their questions.

Table 5. Plants and Their Environment Inquiry Data

Level	Student pairs are...	Number of student pairs
4	Able to plan a simple fair test experiment and present it in detail.	5
3	Able to plan a simple fair test experiment, but presentation lacks some details.	5
2	Able to plan a simple experiment, but it has "unfair" as well as fair aspects.	2
1	Unable to plan a simple fair test experiment.	0
0	Unable to develop a poster that conveys information in which to make a judgment.	0

Another question related to the age at which my students could devise their own fair tests. The plant inquiries were designed by multiage teams in which, presumably, the second graders were directing much of the planning. How able are first graders to make a plan in which only one variable was changed? To find out, I had students plan their investigations individually during our next unit on water. The guiding question was, "How can you speed up or slow down evaporation?" Student questions revolved around the effects of covering water (with wood chips, paper, or blankets), adding other materials (such as pudding, oil, or shampoo), or placing the water in different locations (freezer, window, or heater). Using the same rubric, I judged these investigation plans. The results are shown in Table 6.

Level	The student is...	Number of students	
		First Graders	Second Graders
4	Able to plan a simple fair test experiment and can present it in detail.	3	9
3	Able to plan a simple fair test experiment, but presentation lacks some details.	4	2
2	Able to plan a simple experiment, but it has "unfair" as well as fair aspects.	2	1
1	Unable to plan a simple fair test experiment	1	0
0	Unable to successfully develop a poster to convey information on which to make a judgment.	1	1

Table 6. Water Evaporation Inquiry Data

Again, most of these young students proved themselves very capable of planning a fair test investigation. While the first-grade students were more likely to leave out important details or include complicating elements into their plans than were the second graders, only one did not plan a fair test.

Inquiry Data on Drawing Conclusions

What kind of conclusions do students draw from science workshop investigations? The NSES state that "children in K–4 have difficulty with experimentation as a process of testing ideas and the logic of using evidence to formulate explanations." One goal of inquiry as taught through the science workshop is to allow children to draw their own conclusions, even when those conclusions are not scientifically complete explanations. Knowledge grows from knowledge, and letting children use their individual reasoning abilities to build their own understanding is far better than imposing an adult explanation that they may not be capable of understanding.

Still, if the children's conclusions are too far off base, one has to question the suitability of inquiry as a teaching method for them. To help assess their conclusions, I collected student writing from the portion of their posters in which they were told to answer their question. These responses, with the corresponding question, are shown in Table 7.

All of the students were able to interpret the results of their investigations and come to the logical conclusion to answer their question. For example, a child who investigated the question "Does hot air help water evaporate?" looked at the cup she had placed on the heater and noticed that the water level was below the line indicating the beginning level. On her poster she wrote, "Hot air does help water evaporate." Nearly half of the students added either one or two pertinent comments to their conclusions. These included explanations as to why the water evaporated or did not evaporate ("Heat helps water evaporate because it is sort of like moving air because it's moving up."), predictions about what might happen next ("I think the sun could melt the water to nothing."), and reflections about their inquiry process ("It was hard to see the water because the pudding got on the sides. Next time I will try not to get the pudding on the sides.").

Level	Student...	Number of students	
		First Graders	**Second Graders**
4	Correctly interpreted results to answer the question, and included *two* other pertinent comments (explanation, prediction, reflections on inquiry refinement).	0	2
3	Correctly interpreted results to answer the question, and included *one* other pertinent comment.	2	5
2	Correctly interpreted results to answer the question.	5	5
1	Incorrectly interpreted results.	0	0
0	Provided little or no information from which to make a judgment.	2	0

Table 7. Water Evaporation Conclusions: "Will _____ let water evaporate?"

Inquiry Conclusions and Further Questions

Considering the nature of young children, this ability to plan investigations and draw somewhat logical conclusions is not at all surprising. Children spend the first years of their lives in nearly continuous hands-on inquiry. They are curious about things and figure out ways to satisfy their curiosities. Almost always their plans begin by reaching out and touching. Children then infer relationships from the results of their study. These relationships are continually tested and refined as children discuss their ideas with others and engage in further experimentation. Considered in this way, inquiry is a natural way to learn. It makes sense to give children many opportunities to continue on this path, using the inquiry skills they already are practicing. The NSES allude to this by placing more emphasis on process skills *in* context, instead of out of the context of real inquiry. Certainly the rich discussions and debate my students have during science workshops are very different than those I heard during my preworkshop years. Then, it was all I could do to keep children's attention as I explained the science activity I had just designed and demonstrated.

What effects does the science workshop model of inquiry have on children who are less advantaged then those in my school? How special-needs students perform during science workshop inquiries has not been a particular focus of research. However, other researchers have studied special-needs students who were taught inquiry science. For example, special-education students included in the regular classroom and other lower-achieving students have been found to make gains in conceptual understanding similar to higher-achieving students while being taught through inquiry (Dalton et al. 1997; Palincsar et al. 2001). In another study, students in a district serving primarily poor and non-English speaking families posted significant gains in science scores on standardized tests after the district adapted inquiry-based programs (Jorgenson and Smith 2002).

These studies, plus a summary of earlier research (Haury 1993), generally indicated that special-needs students can benefit from inquiry models similar to the science workshop model.

Summary

Science workshop inquiry capitalizes on the substantial informal abilities that young children have to inquire into their world. Exploration activities and a guiding question encourage students to ask testable questions about important science topics. Students subsequently plan, run, and interpret the results of their own investigations. Knowledge is shaped and extended through the social reflection provided as students discuss and write about their work and about work from the scientific community. Children develop a strong understanding both of science content and of the inquiry process. Data on this inquiry model suggest that many young children may be able to benefit from this type of science instruction.

References

Dalton, B., C. Morrocco, T. Tivnan, and P. Mead. 1997. Supported inquiry science: Teaching for conceptual change in urban and suburban science classrooms. *Journal of Learning Disabilities* 30 (6): 670–684.

Haury, D. L. 1993. Teaching science through inquiry. (ERIC/CMSMEE Digest, ERIC document no. ED 359 048)

Heuser, D. 2000. Reworking the workshop for math and science. *Educational Leadership* 58 (10): 34–37.

Heuser, D. 2002. *Reworking the workshop: Math and science reform in the primary grades.* Portsmouth, NH: Heinemann.

Heuser, D. 2005a. Inquiry, science workshop style. *Science and Children* 43 (2): 32–36.

Heuser, D. 2005b. Learning logs: Writing to learn, reading to assess. *Science and Children* 43 (3), 46–49.

International Association for the Evaluation of Educational Achievement. 1995. *Data almanacs for achievement items: Distribution of responses for TIMSS items. Fourth grade science.* Available online at *http://isc.bc.edu/timss1995i/ TIMSSPDF/pc_alm95/s04alm95.pdf.*

Jorgenson, O., and S. H. Smith 2002. Helping disadvantaged children succeed. *Principal* 82 (2): 38–41.

Marzano, R. J. 2000. *Transforming classroom grading.* Alexandria, VA: Association for Supervision and Curriculum Development.

National Research Council (NRC). 1996. *National Science Education Standards.* Washington, DC: National Academy Press.

National Research Council (NRC). 2000. *Inquiry and the National Science Education Standards: A guide for teaching and learning.* Washington, DC: National Academy Press.

National Research Council (NRC). 2001. *Classroom assessment and the National Science Education Standards.* Washington, DC: National Academy Press.

Palincsar, A. S., S. J. Magnusson, K. M. Collins, and J. Cutter. 2001. Making science accessible to all: Results of a design experiment in inclusive classrooms. *Learning Disability Quarterly* 24 (1): 15–32.

Ridgeway, V. C., and M. J. Padilla. 1998. Guided thinking: Using three-level thinking guides to promote inquiry in the classroom. *The Science Teacher* 65 (8): 18–21.

A Second-Grade Exploration:

Guiding Students in Active and Extended Scientific Inquiry

Elena O'Connell
John H. West Elementary School

Janice Koch
Hofstra University

Setting

What can we hope for as children explore magnets in a second-grade classroom? What are the possibilities for exploration, and how does the teacher facilitate elementary science experiences with magnets that can lead to student understanding? This was the question in Ms. O'Connell's second-grade class as she implemented a second-grade magnets unit and used maglev (magnetic levitation) tracks and makeshift "cars." The cars, made of wooden blocks with Velcro attached to one side, come with small magnets that have Velcro on one side. These materials help the children learn more about magnetic levitation.

Ms. O'Connell's goals were that, by the end of the unit, students would understand that a magnet is an object that contains metal and attracts some other metals, the poles of a rectangular shaped magnet are located on each end, attraction is when an unseen force pulls two objects toward each other, the poles of a magnet are called north and south and opposite poles attract each other, and similar poles of a magnet (north and north or south and south) repel each other. Repelling is when a force, in this case unseen, pushes two objects away from each other.

Ms. O'Connell prepared for this unit by ordering many materials: different-sized and different-shaped magnets, foil, nails, pennies, nickels, dimes, silverware, jewelry, screws, plastic, paper clips, rubber bands, and more. In addition, she ordered 7-foot tracks with a magnetic strip running down the center and a kit of materials that includes wooden blocks ("cars") with four Velcro pieces glued in the corner of one side of the block and many small magnets, labeled N or S with Velcro glued on the other side.

Elena O'Connell's students work with magnets.

This second-grade class was in a middle-class suburban community about 30 miles east of a major northeastern city. The second-grade science curriculum in this district was underdeveloped because most instructional time is spent preparing students for the upcoming third-grade language arts and mathematics assessments. Ms. O'Connell was determined to expand the children's understanding of science concepts, so she developed this magnetism unit, using resources from trade books, journal articles, curriculum guides, and the internet (Murrow 1999; Krensky 1992; Feldman 1996; Iwasyk 1997).

The class had 26 students: 12 boys and 14 girls. The students' needs varied greatly, both academically and emotionally. Three students received remedial reading four times a week, three other students received remedial mathematics twice a week, and one student received services for emotional assistance once a week.

As you entered Ms. O'Connell's classroom, you saw a colorful rug, used for class meetings and small group gatherings. There was a "research" table, covered with books and other print materials used to research the current topic. In this case the topic was magnets and magnetic levitation. There were two networked computers for student use and one classroom printer. The students' desks were set up in four groups. Two groups contained seven students each and two groups contained six students each. There were no rows in this classroom.

As Ms. O'Connell implemented the unit on magnets, there was *More Emphasis* on

- Selecting and adapting curriculum
  As indicated above, this district did not emphasize elementary school science. Ms. O'Connell chose to focus on goals for a unit on magnets with the hope of implementing a culminating activity that models magnetic levitation.
- Focusing on student use of scientific and inquiry processes
  Ms. O'Connell was about to begin a unit on magnets that was developed with the students' abilities in mind. She was interested in engaging them in cooperative group work with magnets and guiding them to use scientific and inquiry processes including engaging the students in a magnet science circus described on p. 38.
- Guiding students in active and extended scientific inquiry
  Ms. O'Connell structured her seating in a way that facilitated group work. She was always walking around the room, as we can see in the description that follows. When she

implemented the science activities, she was busy visiting student groups and individual students, asking them questions and probing their thinking.

- Continuously assessing student understanding

For Ms. O'Connell, assessment was ongoing and usually looked like a good instructional task. Throughout the unit, she employed many forms of assessment, including a pre- and postassessment survey, keeping a teaching journal, using pre- and post-KWL (Know—Want to know—Learn) charts, and interviews. The students would be participating in many hands-on activities that allowed for a variety of results and answers.

During these activities, many forms of assessment were used. Ms. O'Connell walked around the classroom, communicating with children, asking "what" and "why" questions. She recorded these interactions in her teacher journal. The students also kept records of their activities and discoveries to help them during later discussion and comparisons. For the second graders in this class, Ms. O'Connell felt she would not be able to assess accurately what they knew and comprehended by using a paper-and-pencil test. Many of the students had wonderful ideas, theories, and predictions and got good results due to their actions, but became extremely frustrated when they began to put those ideas onto paper. For Ms. O'Connell, being flexible in the assessment process ensured that the assessments were valid. The final activity, creating a maglev vehicle, required a checklist to be assessed. The students created this checklist with teacher guidance and supervision.

Ms. O'Connell believed that the children gained a better sense of the level of expectation and responsibility if they were made a part of the checklist development. Involving the students in the creation of the assessment checklist also helped to ensure that they could read and comprehend the vocabulary used in each section.

Implementing the Unit

To begin the unit on magnetism and magnetic levitation, Ms. O'Connell gave a preassessment survey to the students. Prior to beginning the work, the children met on the rug and Ms. O'Connell stressed that this was not a test and would not be graded. She explained that she was interested in how they felt and what they knew so she could help them to learn. As students completed the survey (see text box), Ms. O'Connell circulated among the students.

Preassessment Survey
1. Do you like science? Why or why not?
2. How do you feel about working in groups? Why do you feel that way?
3. What do you think a magnet does?
4. Where do you find magnets?
5. What do you think magnets can be used for?
6. What do you think of when you hear the word *attract*?
7. What do you think of when you hear the word *repel*?
8. What subject do you think you are the best at in school? Why do you feel that way?
9. What is one question you have about magnets?
10. What is one way you think you can find out the answer all by yourself?
11. Describe your favorite learning experience in school. What made it so great?
12. What do you think a magnet looks like? Draw a picture or pictures of magnet(s).

As the children worked, a few of them needed help reading some words, but all of the children who received reading services were able to finish the entire assessment independently. They were capable of overcoming challenges when presented with them in a nonthreatening environment. The next day, the students gathered on the rug for an informal discussion about magnets. As the students volunteered the information they thought they knew about magnets, it was added it to the KWL chart. Many students said that magnets could stick to refrigerators and other metal substances. One student said that a magnet could be found in a compass. Another told us that magnets stick to each other. Ms. O'Connell posed the question, "Do magnets always stick to each other?" The entire class answered, "Yes." They were able to contribute a lot of different statements and theories. One student told us that magnets stick to things because they are sticky. Certainly there were misconceptions here. The students agreed that they were going to be able to learn a lot of new information about magnets.

At the next meeting, the class began the first day of the two-day magnet science circus. "A science circus consists of several stations at which the visitors are asked to perform certain tasks and record their results or reactions" (Koch 2005, p. 87). A magnet science circus is staged with a classroom set up with a variety of hands-on centers designed to guide students through exploratory discovery and learning about magnets and magnetism. The students were extremely excited about participating in more activities dealing with magnets. They met on the rug to discuss the four activities that they would be doing throughout the circus. The students worked with the other students who sat at the same table during class. Each group spent 20 minutes at each of the stations, giving them enough time to explore as well as finish the task.

Each day of the circus, the students visited two of the centers. During this time, Ms. O'Connell walked around the room asking questions and asking for explanations from individual students. On the first day, as she spent time on the first center, "Mysterious Movements," the children made many exciting discoveries. At this center they were instructed to hold a paper clip on one side of an object and a magnet on the other. The students were to move the magnet back and forth to test if the magnet could attract the paper clip through the object. The children made predictions about the magnet's ability to attract other objects made of other materials and then they tested their predictions. As the children worked with the objects named on the recording sheet, many of them were shocked that magnetic forces could travel through the seat of the chair that they were sitting on. One student decided that she would like to test if the magnetism could go through her arm. Before allowing her to perform this test, Ms. O'Connell asked her a few questions. First she asked what the student predicted the outcome would be. She said, "Miss O'Connell, anything is possible. To be sure, I have to try it." This student demonstrated a beginning understanding of science as process.

Ms. O'Connell continued to walk around and survey the children. Many of them were working very effectively in their groups. At one center the children were working together to test different objects around the room and helping each other to record the data. Some students would question others about the results of the individual testing they did. There were spontaneous conversations. The students were independent learners.

Suddenly, one student called out, "Look what I discovered! Magnets can hold other magnets up in the air!" He was extremely pleased with himself when he came to this realization. His group came to him to see what he had to share. He showed his discovery to his group and they all followed and copied his "experiment."

At the second station, called "Magnet Race," the children had to figure out how to use one magnet to get another magnet from the starting line to the finish line without touching it. As each group worked at this station, it was clear that the students loved every moment they were there. A majority of the students pushed the magnet by holding the other magnet behind it and having it repel the first magnet across the finish line. One student discovered that he could work from the other side and hold the second magnet close to the first so that it attracted and pulled the first magnet over the finish line.

At the third station, called "Create a Magnet," children turned needles into magnets by rubbing them on magnets several times in one direction. Using a new needle each time, the students rubbed it on a magnet 20, 30, 40, and 50 times and then tested its magnetism by trying to attract a paper clip. It was frustrating for some of the students. "It doesn't work. I keep trying," one student said to Ms. O'Connell. Ms. O'Connell asked her to demonstrate how she was doing the experiment and found that the student was rubbing back and forth instead of in one direction. After changing her technique, the student found some success.

At the last station, "Macho Magnets," the students tested how many paper clips magnets of different sizes could hold. They enjoyed piling the paper clips on in many different ways to discover the maximum number a magnet could hold without any falling off. This station allowed the children to do a lot of unstructured experimenting without guidelines or restrictions. "Miss O'Connell, this magnet is so strong that I made it hold 20 paper clips," said one student. The student's focus and intensity had remained strong long into the science circus, making this experience a success.

Ms. O'Connell does a lot of group work with the class because she believes it is important for them to acquire strong group-work skills such as collaboration, decision-making, and listening to others' opinions and ideas. When Ms. O'Connell debriefed the students after the science circus was completed, their answers incorporated many of the concepts that she had wanted the children to learn, such as *polarity, attraction,* and *repulsion.*

Ms. O'Connell again sparked the students' interest in magnetism, this time by showing them a bit of "magic." She taped a bar magnet to the top of a table, allowing the greater part of it to hang over the side. She then tied a string to the bottom of the table's leg and to the open end of the string tied a paper clip. With the string taut and the paper clip centimeters away from the magnet, the paper clip was suspended in air. The students stared in amazement and were all just quiet for a few seconds. She left the materials set up for the children to explore and experiment. Many of the children tried and tried until they were able to make the paper clip remain suspended. It was difficult for them at first, but they learned how to manipulate the string and be very gentle letting go of the paper clip. Ms. O'Connell met with the class again to discuss why and how this could happen. Immediately many children called out, "The magnet is attracting it!" They were using the vocabulary. She asked them why, if the magnet was attracting the paper clip, the paper clip was not touching the magnet. Betty raised her hand first and said, "Maybe it is only attracted to the magnet a little bit."

The class tested her hypothesis to see if that could be the reason. Ms. O'Connell took the same type of magnet and paper clip and held the paper clip close to the magnet. She asked the students to raise their hands if they thought the paper clip would stay in midair when she let go. Six students raised their hands. Ms. O'Connell let go and the paper clip flew up and stuck to the magnet. Ms. O'Connell asked the class the question again, "Why is the paper clip not touching the magnet?" Meghan raised her hand and said, "The string is holding it down, and the magnet is pulling it up. It is stuck in the middle." They went on to discuss that the two forces were pulling it up and down. They were able to see the string pulling the clip down but not able to see the magnetic force pulling it up. The students continued to do this experiment over and over again whenever they found a free moment.

Ms. O'Connell's students worked on many more exploratory activities with magnets and were then ready to do some research on maglev transportation. They researched magnetic levitation trains on the internet and responded to questions in their portfolios such as "Where are the trains found? How do they work? Why do you think they are so quiet?" The students used the "How Stuff Works" website (*www.howstuffworks.com/maglev-train.htm*) to find information about how the trains levitate above the tracks. The students' challenge was to design the placement of magnets on a wooden block ("car") so that their car would "float" or levitate down the two classroom maglev tracks. On the day that the students were to test their cars, the two large tracks were set up at the back of the classroom. The project involved the students' placing magnets at strategic positions on the bottom of wooden blocks so that they would levitate on the maglev track. The goal was for the car to go swiftly down the track and for the children to understand the ways in which to set up magnetic repulsion. The students drew plans for their placement designs and placed their magnets on the wooden blocks to test them.

Ms. O'Connell asked probing questions as the students stood at eye level at the beginning of the track and made observations about whether there was magnetic attraction and repulsion. She asked, "What do you think went wrong? Let's look at the magnets at the bottom of your car—what's happening?" Students were totally engaged in designing and re-designing the placement of their magnets. Ms. O'Connell offered no judgments, only observations, and empathized as the children had to re-think their designs. The amazing part is that, by plodding along, every group came to see that the placement of its magnets would determine if the car would levitate. Several groups observed what "pole" each side of the track was as they lined up north pole magnets on one side of the bottom of their car and south pole magnets on the other side. They said things like, "The poles were the same, so the car kept levitating," or "The same poles will be repulsion."

A few groups decided to try designing their cars to levitate with the least number of magnets possible. When they were successful, they went to their desks and wrote in their design portfolios—needing no urging to do so from the teacher. They were completely self-directed—and they were only eight years old. In the design portfolios students were required to explain why some designs worked and others did not. These second graders were adept at making these explanations about how north and south poles attract each other, and they really understood the concept when the car "worked." Ms. O'Connell asked the students to look at what worked and what was not working each time they came up to send their car down the track. When they were successful, Ms. O'Connell asked, "What did you learn?" Students were engaged in conversation and discussion with the teacher and their peers as they experienced the ways in which like poles repel each other.

Evidence of Student Learning

Much of the unit on magnets and magnetic levitation was driven by the students. The students were able to explore and discover without many limitations. The goals for this unit were that the students would learn about magnetism, attraction, repulsion, and how to use these forces to create a magnetic levitation vehicle. Ms. O'Connell was also interested in learning about the students' attitudes toward science and group work and to see if these attitudes changed due to the way this unit was implemented.

These goals were assessed in a variety of ways. The students completed a pre- and postassessment, class discussions were conducted, and observations were made and recorded in a daily teacher journal. These assessments and the final design portfolio were used to determine the students' learning and attitudes. The assessments showed that the students gained science understandings about magnets and that some students changed their attitudes toward science during the course of this unit. Group work was a significant part of this unit. The students were assigned partners, which in some cases made it more difficult to get started. There were many obstacles and differences to overcome. In the end, every pair was successful and attitudes about working in groups had changed after the conclusion of the unit. Ms. O'Connell administered the same preassessment survey as a postassessment at the completion of the unit. In the 26 completed postassessments, only one student responded that she did not like working in groups. She explained that she did not like it because, "It takes too long, and I got frustrated with waiting for another person." She likely learned an even bigger lesson about cooperation and consideration of others. If she walked away from the unit with a better understanding of how to work effectively with others in difficult situations, then the unit was a significant success for her.

Ms. O'Connell also compared the students' responses to the question, "How do you feel about science?" Five students responded on the preassessment that they disliked science; the other 21 answered that they liked science. The five students who did not like science said that it was too much work. Sixteen of the students explained that they liked science because it was "fun." Five others said they liked science because they "learn new things." Reading through the preassessments and realizing that the majority of the students who enjoyed science enjoyed it because it was fun helped Ms. O'Connell design this unit. The activities and lessons had to be hands-on and centered on self-exploration and discovery. These features helped the students build a sense of control and ownership over their learning.

Although improving attitudes toward group work and attitudes toward science were goals of this unit, Ms. O'Connell also measured the knowledge students gained about magnets. On both the pre- and postassessments, the students were asked, "What do you think of when you hear the word *attract*?" On the preassessment, seven students were able to give an accurate description of the word. The other 19 were unable to define what the word meant. In the postassessment, the number of students who were able to accurately define *attract* rose to 24. The two students whose responses were not accurate wrote that attract meant "sticky things" and "float." Ms. O'Connell had sought evidence of understanding that *attract* means that two different things come together or are pulled toward one another.

The same question was asked of the word *repel* on both the pre- and postassessment. Although some students guessed, their answers were way off, and only one student was able to define what *repel* meant. Seven students related the word *repel* to a helicopter or something that flies. It was interesting to see the process that students used to find the definitions. They thought of a similar word that they were aware of, *propeller,* and connected the meanings. There was a significant increase in the number of students who were able to define the word on the postassessment: Twenty students correctly defined the word *repel*. Of the six students who were unable to define this word, four responded that it meant "floating." Throughout the design activity, Ms. O'Connell often used the words *repel* and *float* interchangeably. Ms. O'Connell concluded that she was overly confident that the students would understand that the "floating" of the wooden car was due to the magnets "repelling" each other. This assessment was helpful in correcting that misconception. The class continued to use these terms and demonstrate comprehension by using them successfully in conversation.

On the postassessment, all of the students were able to draw a magnet and some labeled the north and south poles. The final design portfolios showed the students' drawings of the placements of their magnets on the wooden blocks to ensure that their cars would levitate down the maglev track. This was another assessment of student learning, because the second graders were required to indicate why they made their choices for magnet placement.

When the unit began, it was easy to observe an immediate increase in the enthusiasm of the students. They began to ask, "When are we doing science?" rather than, "When is lunch?" Students were carrying on conversations that were directly related to the magnets unit and were very focused and motivated. Working on this science unit became the students' priority, because this unit was engaging and challenged the students to manipulate materials and make observations on their own. As evidence of their self-directed learning, they were totally immersed in testing and redesigning their maglev cars. They were so engaged that there was no frustration and lots of patience—quite admirable for second graders.

References

Feldman, N. 1996. Challenges of implementing inquiry. *Concept* 10 (4): 3–7.

Iwasyk, M. 1997. Questioning kids: 'Experts' sharing. *Science and Children* 34 (1): 42–47.

Koch, J. 2005. *Science stories: Science methods for elementary and middle school teachers.* Boston: Houghton Mifflin.

Krensky, S. 1992. *All about magnets.* New York: Scholastic.

Murrow, C. 1999. Magnets in the hands of seven year olds. *Connect* 12 (4): 5–9.

Thinking Outside the Box:

No Child Left Inside!

Kim C. Sadler, Cindi Smith-Walters, and Tracey R. Ring
Middle Tennessee State University

Leslie Marrie S. Lasater
Homer Pittard Campus School

Setting

The commitment to "leaving no child inside" began at Homer Pittard Campus School with the implementation of the Ecology, Future, and Global (EFG) Curriculum. The original EFG design was conceived by futurist Joel Barker in the late 1970s and brought to Campus School in 1994 after a Middle Tennessee State University (MTSU) professor from the elementary and special education department attended an EFG Collaborative. Today, 10 of 14 teachers implement a modified form of EFG at Campus School. Since 1995, these teachers have used unique talents and resources to extend EFG beyond its original potential to include an outdoor classroom and nature site with elements such as an amphitheater, student workstations, many diverse wildlife habitats, greenhouse, tracking pit, and a culinary herb garden.

Each year an overarching theme or unit of study is chosen. The National Science Education Standards (NSES) and the Tennessee State Science Standards serve as the guide for inquiry processes. Always interdisciplinary, the theme then coordinates with one or more of the particular EFG domain(s): ecology, future, or global studies. Teachers meet semimonthly to brainstorm and plan projects. Discussion topics include integrating skills, assessment techniques, and varied needs of students at different grade levels. To make the best use of community assets and to facilitate networking of resources, teachers have implemented a Community Connections Council and a Parent Advisory Board. Both groups are composed of experts in the fields pertaining to the theme being studied or the nature trail or both. Communication is consistent because groups meet as needed during the year, or at least twice a year, as projects dictate.

Where IS the Outside?

Campus School is a laboratory school associated with the College of Education at MTSU. Part of the Rutherford County School System for 75 years, Campus School has served students in grades K–6, preservice teachers, and university faculty in a number of ways. Rutherford County is in the geographic center of Tennessee and enrollment in the system's 38 schools has increased from approximately 26,000 in 2000 to 31,500 in 2004. The 2000 National Census figures for Rutherford County indicated a 53.5% population increase in the past 10 years with much of the growth occurring in the urban sector. Although Rutherford County is home to MTSU, the largest undergraduate university in the state, only 18.7% of the residents hold a bachelor's degree or better, and fewer than 74% hold a high school diploma or its equivalent. In addition, more than a quarter (26.4%) of the population is younger than 18 years of age, stressing the public school sector to its limits.

In the Rutherford County system, per pupil spending is at $5,886, below the state average of $6,997, and significantly below the national average of $8,724. These numbers are surprising, because Rutherford County is the 245th largest school system in the United States and is ranked number one in Tennessee in new school construction for both K–12 and non-K–12 public education. Apparently, there is just not enough money to go around, so innovative approaches to science education are needed.

As part of this county system, Campus School serves approximately 300 preK–grade-6 students, 5% of who qualify for a free or reduced-price lunch. The student population is classified as 87% white, 10% black, and 3% other, including Asian and Hispanic. Two teachers are at each grade level for a total of 14 classroom teachers. Campus School is one of several "choice" schools in the RC System, and students from throughout the county attend. Developed as a laboratory school for the university, preservice teacher training is part of the school's mission. The aging three-story red brick building is located in an urban and well-developed historic residential section of Murfreesboro adjacent to Middle Tennessee State University.

The Campus School/NSES Connection

When one reviews the *More Emphasis* areas outlined by NSES, it is clear the constructivist theory abounds. For the teacher, individual student interests, strengths, experiences, and needs are top priorities. In addition, student inquiry, cooperative learning that includes sharing, and continuous assessment of student understanding are also significant. The NSES define assessment as an area of key emphasis, and assessment should be based on rich, well-structured knowledge, scientific understanding, and reasoning. Assessment allows us to gauge what students understand, achievement, and learning opportunities. In keeping with the NSES, it is the intention at Campus School that students understand scientific concepts and develop abilities of inquiry via integrating all aspects of science content. The program is designed so that fewer fundamental science concepts are studied and subject matter disciplines are learned in the context of inquiry, technology, and the history and nature of science. Clearly the NSES stress that students will be engaged in meaningful active learning.

With this in mind, the Campus School program's unique features smoothly dovetail with the guidelines advocated by NSTA related to teaching. Examples include selecting and adapting curriculum, guiding students in active and extended scientific inquiry, sharing responsibility for learning with students, and working with other teachers to enhance the science programs. So many of the *More Emphasis* areas are met that it is difficult to draw a direct line between the campus school model and the NSES. Those related to content include "less is more" by addressing fewer fundamental science concepts in depth. Students do not just know scientific facts about the wetland, but they also have been in the water, observed amphibian metamorphosis, and caught insects or fish at the wetland site they have developed on their campus.

From the perspective of programs, students visit the same outdoor stations year after year but explore different themes related to the station. An example, related to using the Campus School wetland and pond site by grade level, consists of

- kindergarten = study of insect metamorphosis;
- first grade = study of change via tadpole metamorphosis;
- second grade = identification and natural history of birds using the pond as a rest stop during migration or for resident birds;
- third grade = examination of vertebrates living in, on, or near the pond; and
- fourth grade = identification and interactions of invertebrates, specifically insects found in or near the pond habitat and food chains and food webs related to pond inhabitants.

Each outdoor station has depth and breadth that spiral the curriculum from kindergarten to the upper elementary grades. The costs to build each outdoor station cannot be calculated because they are a consequence of student involvement and an active parent volunteer network. In addition to the pond and wetland, students transplanted plants from a rare ecosystem—a cedar glade undergoing development for a shopping center—over a five-year time span. A native tree trail, native flower garden, butterfly garden, herb garden, and Tennessee Iris garden were designed and planted by the students. Thinking of each outdoor station as an environmental center is the result of insightful planning by the teachers, students, and parent volunteers over many years. No Child Left Inside succeeds as a program because it seamlessly incorporates field and laboratory experiences within the schoolyard. Although the emphasis is on science, other subject areas—such as mathematics, language arts, and social studies—are naturally integrated into the inquiry-based learning activities.

Teamwork—Parents and Faculty

Each member of the Homer Pittard Campus School faculty holds a master's degree or higher and has completed at least five years of elementary teaching. More than half participate in EFG, and most have been involved since the program started in 1995. Kindergarten, first, second, third, fourth, and fifth grades participate. The Parent Advisory Board, whose duties are to inform and educate other parents about this learning philosophy and to further community connections, is composed of two parents from each classroom. Outdoor classroom workstations enable students to record data, write observations, or collect samples as they work on assignments. Teachers also work with individuals or small student groups here. Supply trunks of equipment and materials for each habitat along the trail have been developed and are exchanged among classrooms.

Taking It Outside the Box

Campus School faculty believe learning is not confined to within the four walls of a classroom. With experts in various fields, teachers and their students take part in fieldwork and other activities that allow them to transfer and apply new experiences and knowledge to the outdoor classroom. The trail includes 10 varied habitats and an amphitheater. As each habitat changes over time and the Nature Trail evolves, it is important to connect and weave subjects, skills, and experiences, that is, to foster the realization that everything in learning is interconnected. Two examples of this are

- Extending the walking trail a distance of one kilometer: This enables a teacher to integrate larger distances, a difficult concept for young students in mathematics, with the outdoor classroom. Teachers and students walk the trail to experience the length and distance of one kilometer.
- When it was discovered that the campus had only tree species with simple leaves, work began immediately to add diversity by planting trees with compound and doubly compound leaves. A classroom extension asks students to select a tree, identify it, research it, and take data such as height, age, or size. Later, students develop dichotomous keys to aid in identification.

Several unique habitat and learning stations found at Campus School are included and could be easily reproduced at other school sites. Examples of integrating varied subject content, NSES, and mandated skills are included within each narrative.

Native Tree Trail

To introduce students to the trees on the trail, teachers begin with the scientific vocabulary necessary to accurately describe leaves. They use words such as *palmate*, *lobed*, *serrated*, and *entire* to create dichotomous keys. Tree silhouettes are observed, allowing students to classify trees by leaf and branch arrangement and growth. Teachers encourage students to notice and observe distinctive features such as flowers and fruit that also aid in identification. Trees are classified as deciduous or evergreen, and research is conducted to determine if the tree is native or exotic to this region.

A Dichotomous Key Developed by Students to Identify
Trees on Campus School Grounds

1a. The leaf is broad and flat........5
1b. The leaf is needlelike.......2

2a. The needles are round......3
2b. The needles are flat......4

3a. The needles are in bundles of 3, 6–9" long.......Loblolly Pine
3b. The needles are in bundles of 2, 1–3"............. Virginia White Pine

4a. The leaves are scalelike, .06", alternating on branchlets...Red Cedar
4b. The needles are flat, ½", with 2 white lines underneath........Hemlock

5a. The leaf is a compound leaf......Walnut
5b. The leaf is simple......6

6a. The leaf is lobed.......7
6b. The leaf is not lobed.......12

7a. The leaf has spines......Holly
7b. The leaf does not have spines.......8

8a. Leaf veins are palmate......9
8b. Leaf veins are not palmate........Red Oak

9a. Leaf petiole is mostly red, 3-5 lobes......Red Maple
9b. Leaf petiole is not mostly red......10

10a. Leaves droop, at the origin of the petiole there are 2 tiny leaflets, 3 lobes.....Black Maple
10b. Leaves do not droop........11

11a. Leaf usually 5 lobed, most abundant tree around Campus School Grounds.......Sugar Maple
11b. Leaf deeply lobed, silvery underneath, 5 lobes.......Silver Maple

12a. Leaf is fan shaped, foul smelling fruit, a gymnosperm......Ginko
12b. Not like the above, an angiosperm......13

13a. Leaves serrated.......14
13b. Leaves not serrated......15

14a. Leaf veins pinnate.....Elm
14b. Leaf veins arcuate......Sugarberry (Hackberry)

15a. Leaf veins pinnate......Magnolia
15b. Leaf veins arcuate......16

16a. Produces large, juicy, orange fruit.....Persimmon
16b. Produces small, ½" diameter red berries.....Dogwood

One mathematics application is counting tree rings by taking and observing an increment bore sample from each trunk. To further integrate mathematics and make learning relevant, students explore circumference and diameter using tape measures and rulers. After using jar lids to explore the formula for circumference and how it relates to diameter, students, armed with calculators, measure the circumference of the trees and calculate diameters. Students do journaling when studying each habitat to reinforce writing and language skills. Art activities include pressing and rubbing leaves for clothing and portfolio art.

Pond and Wetland

Each year students observe animals such as insects, toads, frogs, and lizards around the wetland area. Students are encouraged to look for eggs, larvae, footprints, and other signs indicative of animal life. From animal study, classes proceed to observing and studying plants. Together they keep journals throughout the year and construct tables on what they found in the wetland during each season. They write class stories about seasonal changes and compare and contrast what they find in and around the wetland area as opposed to their backyard. Teachers guide and assist as students research the need for wetlands. After research, discussion, and fieldwork, children, parents, and experts typically assist in a community wetland cleanup or habitat-enhancement project. Seasonal studies continue with other topics.

The importance of water is one offshoot in which students study the differences between salt, fresh, and glacial water. They find it intriguing that our bodies are made up of about 65% water, just like the Earth's surface. Writing and research skills develop as students begin to study wetland plants and animals in more depth. Questions they pose (or have posed to them) might include: What is needed in a wetland area for these plants and animals to live there? How deep should it be? What temperatures occur and why? What kinds of foods are available? How many of each type (species) can live in a wetland area this size? To answer, students must read, write, and share information with classmates, and teachers continually provide literature, research materials, and relevant internet resources. Students work in pairs or small groups throughout the year to develop presentations to give to classmates and students in other classrooms. They conclude the year by comparing wetland with surrounding gardens. Through this study, children realize how dependent one habitat is upon another and gain the ability to explain how other habitats benefit from wetlands, showing that real learning has taken place.

Butterfly Garden

To attract butterflies, it is important to plant flowers and shrubs that are both hardy and native to Tennessee. Each fall, students experience the garden from the ground up as they sharpen observational skills and they lie on the ground and think about the garden. The teacher poses questions such as: "What do you see?" "What do you smell?" and "What do you hear?". Using their experiences, students construct graphs depicting what they "sensed," write stories, and record their information in journals and observation logs for later comparisons. In the spring, butterflies are raised from larvae. During this time students observe, discuss, and study metamorphosis and species diversity. Later when the butterflies are released, students write stories about them and the travels they may be having.

Through caring for the garden, studying the plant and animal life, and raising and releasing butterflies, students begin to understand the relationship between past, present, and future actions. They are exposed to the impact human actions have on the environment and learn how they as individuals may effect change.

The Homer Pittard butterfly garden.

Cedar Glade

This habitat area was established by transplanting cedar glade plants from areas slated to be destroyed by construction and new development. Each student was assigned a specific glade plant to research and report on. Plant characteristics researched included size and height, scientific and common names, specific glade zone, and time of flowering. This information was presented to a small group and to the class as a whole. Classes traveled to nearby glades and observed glade plants and studied the habitats. An exciting aspect was

Nashville Breadroot

	Historical Info	Our Test Results
Flower:	April—May	Yes—May
Strata:	gravel & grass/shrubs	4% rock 36% gravel 60% small shrubs
Temperature:		76.57°F 24.76°F
Soil Depth:	2–8 in/5–20 cm	4.9 in/12.58 cm
Plant Height:	6 in/15 cm	2.5 in/6.4 cm
Moisture:	medium to low	low
Light:	medium to high	high

Students researched and reported on glade plants.

the extraordinary opportunity to study rare plants. Two examples were Pyne's ground-plum, found only in Rutherford County, and the endangered Tennessee coneflower, found only in Middle Tennessee.

As they studied the glade habitat throughout the year and compared different glades, students used and developed maps, determined stages of succession in glade formation, identified fossils, and used basic tools of science such as magnifying glasses. Questions students asked or attempted to answer included "Why does this area have rocks?" "Where is my flower in this glade?" "Why are they so small?" "Why aren't the flowers colorful?" "Does that make it of less value?" and "What is the purpose of the cedar glades?"

Additionally, a Cedar Glade quilt, picturing a variety of glade plants and the names of students who researched them, is displayed in the hallway. The quilt is made of pictures that cannot readily be found in books or on the internet. It serves as a unique visual prompt of past learning and as a research reference tool for students currently studying these plants. Each spring students visit glades threatened by on-site construction and rescue plants. These are transplanted to the glade area developed on school property. Through habitat study, students gain a sense of connection to the environment, responsibility, and stewardship.

Bird Habitat

When students research birds, and indeed all living things, they find food, water, shelter, and space are needed. With this realization, students do research to determine the types of plants that will provide these necessities and attract birds. Past habitat improvement projects include increasing shelter in the form of an arbor with a berm built with the help of parents, MTSU, and the grounds supervisor. For easy access to water, the bird habitat had to be located near the wetland.

In studying birds, students find that feet, wings, and beaks determine where a bird lives and what it eats. It is not by accident that certain birds have beaks that resemble tongs, while others have spoons, and still others have beaks like tweezers. Because beak shape determines what birds can eat, it also determines the types of plants needed in the school's bird habitat. It is rewarding to hear the students explain the variety of plants and how they are important to birds that feed upon them to a group of invited guests at juried presentations each spring.

Tennessee Iris Garden

The environmental trail mission statement states that all habitats will incorporate organisms native to Tennessee. With this in mind, it was decided to include the Iris Garden—the iris is the Tennessee state flower—planted in the shape of Tennessee. Students were involved from inception to final product. They predicted, then measured the lengths of the sides and determined types of materials necessary for the border. They measured, planted, dug, fertilized, identified, and labeled.

First steps included making a "people outline" to determine garden size. Next, students studied the three grand divisions of Tennessee, east, middle and west; the state bird (mocking-bird); the state tree (tulip poplar); the state flower (iris); and the four main rivers that run through Tennessee (Tennessee, Mississippi, Cumberland, and Stones). Each element was prominently labeled in the garden with stones and a map legend or was planted. The rivers were outlined with landscape tubing stuffed with blue plastic bags. Throughout the year, students maintain the garden with mulching, weeding, watering, general cleaning, and trimming. A similar garden could be designed for any state.

Herb Garden

The herb garden provides opportunities to study annuals and perennials, and students enjoy studying insects, bees, and pollination. Students were intrigued with smelling, touching, and feeling the difference in leaves, stems, flowers, and more in this garden as opposed to the typical vegetable garden. To separate and identify the various herbs, students painted rocks and located them throughout the garden.

The greatest benefit from establishing and taking care of the herb garden has been the cooking. Finding recipes, reading and following the directions, measuring ingredients, mixing student-grown herbs, and then cooking them is a special learning experience. Writing about this in journals, retelling experiences in class stories, and sharing yearly garden changes with other classes is learning at its highest and most enjoyable level. Another feature of the garden is the sundial where students learn Roman numerals and the history of how the Sun was once widely used to keep time.

Animal Tracking Pit

The animal-tracking pit is a simple addition to the trail. Because the trail has been designed to attract animal life, it is beneficial for students to see the evidence of various paw prints of animals we attract. The pit, located on one end of the trail, is outlined with examples of possible paw prints of animals such as raccoon, squirrel, and possum that may come to visit, and students observe these, record findings in journals, compare them to the grid to identify the animal, and even measure the print for use in classroom graphing exercises.

Wildflower Garden

Native wildflowers add beauty and attract wildlife to the surrounding habitats. Butterflies provide natural pollination for annuals and perennials, and students weed, dig, and replant yearly as needed. Studying plants to find scientific names, habitats in Tennessee, and specific growing requirements are just a few of the research activities students undertake in garden studies. During winter months, they raise small cuttings in the greenhouse and then transplant them to the site.

Teaching + Learning + Assessment = Success

Teaching. Curriculum implemented today must prepare young people for successful citizenship and careers in a global environment. This includes instruction in academic content that can be immediately applied to real-world issues via integrated, project-based learning models. Student achievement is advanced when assessment is aligned with instruction and intended student outcomes. The EFG program and NSES provide this foundation at Campus School. Each spring, faculty brainstorm, discuss, and agree upon the following year's theme of study. Project planning begins and subject area skills are integrated. During the summer, teachers gather materials and meet in smaller groups to discuss specific projects or multiage grouping of students for related projects. As the school year begins, they confirm final details and share assessment methods.

Assessment. A number of different assessment techniques, both authentic and alternative, are used in evaluating student progress. Specifics are outlined in the sections that follow.

Authentic Assessment Tools

Data. Data at all outdoor classroom stations are taken and recorded. Water temperature, dissolved oxygen levels, and general water chemistry are taken at the wetlands, and species inventories are taken in each habitat and results are compared to earlier years in a continually expanding database. Teachers have developed dichotomous keys to tree and plant species and share them with students, members who serve on the community council, and the Parent Advisory Board.

Tests. Campus School teachers occasionally give traditional pencil-and-paper exams, but they are not their preferred assessment technique. When possible, they incorporate graphs, pictures, charts, and tables within assessment tools so students use higher-order thinking skills and apply what they know to new experiences.

Alternative Assessment Tools

Portfolios. Students create and develop portfolios to reflect work as projects progress. In some cases, teachers and students confer to decide what will be selected for inclusion in the portfolio. An emphasis is placed on selection of work that represents the student's growth over a period of time.

Presentations. Juried presentations are conducted at the end of each year. After months of studying a particular topic, small groups of students, using a teacher-prepared rubric provided earlier, prepare a presentation for one or more invited guests. Guests might include members from the Parent Advisory Board, Community Connections Council, or the community at large. Guests are paired with groups of students who present their particular topic. On some occasions posters with specific information are needed, while at other times a PowerPoint presentation is the preferred medium of communication. A main objective for these juried presentations is to provide students the opportunity to develop presentation and communication skills. Information delivery, eye contact, clear and complete sentences, partner teamwork and sharing of the presentation, dispensing all information, and more are incorporated within the rubric. Teachers receive additional feedback from invited guests via a survey form, and peers are given the opportunity to provide feedback to peers.

Rubrics/Checklists. Rubrics and checklists are an invaluable way to accomplish the difficult task of assigning grades. A specific example used is one from the wetland study. Students visited Black Fox Wetlands, collected animal and plant data, and took samples and pictures. Upon returning to the classroom, they charted and compared data as a class, then continued research to gather additional wetlands information. To deepen understanding, comparisons and analogies were made within small groups, then as a class. Sample analogies were

- Wetlands are like sponges in that they can save water during wet times and make it available to animals and plants during dry periods.
- Wetlands are like hotels for migrating birds. Here birds stop, rest, and eat while on their journeys.

Using checklists and student-generated information, each pupil receives a "traditional" science, language arts, and composition grade for comparing and contrasting skills, presentations, writing, and data collection.

Unique Assessment Tools

With assistance from the MTSU Digital Media Center, student-generated CDs on various topics have been developed. The cedar glade CD, for example, contains drawings, pictures, interactive diagrams, and plant photographs with scientific names, glade zone, height, size of leaves and blooms, and expected blooming dates of plants studied. The CD includes student comments about what they have learned and individual student journals with notes from guest lectures and research. The creative writing aspect includes haiku and cinquain poems. PowerPoint presentations with music from each class are archived in the school library for future student research.

Videotaped Exit Interviews. As each school year ends, students are asked to participate in a video project. Parent volunteers talk with children on camera about what they have done and learned during the year. This is not only a keepsake video for parents, but it also provides valuable information to teachers about curriculum. The question-and-answer segment consists of 10 questions and takes approximately five to eight minutes to complete.

The questions include

- Who is the most important person in the world?
- What would you like to change about your school?
- What is your favorite activity with your family?
- How can you help the world be a better place?
- What did you enjoy most this year in school?

The number one response from five-year-old kindergarten students to the question, "Who is the most important person in the world?" is "My mom." Most responses change as early as the next year in first grade to their teacher, a grandparent, or a favorite relative. Many kindergarten students mention the herb garden and cooking when asked what they enjoyed most that year in school.

By the time students reach fourth, fifth, and sixth grades, responses to the first question extend further than family. They include sports figures or TV actors or musicians. An interesting note is that students who are most intimately involved with the environmental trail and who experience heavier integration and exposure to science seem to have greater recognition of people and their importance in relation to the positions of responsibility they hold. For example, responses including the president of the United States and senators or other politicians are often given due to the decisions they make that effect change. Many students mention things directly connected to the science experiences on the nature trail, such as taking nature hikes, raising butterflies to release in the gardens, and learning about trees.

Future Assessment and Research

In 2001, the first class to have all seven years recorded (kindergarten through sixth grade) graduated from Campus School. Currently the tapes are part of a research project to explore the impact of this unique program on student knowledge and attitudes.

Project Assessment. A prime example of one positive effect of the Campus School program as it blends EFG and NSES can be seen in its fourth-grade Tennessee Comprehensive Assessment Program's Writing Assessment Summary from 1996–2002 (Table 1).

Table 1 . *Campus School 4th Grade Tennessee Comprehensive Writing Assessment Summary*							
	1996	**1997**	**1998**	**1999**	**2000**	**2001**	**2002**
Three-Year Score Average	0	0	3.7	3.7	4.0	4.03	4.38
Total Tested	52	49	47	50	47	48	48

On a scale that ranges from a low of 1 to a high score of 6 (1=deficient, 2=flawed, 3=limited, 4=competent, 5=strong, 6=outstanding) the yearly average has steadily increased from a low of 3.5 in 1996, when the tests were implemented, to a high in 2002 of 4.75. Tennessee State Guidelines state that schools scoring 4 or higher are noted as *Exemplary*. This is a strong statement indeed, drawing a connection between what is being done in the sciences and its effect upon writing and communication skills. Further data are not available because this assessment was moved to fifth grade in 2003.

Homer Pittard Campus School is unique in that it is a university laboratory school. When comparing its median national percentile achievement scores to those of similar students at other university-related laboratory schools in Tennessee (Memphis University and East Tennessee State University), we find Campus School scores higher in a number of areas (Table 2). The State of Tennessee does not report the scores for first and second grade. Third-grade scores are used in the comparison because the EFG Curriculum and associated NSES are implemented in grade 3.

Table 2. *Median National Percentile 3rd Grade Average (1999 to 2003) Based on Norm Referenced Tests*			
	Reading	**Math**	**Science**
Homer Pittard Campus School	78.50	84.50	74.75
Memphis University Campus School	55.50	57.25	51.50
East Tennessee State University Campus School	66.00	66.00	66.50

Data compiled from *www.state.tn.us/education/mreport.htm*

NSES are not only useful and important in science, but they also support and complement learning in other subject areas. In the reading and mathematics scores of Campus School third graders, a steady increase has been observed over the past few years. These scores and those for science and social studies typically are higher than those of other university schools within Tennessee. Additionally, as scores continue to climb they vary less than 5 points from year to year. The outdoor classroom, curriculum, and NSES have been frameworks for success.

These scores, nontraditional assessment practices, and anecdotal evidence from students, parents, school support staff, and faculty all support that integrated, hands-on, experiential learning tied to real-world application and science process skills works.

Learning Outside the Box

Educators prepare students to be successful citizens in the 21st century. To do this, student learning must be relevant to life. The real world is not divided into stand-alone subjects; it integrates knowledge and skills from all aspects of learning. In addition, greater access is available to a vast amount of information not currently found or available in textbooks today. With this constantly expanding array of information and the importance of real-world application, it is imperative that opportunities for students to experience this way of thinking and learning are present in schools.

Assessment in the real world is based on performance. Students at Campus School are given the opportunity to learn how to learn rather than simply what to learn. All children, regardless of age, grade, gender, handicap, ability, or learning disability participate in each project and the associated habitat studies on the Nature Trail.

Teachers should prepare students for their future, therefore schools must reflect social and intellectual change. Through the implementation of the EFG curriculum and the establishment of the outdoor classroom, Campus School provides integration of science into the lives of students. NSES move educators away from traditional thinking about teaching and learning and reinforce relevant, thoughtful, and useful life learning for their students.

References

Barnes, B. 1998. *Learning architecture for the 21st century*. Torrance, CA: Griffin.

Barnes, B. 1999. *Schools transformed for the 21st century*. Torrance, CA: Griffin.

Enger, S. K., and R. E. Yager. 2001. *Assessing student understanding in science*. Thousand Oaks, CA: Corwin Press.

National Research Council (NRC). 1998. *National Science Education Standards*. Washington, DC: National Academy Press.

Tennessee Advisory Commission of Intergovernmental Relations. 2003. *Rutherford County, Tennessee Selected Statistical Information*. Retrieved June 13, 2003, from *www.state.tn.us/tacir/CountyProfile/RutherfordProfile. htm*.

Tennessee Department of Education. 2003. *Tennessee Science Curriculum Standards*. Retrieved April 18, 2006, from *www.state.tn.us/education/ci/cistandards2001/sci/ciscience.htm*.

United States Bureau of the Census. 2003. *Population Division. Population Paper Listing #47, Population Electronic Product #45*. Retrieved June 13, 2003. Website no longer available.

Empowering Children

Jeffrey S. Englert
Johnson Elementary School of the Arts

Setting

This was written as I was in my sixth year as a first- and second-grade teacher at Johnson Elementary School of the Arts, located in Cedar Rapids, Iowa. My educational background includes a master's degree in early childhood education with an emphasis in science and mathematics. Johnson Elementary School of the Arts is a public school with an enrollment of around 355 students with 69% of the students qualifying for free or reduced-price lunches and minorities accounting for 52% of the total school population. The many learning opportunities available for the students, not only during the school day but also before and after school, include chess club, singing groups, and intramural sports.

Changing Emphases in the National Science Education Standards

When reflecting upon the changes recommended in the National Science Education Standards (NSES), I realized that many of the points identified for greater emphasis were already components of my teaching practice—for example, the emphasis placed on selecting and adapting curriculum. In our district, one of the kits used is the "Life Cycle of the Butterfly." In working with the kit, I wanted the students to experience the facets of inquiry—to question and to wonder—and I wanted to provide relevance for the students.

A second example of greater emphasis in the teaching standards called for the teacher to function as an intellectual and a reflective practitioner. Throughout the entire study of the butterflies unit, I worked to implement an inquiry-learning model as we were studying and learning and at the same time I addressed the district standards. When I reviewed the written records that we kept, I noted that many of the questions that the students generated at the beginning of the unit aligned with guiding questions that were set by the district. Instead of my providing these questions in advance, however, I found the students were capable of posing these guiding questions on their own. What they wanted to know was already in alignment with district curricular documents.

Multiple Process Skills—Manipulation, Cognitive, and Procedural

Throughout the entire butterflies unit, students used multiple ways to express and represent their newly learned knowledge. They used dance and movement, constructed a caterpillar model with food items, used writing, and communicated in various ways.

Through the use of documentation boards, the students shared their scientific knowledge with other students or adults. When students have the opportunity to be involved in the learning process, they become empowered and take ownership. This is a very effective learning technique.

Teaching Lessons

As an educator, I feel that engaging students in the learning process is vital. By using an inquiry method of teaching, you are extending an invitation to all of the students to provide input. Their thinking is validated when their questions are used as research questions for their investigations. Within the Cedar Rapids School District, one of the science kits for second grade is the Science & Technology for Children (STC) unit "Life Cycle of Butterflies," developed by the National Science Resources Center (NSRC). The district selected this kit because it was aligned with the NSES Standard C: Life and Environmental Science. The standards set by the district expect that students develop the understandings that

- All animals depend on plants. Some animals eat plants and others eat animals that eat the plants;
- All plants and animals have life cycles that go from birth, to adulthood, and to death;
- People, plants, and animals live in communities or habitats;
- Changes to the environment of a living organism can be helpful and/or harmful; and
- Plants and animals have special external features that help them thrive in different places.

Every second-grade teacher within the district receives the kit with all of the necessary supplies. They are all given the same materials and manuals for this unit along with directions for ordering the butterfly larvae. Science journals are provided for each child to record his or her information, actions, and questions. The manual is written so that the unit could be completed with very little investigation or inquiry undertaken by the students or teachers.

Believing that students learn better by incorporating their personal knowledge and questions, I decided that I would use this kit as a resource for my "Life Cycle of a Butterfly" unit. Thus the journey to implementing an inquiry approach began in my classroom. Instead of reading a script from a manual, I wanted to determine if, by using an inquiry approach to learning, we would be able to meet the district standards and benchmarks that had been set for all of the district second graders. Throughout this entire process, I noted which benchmarks were being addressed or not addressed. I referred to the manual for ideas and assistance as needed. During the fall of 2004, I began to gather documentation as I began the unit in my classroom. One approach was to keep a journal in which I made notes about the process.

Selected Teaching Journal Entries

These representative journal entries provide evidence of planning and reflection. They are qualitative evidence of my interpretations of the learning experiences in my classroom.

Day 1

The first time I met with the students for their science class, I wanted to elicit their responses to "What is a scientist?" The whole idea behind this process was to see what prior knowledge the students already had about people who do science. I had a piece of chart paper, markers, and made a web and placed the question in the middle. After I asked the question, the students began to raise their hands. Some of the responses that students provided follow.

"What is a scientist?"

- A person who wears a white coat and is old.
- A man who does experiments.
- Scientists know magic.
- They use microscopes to look at things.

After I recorded the students' responses on chart paper, I praised them for having ideas and told them that we were going to hang the chart paper web in the classroom. I began to talk with the students about how I was a scientist, and then I started to list some of the students' names. The students looked at me with confused faces and said, "I'm not a scientist." I explained to them that a scientist is a person who asks questions, does research, and investigates to see if his or her ideas are supported. I then provided some examples of why I classified myself as a scientist. I wanted to find out more about our classroom pet rabbit. I then asked the students if they could think of a time when they had questions about a specific topic or item and did some investigation or research to find evidence that the information was accurate. Students began to raise their hands to share what they had questioned and learned. Each student who shared had a great sense of pride in his or her story. I told the students that when they went home that evening, they should tell their parents or family members about how and why they were like scientists. When reflecting on this lesson, I realize the excitement and curiosity that the students had about science was amazing. By having the students become involved in their learning and allowing them to participate, it opened up a great entry point for my lesson the next day when I introduced our science unit on butterflies.

Day 2

I began the science class by asking the students if they had talked to their family members about how and why they were scientists. Many students raised their hands, and they shared their responses with the rest of the class. Today, I introduced the class to the idea that we were going to be learning more about some creepy crawlers called caterpillars. Their job was to think like scientists and tell us what they already knew about caterpillars as I recorded their contributions under the heading labeled "What we know about caterpillars." This type of recording is also similar to using a KWL (Know, Want to know, Learned) chart within the classroom. After I asked the question, the students wanted to share everything they knew about caterpillars. Some sample responses were

- Caterpillars climb on trees.
- Caterpillars like to eat apples.
- Caterpillars turn into butterflies.
- I found a caterpillar at my house, and I kept him as a pet.

The responses from the students ranged from knowing that caterpillars can be found at home to knowing that caterpillars change into another living creature. After I recorded the students' knowledge, the chart could be revisited when we completed the unit of study.

I labeled the next sheet of chart paper "Questions we have about caterpillars." I feel that a critical piece in inquiry modeling is to have the students verbalize scientific questions for all to use, research, and then investigate. While I was recording the questions, I made sure that I made note of everyone's questions—no matter if the answer were obvious or if it were a more in-depth question. Showing the students that every question is worthy and that each student has a voice is very important. Some questions that students produced about caterpillars were

- How do caterpillars climb upside down?
- How do caterpillars change into a butterfly?
- What do caterpillars eat?
- Do caterpillars swim?
- Where do caterpillars live?

After recording all of the questions, we reviewed both of our charts. The students were very excited about this new unit and were amazed at the information that we gathered from just these two exercises. At the end of the school day, I looked at the questions that the students asked about caterpillars along with the set of district standards. After comparing the students' questions and the NSES content standard, I concluded that the questions that the students raised corresponded to both NSES and district standards. For example, "What do caterpillars eat?" aligns with the standard that covers developing the understanding that all animals depend on plants, that some animals eat plants, and that others eat animals that eat the plants. Another question that aligns with the standards is "Where do caterpillars live?" This question meets the standard that covers developing the understanding that people, plants, and animals live in communities or habitats.

It was apparent to me that my students had identified some great guiding questions that involved higher-order thinking. Instead of my standing in front of the students lecturing on key areas that we were going to be learning about caterpillars, we used student-generated ideas. Too often, we teachers get caught up in teaching the curriculum. If we just slowed down and listened to the students, we would find that various learning skills and opportunities for higher-order thinking are within our reach. Having the students contribute to the curriculum is what I used within this inquiry process. Often teachers seem to fear the use of inquiry, as if they are afraid to give up some of their control, and they are not accustomed to the idea of teacher and students working together to determine the direction of study. But by giving up some control, the teacher can interact with students and together they can build deeper understandings of concepts, topics, and science skills.

Day 3

After reflecting on the questions the students produced on Day 2, I knew I wanted to begin the unit with learning activities about care for caterpillars. In the kit's teacher's manual, I found some basic information and directions, and then I incorporated the questions identified by my students. For example, the second lesson in the teacher's manual described what these particular caterpillars ate and told the students to place mallow food in their caterpillar containers. After working with the mallow, they were to write in their journals what the mallow food looked like, what it smelled like, and what it felt like. Along with this work, they were to color a mallow plant worksheet.

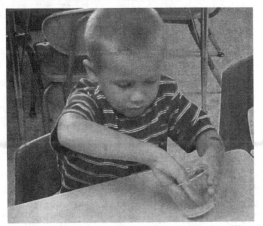

Student puts mallow food into his caterpillar container.

From this information base, I created my own plans regarding what we were going to accomplish. Yes, the class placed the mallow food in their caterpillar containers and filled out the journal page as suggested. But then I moved on to questioning the students for the major part of the lesson. For example, when we talked about what the caterpillars ate, I talked and showed them that some kinds of Iowa caterpillars preferred to eat milkweed plants. I brought in a milkweed plant for the students to see and feel. This led to some great discussions on what would happen if there were not any milkweed plants around and also on what caterpillars eat in the winter. The questions that the students raised were a perfect match with the first district standard: "Develop understanding that all animals depend on plants." Some animals eat plants, and others eat animals that eat the plants. Pulling in real-life material—the milkweed plant—prompted the students to continue questioning and wondering what would happen in different scenarios. In an ideal classroom situation, I would have had students bring in items they could find outside their homes or on the school grounds, so we could have discussed whether or not the caterpillars would eat the items they collected. The school setting I am in, however, is one where most of the children live in apartment buildings with very limited exposure to nature or outdoor living. I knew that, if I did not supply some of the materials, the students would not have had this learning experience.

After the lesson was complete, we had a recess. What do you think the students were looking for? Milkweed plants and caterpillars!

Day 4

I introduced the students to some tools that scientists use. We discussed how people in their different jobs use different tools they need to work successfully. The students offered a great list of items a scientist uses. It included: white coats, microscopes, nets, magnifying glasses (hand lens), and books. I told the students that we were going to be using a tool that some scientists use everyday—a magnifying glass. Here, I showed the students what a magnifying glass was, asked them to use one, and to experiment with it at their desks. After a couple of minutes, I then asked how the magnifying glass works. The students raised their hands to say that you can see things that are very small and things look bigger with a magnifying glass. I then asked, "How do you make sure that the item you are looking at with a magnifying glass is in focus?" One student raised his hand and said that you can move the magnifying glass either closer to or farther away from your item to see it clearly. I then asked the student to come to the front of the classroom to demonstrate this skill.

By doing this, I showed that I value and respect students' thinking. They could see how they are capable of answering questions through investigation and that they could become "experts" on a topic, concept, or skill. While the student demonstrated to the class, the rest of the students followed his instructions. Again, I asked the class if there was any other way to get the items they were looking at to focus in their magnifying glass. Then many students' hands rose because they knew that they were going to be able to demonstrate it to the class. After we learned how to use the magnifying glass, I told the students that our caterpillars had arrived and that we were going to examine them using the magnifying glasses. No suggestions for preliminary experiences with the magnifying glasses were included in the teacher's manual, but considering their use was productive for the students.

In the third lesson, the teacher's manual for "Life Cycle of Butterflies" suggested that students use the magnifying glass to see if they could determine whether their caterpillars were alive. Looking closely was a lead-in to having students discuss the needs of living creatures—for air, water, food, appropriate temperature, and shelter. Finally, I asked the students to fill out a journal page on how the caterpillar received each of these items when the caterpillars were cultured.

If we are to engage students and have them develop into lifelong learners in science, they need multiple opportunities for exploration and discovery. As teachers, we must think about ways to expand and extend student experiences instead of having our students rely on scripted information or facts. Even when we as teachers are implementing quality materials, we need to find ways to implement these materials so they are in alignment with inquiry.

After students had practiced using the magnifying lenses, they examined the caterpillars in their containers. The students discussed with me how they could tell if their caterpillars were living or, in some instances, how they could tell that the caterpillar had already died. We generated a list of descriptive words that I recorded on the chalkboard for the students to see. This also reinforced the use of terms that we had been working on in journal groups.

Practicing Skills

As we continued the unit, the students continued to practice questioning skills and connected the terms or vocabulary words to their everyday lives. We worked together to find out answers to our scientific questions.

It was very interesting to see the differences among classrooms teaching this same unit. Some teachers worked strictly from the manual. I encouraged the use of the inquiry method. When I talked to students in the other classrooms, they often offered very short answers to questions that I asked. The students in my class, on the other hand, loved to share the information that they learned or observed from this project. I feel that using an inquiry method of teaching with the students makes them more engaged and empowered and perhaps more likely to become lifelong learners. A powerful point to remember in science is that we want all students to be able to question, to explain, to show how they figured out a solution to a question, and to provide supporting evidence for their findings.

Assessing Student Learning

The assessments I used with my students varied from the ideas in the curriculum materials in which the assessment consisted of the students' filling in the blank science journal pages and a postassessment writing activity on the life cycle of an egg. I chose alternative assessment plans because I wanted my students to not only be able to write about caterpillars and their transformation into butterflies but also to be able to show their learning through different modes, just as a scientist might.

As noted in a previous section on how I taught my beginning lessons for this unit, I discussed how to use the magnifying glasses. By asking pondering and inquisitive questions about how the magnifying glass works, students were able to do experiments or "try out the materials" to gain valuable information. This procedure allowed for several assessment opportunities later in the unit. Throughout the unit we used the magnifying glasses, so it was very easy to see if students grasped the concept of how to use them correctly.

My second assessment dealt with an extension activity that was noted in the teacher's manual for making a model of a caterpillar. The manual suggested that students make a model by taking apart egg cartons for the body sections and the head. Then students were to join these sections together with yarn or pipe cleaners. Another option was to string cut-up straws, beads, noodles, gumdrops, or marshmallows together for the body segments and head.

I modified this extension for a group assessment for the students to complete. I asked the students to work in their learning groups of six to make a model of a caterpillar. The supplies they could use were: one skewer, mini powdered donuts, rope licorice, mini chocolate chips, dry elbow macaroni, and toothpicks. The groups were cautioned about safety concerns and then asked to use the information they had previously learned about caterpillars—such as segment number, prolegs, true legs, and bristles—to construct the caterpillar model. Students threaded 13 mini powdered donuts on the skewer for the segments of the caterpillar. Next, they cut the rope licorice into the correct numbers for the caterpillar's true legs and inserted these in the caterpillar segments. They used the dry elbow macaroni to represent the prolegs on the caterpillar. Students then placed 12 mini chocolate chips on the first caterpillar segment to represent the caterpillar's 12 simple eyes and used the toothpicks for bristles on the caterpillar segments. Parent volunteers were in the classroom to help supervise this assessment piece.

Most groups used their imaginations and had little trouble matching up the different parts on the caterpillar with the food items. Some groups needed assistance getting started, but, after we discussed what they knew about caterpillars, they were able to complete the task. Throughout this entire project, I documented what the students were doing by taking digital pictures and recording what they said while working. I found my students were using scientific terms that they had learned in this unit. Later, I displayed the pictures and words I had recorded from the students on documentation boards that hung in the hallway. These documentation boards drew a lot of attention from other students, teachers, and adults to work that my students had completed. The students were very excited to share what they knew with anyone who came by the room. This assessment piece provided insight for me and allowed many learning opportunities for my students.

Ideally, I would have liked the students to bring in their own food resources and have them use their imaginations to create their own caterpillars. With 69% of the students on free or reduced-price lunch, my decision was to supply the materials. I would be interested to know what this assessment piece would look like in a school with different demographics.

My final assessment piece was a dance and movement activity that portrayed the life cycle of the butterfly. With this assessment piece, I randomly assigned students to small groups to perform the life cycle of a butterfly for the whole class. Here they were to work together and practice ways, through movement or dance, to show the progression of a butterfly emerging. This was a form of assessment other than the paper and pencil mentioned in the teacher's guide. The students did a great job of showcasing and putting into a performance the information they had learned about butterflies.

Throughout all of the assessment pieces that I used within my classroom, my main goal was to showcase the students' learning and the processes that we used to accomplish that learning. The assessments provided an overall view of the student understandings as they sampled many learning areas: writing, reading, making models, working as group members, investigating, researching, and communicating newly learned knowledge to others. I feel that, by using the inquiry model of learning, the students learned that it is important to ask questions and to investigate answers, to collect evidence for answers that are based on observations. Our classroom experience illustrates how teachers and students can work together to discover answers to questions and that everyone's input is valuable.

References

National Research Council (NRC). 1996. *National Science Education Standards*. Washington, DC: National Academy Press.

National Science Resources Center. 1992. *The life cycle of butterflies*. Washington, DC: National Academy of Sciences.

A Craving for More Science:

Active, Integrated Inquiry in an After-School Setting

Phyllis Katz
Hands On Science Outreach, Inc.

Setting

The American dream, in education as in most other things, is a smorgasbord of choices and the opportunity to choose. The National Science Education Standards (NSES) are a nutritional guide that offers a balance of prime ingredients allowing for individual recipes at the classroom level. For both chefs and consumers, the end goal is a sustaining and sustainable diet. We want healthy, eager, prepared minds in our country. How then do sweet treats, spices, and vitamins (the work of those of us in informal science education) affect the mix? The NSES acknowledge their part on the platter (NRC 1996, pp. 45, 221), but the document could not anticipate how the guidelines would flavor our meals in the years since 1996. Recognition for the general importance of after-school education has been growing (Afterschool Alliance 2004). This chapter examines the impact of extended learning time, focused on quality science learning.

The HOSO (Hands On Science Outreach, Inc.) programs were designed as a vitamin supplement—a chance for children and their families to choose a frequent, convenient science enrichment activity. The HOSO after-school science programs began in 1980 in what was then an affluent Washington, D.C., suburb. Since that time, the original location has undergone major demographic changes as its schools and neighborhoods filled with many immigrants, primarily from Asia, Central America, and the former Soviet Union. With the help of National Science

Foundation (NSF) funding as a catalyst, the same HOSO opportunity for science play has spread to suburban, urban, and rural settings around the country. Some are large and generally affluent, like Fairfax County, Virginia, and some are urban, serving primarily low-income families, like Washington, D.C.; Sacramento, California; and Pontiac, Michigan. A grant brought HOSO classes to farming communities in Iowa.

In each setting, the chance to experiment, make a model, sing a science song, and generally play with the "what if?" of simple materials and tempting questions is a community effort among schools, parents, and teachers. HOSO provides activity guides, inquiry instruction models, and complete kits of take-home materials. Whether fee based or grant supported, the nature of the program is that it brings more people to the table. Sometimes parents organize the opportunity. Sometimes a principal decides to stimulate more science interest. Sometimes an energetic teacher takes the lead. Schools and also churches, recreation centers, museums, or bookstores welcome the use of their sites for community enrichment. Parents offer to register children or lead a group; and teachers, graduate students, retirees, or people released from work for community service learn and practice inquiry teaching and learning. Groups of 10 to 11 children of similar age are encouraged to play with simple materials and wondering questions for an hour a week. Eight-week sessions run fall, winter, and spring on a three-year rotation of themes. The rotation provides a changing menu that allows for sampling without monotony.

There are children who are repeat participants from prekindergarten through fifth or sixth grade, while other children register for sessions on an occasional basis. HOSO, as an informal science experience, is optional, and a major assessment component is the children's and parents' ongoing and continued participation.

Science Is the Prime Ingredient

Each HOSO activity guide has a cover page for parents with the statement, "We hope that your child will have fun while learning to explore his/her world using a science perspective ... helping your child develop skills using the scientific processes of observation, measurement, testing and peer discussion. We want to increase communication skills through new vocabulary ... and help develop a keener awareness of our world and the vast and delicate network of which it is composed" (HOSO 2003). From its inception, HOSO was designed to engage in three of the four science education goals that the NSES later defined: expanding the experience of students in the natural world; using scientific processes and principles in decision making; and engaging in discussion using science experiences. The HOSO target age is young, and attribution is too mingled with the self-selection process to assess whether HOSO participation leads directly to increased economic productivity in later years. It would seem reasonable that positive informal science exposures could help to spark eventual career choices. The sum of a child's environment—consistent exposure and encouragement of early experiences—contributes to life path choices (Andersen et al. 2002; Bergstrom 1985; Bloom 1981; Sprung, Froschl, and Campbell 1985).

The publication of the NSES encouraged HOSO to identify its ingredients more clearly and to include, when possible, the fourth goal in the form of career awareness for the 4–12 year olds in the target audience. Our written guides and training materials have been revised to reflect the inquiry and relevance promoted by the NSES. We have worked to develop appropriate and viable assessments beyond attendance and registration records. We have also taken a stance to support the community feast, but not to lose the excitement and delight that spices provide—to remind us all that informal education provides a different and important role from formal, compulsory education (Katz and McGinnis 1999). HOSO classes add to science time. Depending upon the child's entry point, they allow for practice, exposure, and a connection between science and the fun of learning.

A Premier Chef—The Ideal Adult Leader

In any given neighborhood, the HOSO program is limited only by the available people resources, since activity guides, instruction, and kits can be produced to meet demand. The HOSO adult leader, who may or may not be a classroom teacher, takes time to listen as children talk about their experiences. Whether it is in the opening "think, pair, share" question, the "what ifs" of the activities, or the closing "so what?" question, this HOSO leader finds ways to respond to the children's knowledge. She respects their curiosity, rewards their willingness to risk reasoning out loud, and encourages each child to think toward the current scientific view. She is comfortable learning along with the children as they try something with variables that can make the outcome uncertain. She comes to the HOSO class expecting the children to help manage the materials so that they are always engaged and not waiting for her to give as they take. In short, she treats her hour with the children as a collaborative minicommunity. Each eight-week session has a theme that most often crosses disciplinary boundaries, and each one-hour class explores related concepts in a variety of modalities that include listening, talking, seeing, smelling, and touching. Children practice their observation, data collecting, analysis, prediction, discussion, and other science skills.

HOSO has placed more emphasis on adult science learning through investigation and inquiry during its adult leader orientation and materials training workshops prior to each class series. Although the topics change by session, there is continuity and reinforcement in the integration of theory and practice. Community building also occurs among those who continue to lead groups as they share anecdotes and specific techniques that worked for them. The adult leaders help to generate knowledge about teaching in the HOSO context. Some adult leaders also participate in observations of others, and they help to facilitate change from their feedback.

Recipes and Variations—A Class Series Example

HOSO has centered its programs around questions that respect the children's thinking. To engage the children, activities that make use of simple materials give them playful experiences with the world. These take-home materials are selected to create a starting point for discussion and debate as the children practice science. The sample class series that follows illustrates how HOSO programs pepper the activities with questions to emphasize student engagement and use of prior knowledge during the inquiry process.

In a spring HOSO session, "Waves and Rhythms," children in the second- and third-grade groups have the opportunity to be outdoors as well as indoors while they explore sound and flight.

The eight-week class series, "Swinging Rhythms," illustrates the flow and alignment with the NSES *More Emphasis* indicators. The "What's the Science?" question helps the adult leader understand that the playful design of the program has conceptual development as its core. This question is intended as an advance organizer but is not intended to guide the adult leader's focus for a class.

Class 1: How can one sound imitate another for what we call sound effects? Children begin by pairing or tripling up in different parts of the room and listening very carefully to the sounds around them. They are asked to describe and discuss the sounds and how they determined the source of what they heard. The adult leader creates a sense of mystery and encouragement to explore science by asking the children to support their assertions. Next, the leader introduces a story about camping on a stormy night and asks the children to produce some of the descriptive noises. They are usually creative and playful as they choose ways to imitate croaking, hooting, clanging, crackling, thundering, snoring, pouring, buzzing, and more. When they have finished their noisy story, they work with poster board and onionskin paper to construct a toy that produces a snappy thunder sound. The class ends with children and teacher playing a game of sound production for different intensities of rain and the "so what?" question, "How do the sounds we hear give us clues to life around us, even without looking?"

Class 2: How does your ear help you hear? How can you tell the direction from which a sound is coming? The first question posed to the children is, "How can we feel a sound?" They work in pairs to make a cardboard-and-wax-paper kazoo. Then they explore by humming in different ways against the wax paper to feel the vibrations. They are asked to move a small piece of paper across the wax-paper surface. This is to have them think about how and where their ears might be similar in structure. They create a simple ear model, using their cardboard kazoos to model the eardrum and then look for a pattern to see how the vibrations are passed along a path to their brains for interpretation. Although they cannot see the inner ear directly, they enjoy learning about what goes on: Children have an interest in how their bodies work, and many have had ear infections. The children then play a game where they collect data on the direction from which they perceive another child is making a sound. They try this listening first with both ears and then with only one, and they discuss and compare results. The "so what?" question is, "How might our hearing change if our ears were on top of our head instead of one on each side?"

Class 3: How are some sounds produced? How are high and low sounds produced? The class begins with a question about remembering high and low sounds. The children verbalize high- and low-pitched sounds as they feel their own throats. They then play with rubber bands to produce higher and lower sounds and think about the differences in the adult voices they have heard. How might the vocal chords of women and men differ to make the generally higher and lower pitches associated with females and males? The children are invited to make a model of vocal chords with rubber bands, poster board, and tongue depressors. They are asked to tell how this model differs from the kazoos they had made. The activities move along into speech production as the children play with different components of talking, using tongue twisters, and ventriloquism. Children make puppets as a final activity and try to "throw" their voices. The "so what?" question is, "What couldn't you say without lips, or without a tongue, or without vocal chords?"

Class 4: Does sound travel better through the air or a solid? After the teacher asks about their favorite stringed instruments, the children experiment with plucking a piece of taut string and finding ways to vary its pitch. They compare this with the rubber-band activity of the previous week, and they then use cups, thick rubber bands, precut wooden blocks, thin string, and screw eyes to construct two types of simple musical instruments. They are challenged to try to tune them to one another's creations. The "so what?" question is, "Why do you think that the strings on a guitar are of different thicknesses?"

Class 5: What affects the number of back-and-forth swings a pendulum completes in a given time? To expand their thinking about rhythms and vary the activities, this class provides materials with which children can make and play with pendulum movement. They begin by considering a grandfather clock. Children choose a length of string and use a paper clip to attach the string to a washer. The addition allows the children to explore whether weight affects the pendulum swing later when they can add more clips and washers. First, they play a game in which the adult leader starts them all off with the same conditions, and they all count their swings in a given time. When they line up in a human graph by numbers of swings, what conclusions can they draw? As a final activity, children are given spinner pens that replace the washers. What kinds of patterns do the pens produce as they are subjected to pendulum motion? Children have had the opportunity to make pendulums, to observe what determines the number of swings, to become part of a physical graph, and to explore the connection between science and art. The "so what?" question asks them to think metaphorically with, "How is a pendulum like an ocean wave?"

Class 6: How does the amount of air in a whistle affect its sound? How do three different whistles compare? This class transitions the series from now familiar vibrations made by audible or visible movement to the effects of air. It looks at a common instrument that works by air pressure rather than strumming, plucking, or striking. The class begins as children are asked to think about things, other than people, that whistle. Wherever children live, they may well have heard wind whistling through buildings, birds, or a teakettle. By looking at the pieces of a simple whistle kit and considering how it will work, the children participate in a wide range of science processes: prediction, construction, testing, observation, assessment, comparison, and discussion. They also make less complicated tooters and straw whistles to compare to their wooden models and to see how they can vary the sounds. The "so what?" question is, "How are whistles used for fun or work?" This question again encourages children to consider this particular instrument from both a personal and social perspective.

Class 7: How does air movement make parachutes and propellers stay in the air as long as they do? This class begins by considering what makes leaves float or flutter to the ground. So that all the children become focused on this phenomenon, including those who may not live in an environment with leafy trees, they play a paper-dropping game. In it they compare two identical pieces of paper that they release from the same level. One piece of paper has been left flat, and the other has been balled up. They also play with swooping paper and air pressure as they press the paper against their palms and quickly turn their hands upside down. Will the balled-up paper behave in the same way? The children make parachutes and attach toy figures and play with the descent. They also make paper helicopters and explore the similarities and differences in their motion. What are the variables in directional change? The "so what?" question is, "When might we need to use air resistance to keep something in the air as long as possible?"

Class 8: What do you think makes a kite fly well? After the children answer a start-up question about their experience with kites, they explore lift by blowing on pieces of paper to answer:

Why would a material move upward if you blow down on it? How else would air movement affect object movement? The children are then provided with a simple paper spiral suspended on a string to make a warm-air detector. As they suspend it gently over different areas, perhaps comparing a grassy area and a blacktop, the spinning movement of the spiral gives them evidence of the difference that heat can make to air movement. Next the children make a plastic-bag kite that is strengthened by drinking straws and decorated with streamers. Out they go to try their luck in the air, over and under, warmer or cooler. The "so what?" question concludes the eight-week session by asking, "Where do you find rhythms and waves in the things that you see or do?

In terms of the teaching standards, the HOSO program places great emphasis throughout the eight weeks on children's responding to questions by playing with materials to find out "what happens if?" Because circumstances differ somewhat wherever the program takes place, some outcomes cannot be specified. Adult leaders learn along with the children as they find out how to imitate local noises or where the school's warm air currents are. Children are asked to support their conclusions or decisions with scientific reasoning such as: Were they able to locate sound better with one ear or two? What evidence supported their conclusions? Can they explain why men's and women's voices might generally differ?

Taste Testing

All of us involved in science education want to know how and what the children are learning. In the classroom, tests and other assessments focus on the content and process standards of achievement in various curricula. Within the informal education community, as noncompulsory educators, we are asking additional questions. Do the children and adults enjoy their science experiences with us, increasing the likelihood that they will associate science with pleasure and seek continuing involvement? Are we part of a series of positive experiences that will happen over a lifetime to result in lifelong science appreciation, if not professional work? Do we provide reasonable access to our programs? Do we attract those traditionally underrepresented in science? To continue our metaphor, does the style and flavoring enhance the meal in such a way that we develop a taste for the pursuit of science?

The responses to the spring 2002 parent survey that HOSO conducted indicated that 70% of those who replied chose "more science" as one reason for enrolling their children. Forty-four percent indicated that they wanted their children to try something new. Thirty-two percent of the parents circled "fun with science" as a reason to register their children. In this sample, the responding parents' children were 48.4% male and 51.6% female. More than a third of the parents said that their children were "super enthusiastic" about the HOSO classes. More than half said that the children were "enthusiastic." About 10% were neutral, with no negative choices. It is possible that parents whose children were dissatisfied may not have chosen to return the survey. We continue to seek ways to assess the responses of a wider range within our own time and budget limits—always constraints.

We asked these parents how often the children talked about their HOSO experiences at home. Under a third said, "very often," or "occasionally," with over a third reporting "moderately often." Only two said that their children spoke "infrequently" or "not at all" about HOSO. When asked about their perceptions of their child's learning, many surveyed parents indicated that their children had learned quite a lot, while 22% said "some" and only one said, "not much." We did not have a baseline from which to measure the comparison inherent in different starting points for each child. However, the parents were responding to individual changes for their own children.

In 2002, we also began a series of drawing activities in samples of HOSO classes to try and get closer to the children's notions of what they thought and what they were learning without introducing tests of any sort into the program. We obtained 566 early-session drawings and 378 late-session drawings. We were able to compare these drawings to those of children at the same age and grade groupings who were not enrolled. At first, we asked children to repeat the classic, "Draw a scientist." Those enrolled in HOSO and those not enrolled drew about the same percentage of all-male characters in the drawings. This dropped by 10% in later HOSO children's drawings and rose by 3% in later non-HOSO children's drawings. About 75% of HOSO children drew faces with happy expressions, compared to 96% of the non-HOSO enrolled children. This remained about the same at the end of the session for HOSO children, but dropped down to 75% for the non-HOSO children. About 67% of all children illustrated their scientists with beakers and tubes at the beginning and ending of the session. However, 23% of HOSO children illustrated other tools by the end of the session, compared to 11.5% of non-HOSO children. The following spring, we provided a different prompt: Please draw yourself doing science. The variety of settings and tools increased. We continue to work with drawings. More recently, we have provided prompts more closely related to the HOSO activities. Although we have been unable to develop long-range findings, in the short term many HOSO children show evidence of a pleasant experience that may broaden their views. Our challenge is to look for ways to present a playful learning experience and assess it appropriately in its eight hours spread over two to three months. We expect small influences and need to work on instruments and mechanisms that can help us detect these. This presents quite a challenge!

The National School Boards Association recently commissioned a study of school board presidents' views of after-school programs. As might be expected, after-school activity was not the board presidents' highest priority, but they, like many of us, believe that positive experiences are important for their long-range effects for children (Belden, Russonello, and Stewart 2003). It would be difficult to attribute to one after-school experience the decisions of a lifetime, and so we continue to look for current effects as a way to add to the evidence. There is growing evidence that a mixture of enriched informal learning and inquiry teaching in the classroom leads to increased abilities in scientific reasoning (Cavallo, Gerber, and Marek 1997).

Another challenge in HOSO programming is the development of the adult leaders who lead and teach the children in our program. Busy people who agree to devote an hour a week to children also have limits on the time that they will allocate to preparation or training. We have implemented a system of orientation and materials-training meetings. During the three-hour orientation, prospective adult leaders are exposed to inquiry science theory and methods through activities. They view video clips of children in exemplary programs and view clips of behavior-management situations. In 2000, we did an analysis of our pre- and postorientation workshop assessment sheets from January 1997 through June 2000. There were 219 assessments in this sample. Eighty-two percent were female and 17% were male, with 1% not indicating gender. Half of these people had taught professionally, and half had not. These adult leaders became involved with HOSO because they enjoyed working with children, they were interested in learning about the HOSO approach for themselves, or they wanted to be involved with what their children were doing.

We asked pre- and postworkshop how the adult leaders would respond to a child who asked why a liquid had changed color. Prior to the workshop, 48% said that they would ask a child a question in response. After the workshop, 79% said that they would respond by querying the child, a key HOSO training point that encourages the children to do the thinking. For a second question, involving the use of a rubber band, the number of scenarios that turned the prediction and procedure over to the child doubled. During the workshop, we introduce or reinforce the use of "think, pair, share" and "so, what?" in our activity guides. Many trainees had had misconceptions or no idea of what these teaching techniques were. By the end of the workshop, 84% and 56% respectively were able to describe how to use these questions in HOSO classes. We monitor orientation success by visits to the ongoing classes and discussions with the adult leaders.

The contribution of HOSO's informal science education is that it is most akin to the experience in a small favorite restaurant in each of the locations in which it takes place. The opportunity to laugh among friends, to try something new, to taste a new combination of old favorites reinforces the pleasure of learning science. The NSES encourage all of us to do our best to offer children a rich, nutritious opportunity to learn *how* to learn science and to expose them to the underlying content—the nutrients in this metaphor—upon which their lives depend. As communities, we partake of a varied diet in the hopes of getting the advantages of a diverse consumption in an everchanging environment.

References

Afterschool Alliance. 2004. Working families and afterschool: A special report for America after 3PM. Available online at *www.afterschoolalliance.org/press_archives/Working_Families_ Rpt.pdf.*

Anderson, D., M. Everett, B. Piscitelli, and K. Weier. 2002. The impact of multi-visit museum programs on young children's learning. Paper presented at the National Association of Research in Science Teaching, New Orleans, LA.

Archer, E., C. Fancsali, M. Froschl, and B. Sprung. 2003. *Science, gender, and afterschool: A research action agenda.* New York: Educational Equity Concepts and Academy for Educational Development.

Belden Russonello & Stewart. 2003. School board presidents' views of after-school programs in American schools, results of survey research conducted for the National School Boards Association. Washington DC: Author.

Bergstrom, J. M. 1984. *School's out—Now what?* Berkeley, CA: Ten Speed Press.

Bloom, B. 1981. *All our children learning.* New York: McGraw-Hill.

Cavallo, A. M. L., B. L. Gerber, and E. A. Marek. 1997. Relationships among informal learning environments, teaching procedures, and scientific reasoning ability. Paper presented at the annual meeting of the National Association for Research in Science Teaching, Oak Brook, IL.

Falk, J. H. 2003. A multi-factor investigation of variables affecting free-choice science learning. Paper presented at the annual meeting of the National Association for Research in Science Teaching, Philadelphia, PA.

Hands On Science Outreach (HOSO). 2003. *Swinging rhythms.* 7th ed. Silver Spring, MD: Hands On Science Outreach.

Katz. P., and J. R. McGinnis. 1999. An informal elementary science education program's response to the national science education reform movement. *Journal of Elementary Science Education* 11 (1): 1–15.

Mahoney, J. L., and E. F. Zigler. 2003. The national evaluation of the 21st century community learning centers: A critical analysis of first-year findings. Unpublished Department of Psychology, Yale University Report. Available online at *http://pantheon.yale.edu/%7Ejlm79/Critique-Full.pdf.*

National Research Council (NRC). 1996. *National Science Education Standards.* Washington, DC: National Academy Press.

Simpkins, S. 2003. Does youth participation in out-of-school time activities make a difference? Cambridge, MA: The Evaluation Exchange, IX (1). Available online at *www.gse.harvard.edu/hfrp/eval/issue21/theory. html.*

Sprung, B., M. Froschl, and P. Campbell. 1985. *What will happen if … Young children and the scientific method.* New York: Educational Equity Concepts.

Creating a Context for Inquiry

Janis Bookout
Bertha Arellano, Sara Hilgers, Lucy Alff,
Virgil Anderson, Melissa Madole-Kopp,
Sally Logsdon, and Darlene Strayn
Hornsby-Dunlap Elementary

Setting

ornsby-Dunlap Elementary, a kindergarten through sixth-grade school in the Del Valle Independent School District, is located in a rural community near Austin, Texas. Many of the students enrolled at Hornsby-Dunlap are children of immigrant families in which the language spoken at home is Spanish. Sixty-seven percent of the student population qualifies for free or reduced-price lunch. These children experience a variety of difficult life circumstances outside of school, but the Hornsby-Dunlap Elementary staff is committed to excellence for each and every child. In keeping with the district motto of "Whatever It Takes," Hornsby-Dunlap staff members do what it takes to provide these students every educational opportunity. Because of the hard work of our community liaison, our administrators, and our Parent Teacher Organization (PTO), Hornsby-Dunlap has some wonderful community partnerships and a wealth of educational resources. Every classroom houses a television and an internet-ready computer, as well as full sets of textbooks and manipulatives, and the school has a science lab, a computer lab, and a well-stocked library. Standardized test results reflect the commitment of our staff and the utilization of our excellent resources, as well as the commitment of our principal, Bertha Arellano. Our school has earned "Recognized" status for schoolwide performance on these standardized tests. With the leadership of Ms. Arellano, Hornsby-Dunlap's teachers are at work adapting the school's curriculum to provide authentic learning experiences and meet the individual needs of each and every student. The ever-expanding science program is no exception.

Supporting the NSES Four Goals of Science Education

At the elementary level, teachers lay the foundation for meeting the NSES Four Goals of Science Education (NRC 1996, p. 13). At Hornsby-Dunlap Elementary, we have addressed these goals through our collaboration in the implementation of a curriculum timeline centered on science concepts, development of an extensive outdoor education project, and use of an inquiry approach in our classrooms. NSES calls for *"More Emphasis"* on certain objectives. Through our collaborative efforts, we are meeting many of those conditions, but we are placing special emphases on the following:

- teachers as members of a collegial professional community,
- integration of theory and practice in school settings,
- studying a few fundamental science concepts,
- learning science through investigation and inquiry,
- sharing responsibility for learning with students,
- supporting a classroom community with cooperation, shared responsibility, and respect,
- process skills in context, and
- public communication of student ideas and work to classmates.

Exemplary Teachers in Collaboration

Collaboration is the single most critical component of our program. Also known as the Hornsby Outdoor Education Project (HOEP) Committee, Hornsby-Dunlap's vertical planning team is composed of teachers from each grade level, the school principal, the physical education teacher, our in-house mathematics specialist, the gifted and talented teacher, a PTO representative, and an on-site gardening and environmental specialist.

The teaching garden has applications for math and science.

Strong leadership makes this collaboration possible, and the fifth-grade science teacher Sara Hilgers, founder of our "Teaching Garden," leads the group. Ms. Hilgers has established numerous community contacts and partnerships, including partnerships with the business community, the University of Texas, the Wildflower Center, and various community plant experts. These partners have been involved in the expansion of the Teaching Garden, the construction of a new greenhouse, and the development of our courtyard, among other projects. Ms. Hilgers was awarded more than $30,000 in grant money from Texas Parks and Wildlife and other organizations in the last year alone, and this grant money has been used for expansion of the outdoor education project and for training teachers in such topics as environmental education and in inquiry approaches. Her ongoing commitment to hands-on learning has inspired the staff for years and has stimulated increased participation in the science program. On-site gardening expert and consultant Jefferson Ryan, also a critical contributor to the program, continually works with and trains students, parents, and teachers and provides support in planning effective lessons for the Teaching Garden.

Our team accomplishments would not have been possible without the support and participation of our school principal, Ms. Arellano. Ms. Arellano has been committed to this project and has repeatedly sponsored extra training for our teachers. She has not only supported the Teaching Garden, but she also has led efforts to transform our entire schoolyard into a learning environment. In the interest of enhancing a growing environmental education project, the collaborative team designed a curriculum that has created a context in which new, in-depth learning experiences can occur. The remainder of this chapter will focus on this program and how it is implemented in our classrooms at Hornsby.

Features of the Hornsby-Dunlap Environmental Program

This section will highlight the components of an exemplary program in development through examples from different classrooms. The third grade is the example class used to illustrate how the various components come together.

Collaboration Brings Vision to Life

Members of the HOEP Committee have been working together over the past several years to develop practices that use and expand our existing outdoor education program and to build on partnerships with Texas Parks and Wildlife, Blue Bell/Lady Bird Johnson Wildflower Center, the City of Austin, the University of Texas, Master Gardeners and Naturalists, the Audubon Society, and Hornsby Bend Center for Environmental Research. These partnerships have provided us with funding, volunteers, materials, guidance, and expertise. Graduates from the University of Texas have come from various departments to provide expertise in entomology, plants, and soil analysis, and Hornsby Bend has hosted the Living Lab, a program designed with the help of fifth-grade science teacher Sara Hilgers.

With the encouragement and support of the principal, our team worked to align our grade level–specific environmental curriculum with state and national standards. The approach used was informed by resources from the Charles A. Dana Center at the University of Texas and a presentation to the Hornsby-Dunlap staff by Dr. Paul Slocumb. He suggested creating a context for learning by identifying several unifying concepts to be reinforced throughout the year. Based on exemplary practices in science, we reorganized our curriculum timelines to emphasize four unifying scientific concepts or themes—*Parts and Properties, Systems, Change,* and *Cycles*—throughout the year, one for each of the four nine-week periods. Although the curriculum for each grade level is still aligned with the district curriculum and state requirements, the sequence and context were re-designed to fit inside these four themes.

Our intended student outcomes are to
- encourage students to deeply consider these scientific concepts,
- provide contexts in which students can make connections among concept topics,

- familiarize students with scientific concepts rather than just disconnected content,
- encourage students to feel connected to the process of learning and to the world around them, and
- generate excitement about science across grade levels.

As a team, we created timelines to reflect the four themes and we established teaching partnerships to support ourselves in implementing the curriculum. These partnerships, or buddy pairs, included a representative teacher from each of two grade levels. We partnered older grade-level students with younger grade-level students so that peer tutoring could be an effective option. These buddy pairs worked together throughout the year, planning and creating activities that included students from both grade levels.

Throughout the year we also planned events that encourage student, teacher, and parent participation. Most of these events have centered on transforming our schoolyard into a learning environment, and these have included such activities as weeding, greenhouse preparation, and tree planting. During PTO Fun Days, parents, teachers, and students come on a Saturday to plant the garden. These activities have led to further involvement. One parent has not only assisted in planting trees but also has donated the services of his landscaping team to help with our schoolyard project. Scott Harris, owner of a local tree nursery and a parent, has donated many trees as well as his time and energy. Throughout, the PTO has helped organize parent volunteers and has contributed gardening supplies. It donated more than $2,000 to the project. Plans for expansion of this project include a sensory garden, a sunflower garden, an observation deck, a set of small ponds, and a rainwater recycling system.

Students walk a nature trail constructed with the help of a Boy Scout troop.

Students from all grade levels have been involved. Kathy Sane, physical education teacher, organized a bucket brigade to bring gravel into observation areas of the courtyard, with kindergartners carrying the smallest buckets. As we continue to expand our program, parent involvement continues to be an important piece of our success.

Collaborative Classroom Environments

Such a collaborative environment makes a difference only if classrooms are prepared to participate and contribute. Hornsby-Dunlap teachers work to establish such classrooms. Collaboration in the classrooms creates a synergistic learning environment in which teachers and students can learn from one another.

Third-grade teacher Janis Bookout's students are expected to be 100% responsible for monitoring their behavior. They are asked to add to an anonymous class bar graph that shows positive and negative behaviors in each of five categories: communication, cooperation, respect, responsibility, and trust. As they earn positive or negative consequences, they track their individual behaviors, making notes in their own folders or filling out a "time-out for reflection" sheet that they place in their records folders. A student monitor helps remind students to mark their folders and keep track of their behaviors. A student who is having difficulty with another student can fill out a "work it out" form and request the counsel of a mediator.

In addition to structures that encourage citizenship, Ms. Bookout uses methods that encourage participation. For example, she has a sign on her wall that reads, "Mistakes are great because we learn from them." She asks students to share their biggest mistakes from assignments or experiments and explain how they made the mistake, what they learned, and what they could do next time. The class always applauds the volunteer, acknowledging the courage it took to risk sharing their mistakes. Ms. Bookout has made the students aware that many scientific discoveries were made because someone observed the outcome of a so-called mistake and learned from it.

As a result of these practices, students work well together in groups. During science laboratories and observations, students almost always work in collaborative groups or partnerships, and they are often required to turn in a group assignment rather than individual ones. So they must collaborate to make their decisions, observations, and conclusions. Although the activities are less structured than direct teaching, student behavior is rarely a problem during these activities, perhaps because the consequence for misbehavior in science activities is not being allowed to participate.

Integrated Timelines

The sixth- and third-grade science representatives, in order to make their lessons and partnership more effective, decided to cycle through all of the content areas each time a theme was presented. During Parts and Properties, the third-grade curriculum addresses the parts and properties of plants and animals, parts and properties of the atmosphere, types of clouds, properties of different soil types, types of rocks, parts of the solar system, and properties of matter. At the same time, the sixth graders were studying parts of plants, types of stars, dichotomous keys, and parts of matter. This made team-teaching possible. In one team-teaching experience, the sixth graders led a guided tour for the third graders, in which they used plants in the garden to explain to the younger students the parts and properties of plants.

SYNERGY: 2003-04 Third-Grade Science Timeline

	1st Nine Weeks PARTS and PROPERTIES	2nd Nine Weeks SYSTEMS	3rd Nine Weeks CHANGE	4th Nine Weeks CYCLES
ASTRONOMY	*One Week*	*One Week*	*One Week*	*One Week*
	Parts of the Solar System	Sun's Energy	Position of the Sun	Earth's Rotation
	Properties of the Sun	Solar System	Star Journal	Star Journal
	Star Journal	Star Journal		
BIOLOGY	*Two Weeks*	*Two Weeks*	*Two Weeks*	*Two Weeks*
	Parts/Properties of Plants	Plant/Animal Interactions	Adaptation	Life Cycles: Butterflies
	Parts/Properties of Animals	Ecosystems	Genetics	Tree Project
	Needs for Survival	Habitats	Changes in Resources	Nitrogen Cycle
	Classification	Competition	Tree Project	Respiration/
	Tree Project	Tree Project		Photosynthesis
EARTH	*One Week*	*One Week*	*One Week*	*One Week*
	Types of Rock	Plate Tectonics	Forces Shaping Earth	Rock Cycle
	Properties of Soil	Groundwater		
METEOROLOGY	*One Week*	*One Week*	*One Week*	*One Week*
	Types of Clouds	Weather Systems	Weather Patterns	Water Cycle
	Atmospheric Layers	Weather Journal	Fronts	Weather Cycles
	Weather Journal		Weather Predicting	Weather Journal
			Weather Journal	
PHYSICS/	*One Week*	*One Week*	*One Week*	*One Week*
CHEMISTRY	Properties of Matter	Mixtures/Solutions	States of Matter	States of Matter
	Solid, Liquid, Gas	Electricity/Magnetism	Motion/Forces	
			Energy	
			Light and Sound	
RESOURCES	*One Week*	*One Week*	*One Week*	*One Week*
	Types of Resources	Role of Resources in Ecosystem	Changes in Our Resources	Recycling

During the Systems unit, both grades again explored each of these content areas within the context of systems. Furthermore, our timelines resemble each other in format to facilitate placing our classrooms together. Third graders studied content such as the solar system, ecosystems, soil as a system, weather systems, and water systems, while sixth graders studied the universe, cells, magnetism, ecosystems, groundwater, and storm systems.

In each nine-week period, both grade levels continued to revisit all content areas, layering knowledge learned within one context with knowledge learned in the next. Each content thread was repeated within each theme. During Parts and Properties, students learned about the parts of the environment, and, in Systems, they learned about how these parts interact. During Change, they studied competition and adaptation. In Cycles, they studied life cycles. All other content threads follow a similar pattern, with themes reinforced after every lesson as students add to a concept map representing how various content and concepts connect to the theme. In this way, not only are students gaining a rich understanding of science concepts, but they also are deepening their understanding of each content area as these areas are revisited throughout the year.

Comprehensive Lesson Planning

For students to gain the most from this theme-based approach, they need time to wonder, to explore, to observe, to reflect, to share, to process, to synthesize, and to evaluate what they are encountering. Effective lesson planning allows all of this to happen. The third-grade teachers use a model that incorporates these aspects of learning. In developing this model, Ms. Bookout used online resources from the Eisenhower National Clearinghouse (ENC) and communicated with a consultant at ENC to verify the effectiveness of the model.

In a lesson series, students begin with an inquiry-based investigation, which may or may not include teachers' asking students what they know about the subject area and introducing relevant vocabulary. Typically, students are given little, if any, content prior to the investigation. Following an activity, students share observations and conclusions in a class discussion. The class begins to build understanding of a new topic when the class discussion is followed by the presentation of content. Another activity may follow to apply the concepts students just learned. Culminating activities that synthesize and connect the lessons to the theme end the lesson series.

Wanting to explore a topic in depth, the third-grade teachers have reorganized blocks of instructional time to allow for an extended series of science lessons each Friday. What follows is a detailed description of plans for one of these days, but these plans could be implemented instead in five 30- to 45-minute periods.

Ongoing Investigation

Each week student groups devoted time to a yearlong investigation of a tree they adopted at the beginning of the year. Students recorded weather information for the day and made observations about their tree. As the year progressed, students saw changes in their trees, compared these changes with the changes of others' trees, and eventually made generalized conclusions about the effect of environmental conditions on an organism.

Inquiry-Based Investigations

Each science lesson series begins with an investigation. These investigations are identified from sites provided online by ENC or, in some cases, from activities in the state-adopted textbook. Inquiry-based lessons are selected and modified as needed for third-grade classrooms.

From 45 to 90 minutes are spent on one or more inquiry-based investigations that, as often as possible, make use of the Teaching Garden or another aspect of our schoolyard environment. In these investigations, students are encouraged to draw their own conclusions. Assessment at this stage usually comes in the form of a laboratory write-up.

Students study plant parts.   A third grader conducts a soil experiment.

In one lesson students were asked to compare the properties of sand, loam, clay, and local soil samples in a series of observations. The local soil sample was taken from the native-plant section of the garden. After recording their observations, students were asked to decide what the soil was made up of and were told that the soil could be composed of one, two, or all three soil types. Students were told that they would not be given the answer but would have to make decisions and defend those decisions with evidence. The teachers explained that, when scientists are at work, they are not given an answer key. Students were asked to write a paragraph defending their decisions based on the observations that they made. The papers were used as an informal assessment of their observation skills as well as their scientific reasoning. Nearly all students correctly identified that the local soil was a combination of two soil types, and the large majority of students presented their arguments effectively. In the lesson, students connected to the local world around them. In two years, these same students will encounter soil samples again as they take field trips to the Hornsby Bend Center for Environmental Research where they will conduct more extensive soil tests in the Hornsby Bend Living Lab.

Class Discussion Example

At least 20 to 30 minutes are devoted to a discussion of the completed investigation, and students are asked to share what they have learned or decided based on evidence. These conclusions are used as a bridge to presenting relevant vocabulary and content. A vocabulary wall is kept nearby so that the class can add relevant words. It was during one of the guided discussions that the students in Ms. Bookout's class, after doing an experiment showing convection, came to the conclusion that convection had a lot to do with causing weather.

Expanding the Knowledge Base

After students have investigated a topic and have had time to draw some of their own conclusions, content is presented in a more formal way. These lessons are brief and varied in structure. Presentations of content have included cooperative reading assignments, watching a short film from *BrainPop.com* on the internet, reviewing a PowerPoint presentation, or a giving brief direct lesson. The third-grade teachers take care to present the content in a way that does not overtly validate or invalidate students' conclusions but rather gives them an opportunity to anchor their observations and reassess their own conclusions.

Closing the Lesson and Connecting to the Theme

Lessons are ended with a collaborative activity and then connected to the larger theme by adding to a theme-based concept map. These collaborative activities usually involve displaying what students learned in a graphic format that can be placed in the hallway. This might be a student-made mural such as a depiction of the parts and layers of the atmosphere, or a KWL chart, in which students have listed what they know (K) and want to know (W) and, following the lesson, what they have learned (L).

Lessons are then connected to other lessons and to the theme by adding to the class concept map, which illustrates what students have learned in the nine weeks and the

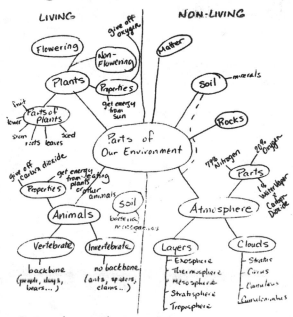

Parts and properties concept map.

relationships to the theme. The Parts and Properties concept map, for example, showed parts and properties of living and nonliving components of the environment. The concept map is an excellent opportunity to assess student understanding at the classroom level. After encountering misconceptions, the teacher can re-teach as the concept map is constructed and make notes for things to review or teach in future lessons.

Synthesizing and Evaluating Ideas and Sharing Student Thinking

At the end of the science lesson series, students are often asked to write in journals about what they learned and, if time permits, share their thoughts with the class. This practice presents opportunities for informal assessment of individual performance and helps students strengthen their speaking skills.

Connecting to Other Disciplines

Whenever possible, the lesson series is followed by social studies lessons and activities that emphasize the day's science lesson. For example, when the third graders studied the atmosphere and clouds, students were asked to examine a teacher-designed worksheet that presented two world maps—one showing global rainfall patterns and the other showing global population density. Students were asked to compare the two and make conclusions about how they were similar. In this way, students were able to connect what they had learned in science to a sociological phenomenon.

Assessing Learning

Learning is assessed throughout the lesson with lab reports, concept maps, journals, practice sheets, and discussions. Assessment is also addressed more formally through teacher-made and standardized tests.

What Other Grade Levels Are Doing

Virgil Anderson, the sixth-grade science teacher, has used a "learning wall" to have students write what they have learned in each topic area. According to Mr. Anderson, "Students were able to easily see the relationships between various topic areas and how the themes tied everything together. Also, Parts and Properties flowed nicely into Systems. During the first nine weeks, the class studied different types of clouds and their properties. They then examined weather systems during the second nine weeks, and the kids saw what clouds fit with what weather systems." He added that using the thematic approach has increased cooperation with other teachers, such as the special area teachers, who have planned activities to support what his classes are doing within each theme.

Encouraged by the principal to use these themes to address other content areas, teachers not only organized science timelines, but also aligned reading, language arts, math, social studies, and special areas timelines around these themes. Under the guidance of HOEP committee member Darlene Strayn, the second-grade team has done an especially thorough job of tying lessons to these themes. According to Ms. Strayn, "All content areas are tied to unify to the themes." She reported that second graders have begun to see the connectedness of all aspects of learning and that her grade-level team members highly support the thematic approach.

Under the guidance of Ms. Alff, the first-grade teachers have students observing seasonal changes, life cycles, and plant growth throughout the year. Their fifth-grade partners assist them in making these observations in the Teaching Garden. Ms. Alff notes that, "The garden is very rewarding for almost all students," although, she admits, some first graders have trouble staying on task in the freedom of the outdoors.

In a truly hands-on approach, Ms. Hilgers's fifth-grade science classroom takes place primarily outdoors. For years her classes have been the stewards of the Teaching Garden and the school's environmental experts, and they even partner with the sixth graders as our "recycling rangers," students who pick up the weekly recycling from every classroom. In Ms. Hilgers's class, students conduct scientific studies as they develop and tend the garden. As a result, the students' experiences of science are relevant, timely, and hands-on, and math and science are integrated. During the Parts and Properties unit, Ms. Hilgers's students studied the properties of plants by measuring their height and preparing comparative graphs, and, during Changes, her class studied seasonal changes and used mathematical approaches to interpret observation.

Students maintain a compost pile.   Students chart plant growth in the Teaching Garden.

Melissa Madole, Hornsby-Dunlap's gifted-and-talented teacher and 2003–2004 Teacher of the Year, says that the use of themes has had a very positive impact on student interest in science. She uses the themes in many ways and finds that her students are making more connections.

Evidence of Success

As the themes-based program was in its first year at Hornsby-Dunlap, it was a work-in-progress, and its effectiveness was difficult to measure. The program was built, however, upon the shoulders of solid research and reputable recommendations, and the preliminary evidence has been positive.

Research-Based Practices

According to Ruby Payne, teaching through conceptual frameworks is especially important to reach students who live in poverty (Payne 2001). She suggests using graphic organizers and "teaching content in an associative way," linking it to what students have experienced (p. 135). Paul Slocumb, author with Payne of *Removing the Mask: Giftedness in Poverty,* has also advocated this approach, and, in a 2003 workshop with Hornsby-Dunlap teachers, suggested a tiered approach to organizing content, beginning with a broad concept and branching down to themes and then presenting content within the context of a broader theme.

In *Best Practice: New Standards for Teaching and Learning in America's Schools,* the authors suggest that, "Science study should involve doing science, that is, questioning and discovering—not just covering—material." They encourage a "constructivist approach, which means activating children's prior knowledge about a phenomenon, encouraging their questions about it, and helping them gather information hands-on and build their own concepts." The authors also encourage a series of steps that includes questioning, observation, organizing data, explanation, reflection, and taking action (Zemelman, Daniels, and Hyde 1998, pp. 111–114). Our program uses approaches and practices consistent with these recommendations.

Student Feedback

We surveyed 37 third-grade students to find out about their experience with this science program. Although the results are by no means definitive, they are positive. Ninety-seven percent of the students surveyed said that they enjoyed the year's science lessons, and 97% said that they learned a lot from working in groups. Eighty-nine percent reported positive feelings about science in general; 80% of students agreed that this year's science activities were either a little or a lot more interesting than last year's science activities. When students were asked to write what they learned from working in groups, these were some of the comments:

- I learn to get along with kids I don't know.
- I have learned that I have to work with everybody in the class.
- Everybody has a part.
- I don't know.
- I learn that if you work in groups you get done faster.
- It takes a lot of courage to be nice and work together.
- When you work in a group you learn more and get more work done.

The survey also asked students to describe how they grew as scientists and what skills they developed. One student wrote, "being interested in stuff a lot and having fun being interested in stuff." Overall, the third graders seem to have a positive experience in the program. Future plans call for schoolwide teacher and student surveys that will provide more telling information.

Teacher Feedback

In an effort to evaluate the program's early impact, members of the HOEP committee were recently surveyed about the program.

- Six out of seven teachers surveyed said that using the themes had a positive or very positive impact on their students' interest and success in science.
- Six out of seven teachers agreed or agreed strongly that students were learning primarily through investigation and inquiry.
- Six out of seven teachers agreed or agreed strongly that focusing on a few fundamental science concepts made a positive difference in the classroom.
- Six out of seven teachers reported implementing the integration of science content.
- One teacher expressed difficulty implementing the program at the kindergarten level, but she qualified this by expressing her interest in getting support to modify for the following year.

- All teachers reported that using the garden had a positive or very positive impact on student interest in science.
- All teachers reported that being on the science committee enhanced their experience of being a part of a professional community.

Standardized Tests

In 2004, Hornsby-Dunlap Elementary's fifth graders took the first run at the statewide standardized science test. We had an 82% passing rate—11% higher than the state average of 69%. The next highest passing rate in our district was 73%. The test scores also showed an improvement from the previous year's mock test scores.

In Summary

The Hornsby-Dunlap HOEP committee has expanded upon our existing outdoor education project to develop an innovative, research-based, schoolwide science program. Organizing our science timelines around a few fundamental scientific concepts has not only enriched the learning experiences of our students but also our own teaching experience. We are beginning to see our intended outcomes met, and, as we develop this program in future years, we will continue to seek appropriate training, monitor our success, and support one another in developing powerful, inquiry-based lesson plans and more effective assessment techniques. At the same time we continue to develop and enhance the Teaching Garden and courtyard. "We don't want to ever finish it," says Ms. Arellano. "It's a learning environment—a work in progress."

Note. Bertha Arellano is no longer the principal at Hornsby-Dunlap Elementary, and the school has stopped using the integrated themes schoolwide, although some of the teachers still use the themes in their lesson planning. The Teaching Garden and associated programs are flourishing, and students continue to profit from them.

To find out more about this program or to contact the author, e-mail Janis Bookout at *janisgbookout@yahoo.com*. To find out more about the teaching garden, visit the website at *www.del-valle.k12.tx.us/DVISD/Hornsby/teachgarden/index.html*.

References

National Research Council (NRC). 1996. *National Science Education Standards.* Washington, DC: National Academy Press.

National Research Council (NRC). 2001. *Classroom assessment and the National Science Education Standards.* Washington, DC: National Academy Press.

Payne, R. K. 2001. *A framework for understanding poverty.* Highlands, TX: aha! Process.

Slocumb, P. D., and K. A. Payne. 2000. *Removing the mask: Giftedness in poverty.* Highlands, TX: aha! Process.

Zemelman, S., H. Daniels, and A. Hyde. 1998. *Best practice: New standards for teaching and learning in America's schools.* Portsmouth, NH: Heinemann.

Other Resources

Audubon Society: *www.audubon.org*

Charles A. Dana Center: *www.utdanacenter.org*

Eisenhower National Clearinghouse: *www.goenc.org*

ENC Focus, A Magazine for Classroom Innovators, Vol. 9, Number 1, 2002.

Hornsby Bend Center Bird Observatory: *www.hornsbybend.org*

Lady Bird Johnson Wildflower Center: *www.wildflower.org*

Master Gardeners: *www.texasmastergardeners.com*

National Parks and Wildlife: *www.npws.nsw.gov.au*

Tree Folks: *www.treefolks.org*

University of Texas: *www.utexas.edu*

Is Your Classroom Body/Brain-Compatible?

Shelly Kennedy
Burnett Creek Elementary School

Setting

urnett Creek first opened its doors for the 1999–2000 school year. The school site occupies 24 acres of land bordered on three sides by cornfields. Burnett Creek Elementary School is located approximately 60 miles north of Indianapolis, Indiana, and four miles north of West Lafayette, in Tippecanoe County. The school has a varied student population ranging from children of students and faculty members at Purdue University to office and retail workers, managers, blue-collar workers, and farmers. The student population encompasses 12 nationalities with an enrollment of 580 students in kindergarten through fifth grade. About 15% of the students qualify for free and reduced-price lunch. Burnett Creek has 80,000 square feet of educational space.

Goals of Science Education

Textbooks and packaged programs used to carry out a district's science standards should be a viable resource, but they tend to drive classroom science. This can be detrimental for two reasons. The first is that the resource may not address the appropriate standards set forth in the National Science Education Standards (NSES). Even as improved as textbooks are, they likely are not in exact alignment with the school district grade-level assignment of science concepts and topics. The second is that, if only textbooks are used as the vehicles to teach science, science becomes reading instruction. Students must be actively engaged in hands-on science using process skills and doing science rather than just reading about it.

Teachers select and adapt curricula to meet the needs of the students in their classrooms. Science, a content area that engages students, is the most logical content area to use as a framework for "theming" or integration of all the subjects. Science experiences are natural because students have already spent their lives trying to make sense of the world in which they live. Science can be experienced firsthand through the senses with an *emphasis* on learning through investigation and inquiry. Kovalik and Olsen (1991) noted that all curricula other than science are human constructions. Students must learn how to learn about mathematics, history, reading, or language mechanics. Science, however, provides real-life experiences for students to easily understand. Kovalik and Olsen share the following anecdote:

It should come as no surprise, for example, that a majority of our early astronauts were Midwest farm boys who grew up "doing science" as a natural aspect of growing up in the backyard and the south forty. They had hours of practice, on a daily basis, with the science behavioral processes: 1) observing (animals and plants growing and reproducing), 2) communicating (how best to care for them and when), 3) comparing (examining similarities and differences between two breeds of cattle kept as a 4-H project), 4) organizing (repeated replacing of tools and materials for easy access on the next task), 5) analyzing (bushels per acre and weight gain of various strains and breeds), 6) relating (analyzing why the new harvester broke down in light of knowledge of the quirks of the old harvester), 7) inferring (estimating international market prices for one's products and the possible effect on one's own sales), and 8) applying (being able to fix any and all equipment on the farm while out in the field with limited resources). Again, "doing science" in such natural world settings was natural and automatic, a "kinder's garden" for many of the best scientists this country has ever known. (p. 1)

By integrating all aspects of science, the other disciplines begin to naturally emerge. As adults we do not walk around breaking life down thinking, "OK, this is math, or this is a language arts skill that I am doing now." Life is integrated just as a curriculum should be.

Teacher Background

I received my bachelor's degree in elementary education from Purdue University and taught for five years in the Metropolitan School District of Lawrence Township Schools in Indianapolis, Indiana. I left the classroom for Purdue to become a full-time student studying for a master's degree in science education. While working on this degree, I served as a Connected Learning Assures Successful Students (CLASS) coach, training teachers around the state of Indiana about creating body/brain-compatible classrooms. CLASS is a recognized professional development model. CLASS principles are founded upon Susan Kovalik's nationally recognized model, Integrated Thematic Instruction (ITI), which is recognized as an accepted school reform program. The focus of ITI is to create a body/brain-compatible learning environment. In 2000, after receiving my master's degree, I returned to the classroom, and I am now in the Tippecanoe School Corporation in Lafayette, Indiana, working with fifth graders in a heterogeneous classroom. This last year's class had 21 students, aged 10 to 12. Four students were identified for Program for Accelerated and Creative Enrichment (P.A.C.E.), and one student was identified as emotionally disabled. My classroom projects a relaxed atmosphere. A nautical theme pervades throughout with lighthouse decor and a comfortable sofa for students. Students sit at tables and share supplies while having the opportunity to collaborate as needed. Soft music is often playing in the background to add to this relaxed environment. Depending on what topic we are studying, you might find a solar system mobile and celestial globes, a motorized solar system for space, or rock specimens, thermometers, and beakers. It would be evident to an observer that the students are engaged in some sort of project or scientific inquiry.

Brain Basics

Brain biology and neuroscience on how the brain learns are hot topics in education. Ninety percent of brain research scientists are still living, making it is a very young science. Great discoveries are being made about how the brain learns. Although scientists have generated ideas about the brain since the early 1800s, they have learned more about it in the past 50 years than in all of history. Some educators are taking this research and making it applicable to classrooms. Interestingly, others are saying that the findings have no implications for schools at this time and that teachers should be very cautious of classroom applications and implications posed by anyone. Researchers do credit teachers, however, as being the people who can and will turn the research into applicable pedagogy.

CLASS (Pedersen 2005) provided me the framework as well as a philosophical match for teaching the standards in a brain-compatible way:

Climate. Building relationships with students and among students to create a trusting environment is imperative for teachers. During the preparation period inclusion activities and energizers serve as a foundation for creating a nonthreatening environment. In addition, using agendas and procedures with students helps the teacher develop rapport with the students and helps students establish organization for the day while the teacher weaves literacy throughout everything. A daily class meeting, called Community Circle, begins as a sharing and getting-to-know-you time and builds into a strong curriculum discussion in which everyone has a front row seat, the opportunity to talk, and valued contribution. Character skills known as *life goals* lay the foundation in a brain-compatible classroom in which teachers "Do The Right Thing!" and "Treat People Right!" Additional character skills—cooperation, curiosity, and responsibility among them—promote appropriate behaviors and respect and permeate throughout interactions, discussion of literature characters, hallway behavior, and science project collaboration. Another contribution to the classroom climate is the physical environment, which should stimulate thinkers to make connections to the curriculum. When entering an enriched classroom, it is obvious what is being studied because there is immersion in the topic through displays, books, pictures, and exploratory stations.

Community. In my classroom we define *community* as a group of equally significant members working toward a common goal. Students *must* collaborate or work together toward a common goal—learning. By using teamwork and cooperation, students can work together to achieve that goal. Working with others builds a sense of community within the classroom that will help cultivate responsible citizens of the future. Going a step further, while using Collaboration Structures (or processing strategies), students can process concepts and ideas in a meaningful way, a brain-compatible way. One example of this is a *think/pair/share*. The teacher poses a question. Students collaborate with a partner, come up with the answer, and then share it with another pair or the teacher. Students need the opportunity to process what they are learning both during and after a lesson.

Curriculum. The learner determines meaningful curriculum. So, as educators, how do we determine what to teach? It must have real-life significance, be based on prior experiences, and be relevant. Through experience, the brain grows dendrites—the physiological connection between neurons when something new is learned. "Experience—what children do every day, the ways in which they think and respond to the world, what they learn, and the stimuli to which they decide to pay attention—shapes their brains. Not only does it change the ways in which the brain is used *(functional change)*, but it also causes physical alterations *(structural change)* in the neural wiring systems" (Kovalik and Olsen 1991). By providing students with natural science and real-life experiences and the opportunity for dendrite growth, we are also placing *more emphasis* on learning disciplines in the context of inquiry, technology, and science. The Curriculum Strand of the CLASS model organizes state standards into a Yearlong Curriculum Plan with Knowledge Key Points connected to those standards. The processing of the skills and content is assessed through collaborative activities called *Say It, Play It, Relay It, and Weigh It*. After learning is assessed, students are evaluated with various tools through Student Performance Tasks.

More Emphases

Learning involves a conceptual change of some sort by the learner, and what is a conceptual change? Posner et al. (1982) researched scientific misconceptions and conceptual change and arrived at a theory of conceptual change. In their theory, as students are introduced to new information, they attempt to organize, comprehend, and accept the ideas. The first phase of conceptual change is related to regular science—the explanation of experiences, general research, and generally accepted information. Thomas Kuhn (as cited in Posner et al. 1982) called these *paradigms* or *normal science*. The second phase of conceptual change is reached when the current thinking in science is challenged with conflicting information. Learners must reorganize their existing schema to accommodate the new information. This epistemological base of conceptual change can be related to current brain research previously discussed in this chapter. The new information about how the brain learns does not fit with the way many teachers instruct. As teachers learn and implement more body/brain-compatible practices into their classrooms, however, they are accommodating their teaching styles and curriculum. Brain research has tremendous implications for teaching and learning in our schools. At present, however, it conflicts with some of our current beliefs and practices including lecture versus discussion, activities versus inquiry, and teacher-driven curriculum versus student-driven curriculum.

Constructivists such as Ernst von Glaserfeld believe that learning is a process in which the learner takes new experiences and fits them into existing knowledge. Constructivist classrooms take the limelight away from the teacher and transfer it to the students. Constructivists have shifted from traditional classrooms, in which the teacher disseminates information and students participate only in rote learning for "right" answers, to inquiry classrooms, in which students direct the curriculum and pursue their own questions. Through this process, students experience conceptual change (von Glaserfeld's study as cited in Tobin, Tippins, and Gallard 1994). Students can pursue their own questions and drive the curriculum in an inquiry-based classroom. True inquiry and a truly integrated curriculum rather than an interdisciplinary curriculum begins with the learner's pursuit of his or her own individual questions. Through this pursuit, the necessary skills and concepts emerge (Beane 1997). Thus, the curriculum is not and cannot be completely established in advance. Districts adopt curricular standards that teachers must use as the guidelines for their planning, and this limits true inquiry by students. National science educators set these standards, but, because these are guidelines only, they provide for freedom and flexibility within each classroom, and then students can have the opportunity to pursue individual pursuits, while in turn meeting science standards.

Science instruction that promotes conceptual change must parallel meaningful curriculum. What makes curriculum meaningful? Areas of teaching, learning, problem solving, curriculum, and context have been researched in science education to measure conceptual change. Conceptual change is improved and enhanced through meaningful learning, and the two cannot be separated. Rather than having students memorize countless facts that can be obtained from another source in a moment, students should learn processes and concepts that are transferable to other learning situations. For this to happen, teachers must promote conceptual learning rather than facts and science processes rather than formulas. Each of these things must happen in a body/brain-compatible environment.

Teaching Rocks and Mineral: From Theory to Practice

To begin any "body/brain-compatible" unit, students must first have an experience with which to connect. Rather than using a field trip as a culmination to a unit, it is imperative to go on a "study trip" before beginning a unit so that every student has the opportunity to learn as much as possible. For my "Rocks and Minerals" unit, students visit a quarry to collect rock samples. I arrange for someone knowledgeable in this area of study to accompany us, and she even dresses like Mrs. Frizzle in the book, *Magic School Bus Inside the Earth*. The purpose of the study trip is to provide students with a firsthand experience of how and where rocks are found in nature. On this trip, students ask questions about the environment around them and record observations in their geology journals. Students might note patterns of reshaping of the Earth either by erosion or by some unnatural means. Students might develop questions about how the rocks formed or about their composition. Back in the classroom, students engage in a variety of activities, discussions, and inquiries, most of which incorporate collaborative group skills. The class develops a procedure for cooperative and collaborative groups. Ideas that evolve include

- All members work together to accomplish the task.
- Each group member should contribute ideas and responsibly fulfill duties.

Additionally, some roles that might be established—just like in the "real geology world" include

- *The Team Leader*—scientist in charge of reading directions and setting up equipment,
- *The Geologist*—scientist in charge of carrying out directions,
- *The Stenographer*—scientist in charge of recording all of the information, and
- *The Transcriber*—scientist who translates notes and communicates findings.

Opportunities for collaboration are offered through stations and whole-class activities.

The curriculum begins with Key Points (See Appendix B). The key points are a brain-compatible format for both teachers and students, clearly defining what the concepts and significant knowledge are within the unit. The conceptual key point serves as the overarching idea for the unit. This model of curriculum writing successfully reinforces what can be found in the literature about teaching with concepts versus isolated facts. In a brain-compatible curriculum, key points can by predetermined by the teacher or developed by the students. Certainly with the standard accountability in public schools, standards must be connected to established curriculum units while allowing for flexibility within and for more key points as students pursue their own individual inquiries. Overall, key points drive the curriculum planning.

Each day begins with a community circle, giving students the opportunity to discuss questions ranging from where they find rocks to their ideas about cycles. Secondly, a focus question is assigned to students individually to write about in their geology journals. Through the journal, teachers will have a written record of progress of science values and attitudes, knowledge, understanding, and skills. Posing the questions is crucial to this process of learning. Students should be encouraged to use their journal like a "diary," writing down their thoughts as they "do" science. Students are also given specific writing tasks by the teacher. Spelling, punctuation, and grammar should not be graded in these journals. Here is one example journal task: "Describe your special rock. Tell where you found it. Describe its physical characteristics and what makes it special to you." A focus question might read: *Where are rocks found?* Students need time to discuss their thoughts with their learning club or collaborative group. The idea is to set the stage for a possible accommodation or conceptual change opportunity. Community circles and geology journals aid in developing a classroom environment that appreciates communication about science ideas through both verbal and written speech. From a Vygotskyian theoretical perspective, students talk about science in order to help develop scientific ideas. Also through group experiences, students will construct knowledge and develop conceptual understandings (Reddy et al. 1998).

After community circles and journal writing each day, students participate in a hands-on/minds-on science experiment of an inquiry nature. Some of the lessons include embedded assessments (See Appendix C.) However, the overall assessment of the unit comes from analyzing a pretest/posttest concept map about the rock cycle. Concept maps, first introduced by Joseph Novak of Cornell University, are graphic organizers that aid students in demonstrating their knowledge about concepts, specifically science concepts. These hierarchical diagrams illustrate concepts with connectors among concepts (Novak, as cited in Starr and Krajcik 1990). Though they seem simple at first glance, concept maps are actually quite complex. Not only must students make links between concepts, they must also identify crosslinks. By using concept maps, teachers can see readily what students know about a concept and identify misconceptions. When used as a pretest, the maps allow students to demonstrate prior knowledge about a concept. This gives teachers a starting point for curriculum development. Concept maps are scored based on how concepts are linked together by propositions, examples, crosslinks, and their hierarchical nature (See Appendix D).

Assessment Practices

Learning is measured within the unit in a variety of ways. Pre- and posttest concept maps represent one way: Comparing the concept maps is evidence that students demonstrated learning and a conceptual change. Scoring the concept map can be challenging, but it serves as a valuable portfolio piece. Developing a valid scoring system presents the first problem. Also, one student may score lower than another because of limited links and cross-links, but he or she may demonstrate a greater understanding of the rock cycle. This problem illustrates the need for using more authentic assessment rather than using "scores" placed upon things. Another means of providing feedback is the experiment rubric. In my classroom, I continually teach how to use scientific methodology as a way of thinking for investigating problems. By reinforcing this approach, students show growth through the year as we progress through the curriculum. This is noted as students begin to formulate their own questions, make plans, gather materials, write procedures, and conduct experiments of their own designs.

Throughout the geology study, thorough documentation showed that all students had conceptual changes about the rock cycle, as demonstrated on the concept map pre- and posttest. Examples of growth based on the random sampling include the following:

- All students identified the three rock types: igneous, metamorphic, and sedimentary.
- All students identified rock properties or ways to describe and identify rocks.
- All students identified that rocks are made of minerals.
- All students indicated either an erosion concept, or heat or pressure, as a concept relating to how rocks are formed. Two of the four sampled also indicated cycles but did not have a well-thought-out proposition to indicate understanding.

Conclusions

A total body/brain-compatible unit cannot be developed overnight. Teachers must have a personal "conceptual change" about how to teach science. Perhaps I can best relate the idea of creating "body/brain-compatible" classrooms to experience with Posner's et al. (1982) theory of conceptual change and conditions for accommodation. Anderson and Smith (1987) write about the characteristics of conceptual change of teachers as they help students overcome scientific misconceptions. For teachers who are comfortable teaching science only from a textbook or even doing recipe activities, the ideas presented here might relate to the first rule of conceptual change. These ideas might conflict with what is currently happening in some rooms. Perhaps teachers will recognize that they have not been doing inquiry science and would be willing to change. This willingness to change fits with Posner's et al. (1982) conditions for accommodation:

- There must be dissatisfaction with existing conceptions.
  Teachers must have a realization that students will not necessarily discover science concepts on their own through activity-oriented science and certainly not from a textbook only.

- A new conception must be intelligible.
  Teachers must possess or develop an attitude of "I can do hands-on/minds-on inquiry science."
- A new conception must appear initially plausible.
  Teachers must know that these ideas are conceivable and see themselves applying inquiry in more situations.
- A new concept should suggest the possibility of a fruitful research program.
  Hopefully, teachers see themselves in their body/brain-compatible classrooms developing programs and curriculum units that incorporate total inquiry science and find this idea enticing.

References

Anderson, C. W., and E. L. Smith. 1987. Teaching science. In *Educators' handbook: A research perspective*, ed. V. Richardson-Koehler, 84–111. New York: Longman.

Beane, J. 1997. *Curriculum integration: Designing the core of democratic education*. New York: Teachers College Press.

Gardner, H. 1983. *Frames of mind*. New York: BasicBooks.

Kovalik, S. 1994. *Integrated thematic instruction: The model*. Kent, WA: Books for Educators.

Kovalik, S., and K. Olsen. 1991. *Kid's eye view of science: A teacher's handbook for implementing an integrated thematic approach to teaching science, K–6*. Village of Oak Creek, AZ: Center for the Future of Public Education.

Pedersen, B. 2005. The joy of CLASS: A journey toward exemplary schools, extraordinary teachers, and successful students. Indianapolis: CLASSWorks.

Posner, G., K. Strike, P. Hewson, and W. Gertzog. 1982. Accommodation of a scientific conception: Toward a theory of conceptual change. *Science Education* 66 (2): 211–227.

Reddy, M., P. Jacobs, C. McCrohon, and L. Rupert-Herrenkohl. 1998. *Creating scientific communities in the elementary classroom*. Portsmouth, NH: Heinemann.

Starr, M., and J. Krajcik. 1990. Concept maps as a heuristic for science curriculum development: Toward improvement in process and product. *Journal of Research in Science Teaching* 28 (10): 987–1000.

Tobin, K., D. Tippins, and A. J. Gallard. 1994. Research on instructional strategies for science teaching. In *Handbook of research on science teaching and learning*, ed. D. Gabel, 45–93. New York: Macmillan.

Appendix A

Rocks and Minerals Project Choices

Knowledge

Make a chart identifying the different types of rocks. Identify each type and give examples.
Chart the different types of rocks and illustrate your findings.

Comprehension

Write a report about a specific rock or mineral.
Research how different cultures have used rocks and minerals to build and/or create. Share your findings creatively.

Application

Make a model of the Earth and label its layers. Thoroughly discuss each layer and the types of rocks found there.

Pretend a rock has feelings just like you. Write about its life from his or her perspective. How might it feel to be picked up and thrown down all the time?

Make a card/board game that teaches others about rocks and minerals.

Analysis

Make a graph showing the different rocks and their usages.

Make a Venn diagram comparing the three different rock types.

Create a database on the computer showing the different rocks, their types, properties, and uses.

Synthesis

Write a song that includes facts/concepts about rocks and minerals. Write it to a familiar tune or create your own.

Create a new use for a rock and show it in some sort of display. Be sure to incorporate how the rock properties will be good for this new use.

Evaluation

Participate in a debate about which rock is the most important and why. Act it out with a friend.

Decide, after research, which rock has the highest values. Rank your results of your top five rocks. Defend your conclusions.

Design your own project…investigate your own question…get teacher approval!*

Appendix B
Rock Cycle Key Points

Conceptual Key Point—A cycle is a complete round or series of events that is repeated. It is important to understand cycles because many things in nature transpire in a repeating pattern.

The rock cycle is the gradual and continuous change that rocks go through to change from one type of rock into another.

The Earth has three layers: the crust, the mantle, and the core.

Rocks are made of one or more minerals. Minerals are pure, solid materials found in the Earth's crust. Minerals in the rock form crystals that have a definite geometric shape.

The three types of rocks are igneous, sedimentary, and metamorphic.

Sedimentary rocks are formed from layers of sediment (mud, sand, and gravel) compacted together.

Igneous rocks are formed when molten rock cools and becomes solid.

Metamorphic rocks are formed from igneous and sedimentary rock that has been put under heat and pressure.

Erosion is the process of water, glaciers, winds, waves, and other forces wearing away the surface of the Earth.

Smaller rocks come from the breakage and weathering of bedrock and larger rocks. Soil is made from weathered rock, partly from plant remains, and also contains many living organisms.

Appendix C
Science Experiment Rubric

Criteria	Ranking/Score	Score	Comments
States problem or question	Outstanding Essentially complete Partial statement Not at all	Score 3 Score 2 Score 1 Score 0	
Formulates a hypothesis	Outstanding Essentially complete Partial statement Not at all	Score 3 Score 2 Score 1 Score 0	
Formulates experiment (materials and procedure)	Outstanding Essentially complete Partial statement Not at all	Score 3 Score 2 Score 1 Score 0	
Carries out experiment (Follows directions)	Outstanding Essentially complete Partial statement Not at all	Score 3 Score 2 Score 1 Score 0	
Makes logical conclusions based on results. (Results—You should discuss your results based on your data and evidence; you must logically discuss why you think you obtained the results that you did.)	Outstanding Essentially complete Partial statement Not at all	Score 3 Score 2 Score 1 Score 0	
TOTAL			

Appendix D
  Student Pretest and Posttest Concept Maps

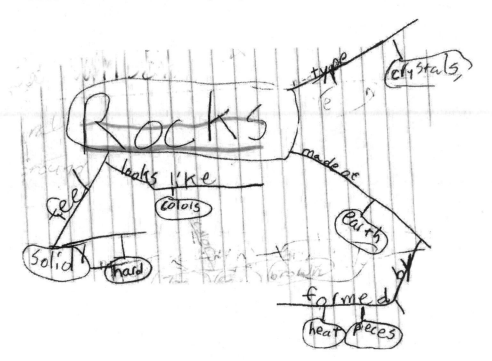

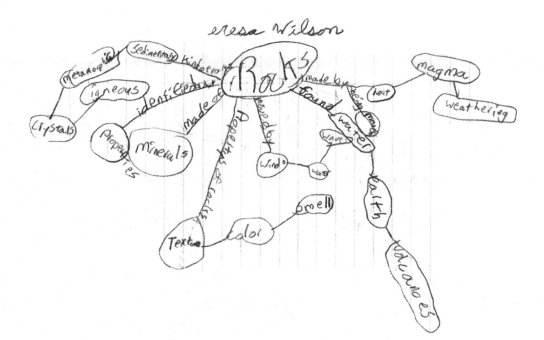

The Primary Classroom:

Science, Literacy, and Inquiry

Lee Ann Cervini
Terry A. Taylor Elementary School

Peter Veronesi
State University of New York, College at Brockport

"Inquiry is the process of exploration which is guided by a personal interest or question. It involves risk taking and experimenting which can lead to pathways where the learner may discover meaningful concepts and understandings."
— *Marilyn Austin, Teacher in Residence, The Exploratorium, San Francisco*

Setting

Questioning is the driving force behind the innate desire to learn what it is we seek. As teachers, we strive to provide a learning environment that embraces our students' quest for knowledge yet is responsive to the curriculum-driven mandates of our district and the state. How do we effectively bridge the gap between what we intuitively know is best for students and the demands of our profession, especially in the realm of content teaching? The answer lies in engaging students in the use of the inquiry process and hooking them at the point of their interests.

Children learn best when they are engaged in meaningful projects that are relevant to their own design and when they are enthusiastically involved in explorations that interest them.

Students engage in inquiry about the properties of water.

Taking this to heart, I designed primary inquiry boxes, focusing on the big ideas and content in science and integrating these with literacy skills and developmentally appropriate work (see p. 107 for a description of one inquiry box). Well-known literacy guru Reggie Routman (2000) said it best: "Believe that questioning and investigation are at the heart of meaningful curriculum and learning. A question-centered curriculum includes question-posing, exploring, negotiating, clarifying, extending, seeking, and answering … all of which lead to more questions as students engage in authentic activities."

Students during reading of expository text material.

At the primary level, literacy is a critical component of science instruction, and building literacy skills through high-interest science investigations helps to build student success in both science and literacy. To be successful, educators must first recognize the critical role that literacy plays in science instruction. Students need to be immersed in reading, writing, thinking, and speaking about science just as an authentic scientist is. In the real world, scientists are engaged with science in tandem with literacy, and they read relevant literature. They write about their investigations and conclusions, and they document and present their findings to colleagues. Students must pursue science with the same multidimensional approach.

"One engages in science-related reading and writing as one does science. To put it differently, it is the doing of science, not just reading about it, that students learn to master the concepts that will enable them to better understand both the reading and writing of expository and procedural text. To teach science reading and writing and talk about it without hands-on work makes as much sense as learning to play the piano on a paper keyboard," says E. Wendy Saul (2002).

Fluency in both reading and writing are needed for success in each discipline. With inquiry, students use language to solve real science investigations. They must engage with a text and think critically about what they are learning so that they can relate it to the science investigation they are trying to solve. Incorporating literacy with inquiry encourages purposeful use of language and enriches formal and informal discourse. Finally, literacy is a means by which students can build self-reflective practices through a variety of techniques such as journaling and oral sharing. As a result of combining literacy with science inquiry, students are engaged with purposeful communication that promotes authentic language usage.

Students with text material from an inquiry box on the properties of solids.

Teachers can use specific strategies to develop students' ability to read, ponder, and comprehend science as a means of becoming successful with their inquiry investigations (see Figure 1). Before students can be expected to apply strategies on their own, teachers must instruct them systematically in how to use the strategies, monitor them as they are learning, and spot-check them as they transfer the strategies to independent use: Teachers must first model using various strategies until students are able to use them on their own. One effective strategy is to teach students about *metacognition* or thinking about their own thinking. With this technique, students learn how to process information by making connections and self-questioning while reading and reflecting upon what they just read. When students are making connections, it helps them to build schema that enhance reading comprehension and memory.

Tell them: While reading, make connections

- to what you have learned or know,
- to what you have experienced or done, and
- to other books or stories you have read or heard.

Other effective balanced reading strategies are covered in the appendix (pp. 110–117). The goal is to provide students with a variety of strategies that balance their approaches to learning about science through literacy as they investigate with their inquiries, research their questions, and pull together their conclusions. Teachers can, for example, conduct small, guided reading groups using science text material or science-based big books for shared reading experiences.

Figure 1. Balanced Reading Strategies to Use With Nonfiction and Fiction Text

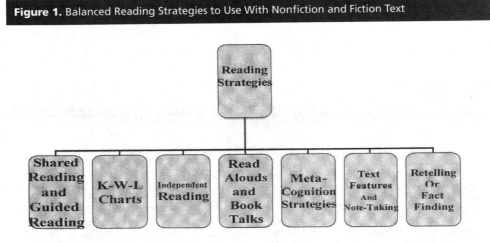

Students must learn how to be independent and effective strategic readers. The ability to find key ideas and important information and make connections is a necessary and important skill for success with science texts. To navigate effectively and glean information from expository text, young readers must know what to do before, during, and after reading, and when reading breaks down. Strategies that promote the development of these reading skills include the following things good readers do before, during, and after reading:

- Look through the book and think about what they see,

- Ask themselves questions about what they are reading and make connections, and
- Check themselves to make sure that know what they read by retelling.

What good readers do when reading breaks down into the following:
- Look at the picture,
- Say the beginning sound(s),
- Stretch the word out,
- Skip the word, and read to the end of the sentence,
- Go back and read again fixing their reading, and
- Ask for help.

Research finds that using nonfiction texts to scaffold science inquiry builds a strong foundation for science achievement and informational reading and writing. This helps to build valuable prior knowledge from which students can develop questions to launch inquiry investigations. Using nonfiction text is attractive to students, taps into their natural interests, and provides authentic opportunities for them to read and write. Using informational science texts provides modeling opportunities for teachers' "read alouds" to build student questioning techniques, content understanding, and understandings of new or unusual text features not yet explored by young readers.

In selecting texts, teachers should search for books that are more than just collections of facts and information. Books that show science in action—real scientists working in their fields—should be included. Whenever possible, a variety of books showing the vast array of real science taking place in the real world helps students contextualize science.

In addition to reading about science, writing plays an active and intricate role in the process of inquiry science in the classroom. There are a variety of balanced writing strategies to use with nonfiction text to support science inquiry and development (see Figure 2). It is essential to use a variety of strategies with your students to help them develop into more confident and able writers.

Figure 2. Balanced Writing Strategies to Use With Nonfiction and Fiction Text

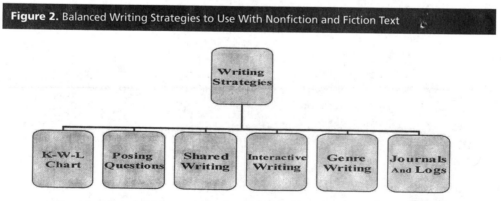

Too often students struggle with their writing because they lack passion and the content upon which to base their writing, but, with inquiry science, students have a defined purpose and audience for their writing. Embedding writing in inquiry science to access the content is an effective learning strategy. Writing to learn science is a excellent way to enhance thinking and learning about science. Writing helps students extract more of the content and pushes them to think about the big picture of science concepts rather than to learn just basic facts. Writing is student driven and allows for a student's "science voice" to sing. This process helps students internalize learning for better understanding and recall. Having students write in science encourages higher-level thinking, resulting in more abstract thought and connections. Writing to learn is expressive, personal, and exploratory by nature and allows students freedoms that lead to greater understanding and richer learning.

When writing in the inquiry science classroom, remember the following guidelines:

- Set your expectations for student writing and stick to them.
- Make use of frequent minilessons and modeling to ensure student success with various writing tasks.
- Keep students focused on authentic writing based on their inquiry investigations.
- Provide time to confer with individuals and small groups of students and opportunities for students to share and celebrate their writing successes.

Science inquiry in the primary classroom is a different approach to teaching science and follows constructivist teaching theory closely. The least constructivist approach is the traditional use of textbook and company-supplied materials to teach science. Next in the sequence are demonstration lessons and hands-on activities that are more student-centered approaches—but learning outcomes are still controlled by the teacher. Finally, the most constructivist approach is the inquiry method.

Students use guide sheets for fact finding.

In a science inquiry classroom, student interests, curiosities, and experiences falling within the curriculum can form the basis for generating a multitude of questions to be investigated and shared following the scientific process. The key to making the inquiry cycle a success in the primary classroom is early student engagement with science and purposeful linkage to literacy.

One of the most valuable aspects of using inquiry-based science teaching in the classroom is the rich and authentic discussions that drive conversations during an investigation. Students are immersed in science, and science becomes their passion. They can be heard reflecting and discussing with each other—genuine science. They listen to one another and translate what is happening into their own words, reflecting their own abilities to explain and express their new understandings of science.

These scientific conversations become the shared understandings of concepts and ideas behind all the work and experiences of the students. Through discourse, students reflect on the nature of science and are exposed to their own thoughts and conclusions. It is a part of the scientific community to share and critique each others' ideas. This is engaging in real science, and this helps to build strong involvement in science skills, such as relying on data, engaging in logical thinking, and being open to the conclusions of others that can cause one to reflect and change.

Science begins with a simple curiosity about the interactions of our world and leads to creative, imaginative, and wondrous thoughts about those interactions. Young children come to school with a head full of thoughts and questions. They are true scientists but all too often lose that natural curiosity. Using inquiry in the primary classroom nurtures and supports the natural momentum of young, budding scientists.

Inquiry Boxes in the Primary Classroom: The Nuts and Bolts

My students respond well to knowing ahead of time my expectations for behavior and appropriate conditions for a positive learning environment. Establishing and teaching these conditions early in the process is crucial to the success of an inquiry-based classroom. This proactive approach reduces disciplinary issues, because all you need to do is point to a chart as a reminder for students to keep themselves in check or as a positive reinforcement when students are following your conditions.

One of the first conditions I set with my students is that doing science is active, loud, and mind engaging. I always preface this with "doing the work of a real scientist," and my students truly enjoy thinking of themselves as young scientists. I have them hooked right up front, so it makes addressing "working conditions" very enjoyable.

We brainstorm descriptors for the active, loud, and mind-engaging working conditions of a scientist, and I model what each one of the descriptors that we come up with looks like in my classroom. Then the fun begins with some role playing. For example, *active* means doing, not running around the room, and we role-play what *doing* looks like. When I am finished, students have a strong sense of my expectations for the working conditions of doing science inquiry boxes in my classroom.

Following a Scientific Process

I want my students acting and thinking like scientists, and my students buy into this. My commitment to them is to teach them the skills a scientist needs for success and to build within our practices structures that ensure they are transferring these skills to the work they do with the inquiry boxes.

I teach and model each step of the scientific process that I expect my primary students to include in the science work that they do. I label this on a poster as "The Work of a Scientist" and display this in the classroom because I refer to it frequently as students are engaged in inquiry.

The steps I include on the poster are
- developing questions,
- selecting one question to pursue and making a guess as to what will happen,
- researching the content of the question and experimenting to find an answer,
- recording information every step of the way, and
- writing a conclusion.

I provide students with guide sheets for each of the steps, and, when they are all done, I bind their work into a book to be placed in our "science research library" but only if their work passes the peer review process.

Successful First Steps With Inquiry Boxes

Inquiry boxes house a collection of resources that students can use as they investigate a question. The secret is to try and place in the boxes as many resources as you can that students may need. I always include a variety of expository text materials at various reading levels, hands-on science experimentation tools, and any media or software programs that might help as well. You will find that you cannot be prepared for every single question that students want to investigate, but you can have a wealth of materials on hand that will make it easier.

For example, in an inquiry box on the properties of air, I included various expository text reading materials, a small fan, a hot-air popcorn popper, and a blow dryer. Students use these only with supervision to maintain a safety-conscious environment. I also included a variety of items students could use to collect or experiment with such as plastic bags, balloons, small kites, chimes, wind socks, weather vanes, a small tarp, toy sailboats, and cotton balls. Of course, I did not think of everything. A group of students wanted to in-

Students explore materials from an inquiry box on the properties of air.

vestigate how sails capture air to move a sailboat. They decided that they needed a wading pool for the sailboat to be able to conduct their experiment. Luckily, that was not a difficult request to fulfill.

As with any new topic of study, I like to begin with a KWL (what I Know, what I Want to know, and what I Learned) chart. This gives my students a chance to tap into their prior knowledge about a subject and share their experiences. It also gives me a baseline of information about my students' readiness levels before we move forward. I get a sense of my students' strengths and weaknesses and of the general direction in which to start.

I have found that different students begin in different ways. Some students need time to read the science expository text to develop a deeper understanding of the science content and build their background knowledge. Other students need the time to "play" with the science materials within the inquiry box before interacting with text. Either way, students direct their own learning and begin to develop their own questions that they wish to investigate in their own unique ways. My role lies in knowing my students and being able to facilitate their learning from the point at which they begin.

Often, after developing their own testable question to investigate, students would find that they needed to go back to the text for more information. This is where I found my facilitation critical for moving students to a higher level of thinking. Students would read, question, test, and have more questions. At this point, sending them back to the text or even contacting an expert in the realm of their investigation proved helpful. Repeated exposure provides understanding, and engaging in text material supports deeper understandings.

Embedding Literacy for Student-Driven Investigations

Primary students have a wide range of literacy skills. Often this is a big challenge for a teacher who is beginning to use inquiry boxes with young learners. You must first know your students' literacy strengths and weaknesses because you will have to support varying levels of literacy development while your students are engaged in scientific inquiry. Unfortunately, there is no easy or quick way to get to know your students, so inquiry boxes are not something you start right away.

Before my students begin working with an inquiry box, I review with them the scientific process that I termed "the work of a scientist." The first important task they have to complete is determining and journaling what questions they have about a topic. I model this process for my students, and they work independently to complete the various tasks, but I must circulate and help as necessary.

While groups of students are engaged with inquiry, I go about observing, teaching, and giving feedback to individuals or small groups of students who are using, confusing, and learning literacy skills. This is when I must draw upon my knowledge of my students to support their acquiring these skills.

For instance, when I notice a small group generating few questions and I determine that they do not have much prior knowledge about their topic, I pull them aside. I do an interactive read-aloud using an expository text from the inquiry box that has a reading level a little above the reading level of most of the students in the group. Then I release the students to continue building their list of questions. If they still have trouble, I work with them on how to brainstorm questions and give them a list of question stems from which to draw some ideas.

Once students have generated a variety of questions, they must decide which one to pursue. My students know the difference between "testable" and "nontestable" questions, and they use this knowledge to make a decision and select a "testable" question. Again, I monitor each group's choice and facilitate appropriate choices when necessary.

When the groups are designing their investigations, I make sure they have appropriate materials. If groups do not have what they need listed on their guide sheet, I let them discover this on their own. This makes for interesting group dynamics.

Sometimes I have to teach a minilesson to students about the writing involved with doing inquiry. One area that is often a target is keeping that daily log sheet. Sometimes students do not know how or what to write, and this is a productive opportunity for students to learn that writing is communicating.

Next, I might encourage another group to complete a shared reading experience using one of the science expository "big books" in their inquiry box and have them use this experience for research and to find facts about their topic. Because I have frequently modeled this technique with all my students, I let them take charge. I might join the group as a participant and look for how the students interact with the content.

I also like to pull aside small, guided reading groups if I have multiple copies of a text for a particular inquiry box. I usually make this quick and focus on two very important aspects of reading expository text—understanding vocabulary and using text features. Once I finish a quick guided reading, I always chart with the students the key facts they learned from the reading and remind them to record this in their daily logs and save to use in their research.

As inquiry moves on in my classroom, I ensure that students are using the guide sheets to keep them on track with "the work of a scientist." I monitor and facilitate this process to ensure success.

Each student must synthesize his or her investigation and include all he or she learned while engaging with the expository reading materials. He or she then must present this information as a written report. As this time approaches, I do whole-group minilessons if everyone needs instruction. If not, I do small-group minilessons. Graphic organizers help students pull together all the information into one written report.

Pulling It All Together

When it is time to wrap up the inquiry boxes that support a particular unit of study, I bring my students back together and we revisit the KWL chart we created to kick off this study. It is an empowering experience for students to confirm what they wanted to learn, the *W* in KWL and to share what additional learning has taken place, the *L* in KWL.

One of the most positive outgrowths of this process is the establishment of our "science resource library." Students know that, when they finish their investigations, their peers will review their work. We use the following questions for the review:

- Did the scientist have all of the steps in his or her work, including a log?
- Did the scientist design an experiment that tested a hypothesis?
- Did the scientist reflect what he or she learned in his or her final research paper?

If their peers agree with and approve of a student's submitted work, it is laminated and bound into a book for our science resource library. My students think this is a big deal, and they love sharing their work and ultimately having it placed with such esteem in our renowned library.

Conclusion

My success with inquiry boxes is evident on the faces and in the work of my young true scientists. They remind me every day why it is important to teach science through inquiry, not in the words they say but rather in the products of their experiences. Inquiry taps into their interests. This builds upon their natural curiosity and desire to question everything around them. The experiences provide them numerous opportunities to engage in their own learning, and the interactions promote higher-level thinking and problem-solving skills.

How about you? Are you ready to discover the power of your own enthusiasm? Are you willing to take time to share and wonder with curious young minds? Can you handle the unexpected? And are you ready to watch your students soar to new heights? If the answer to any of these questions is yes, then go for it. Go implement inquiry science in your classroom. I guarantee you will be surprised by your own flexibility and delighted by the reception of your students.

References

Akerson, V., and T. Young. 2004. Non-fiction know-how. *Science and Children* 41 (6): 48–51.

Austin, P., and C. Buxton. 2004. Better books, better teaching. *Science and Children* 41 (2): 28–32.

Butzow, C., and J. Butzow. 1989. *Science through children's literature: An integrated approach.* Englewood, CO: Teacher Ideas Press.

Bybee, R. 1997. *Learning science and the science of learning.* Washington, DC: NSTA Press.

Chalufour, I., C. Hoisington, R. Moriarty, J. Winokur, and K. Worth. 2004. The science and mathematics of building structures. *Science and Children* 41 (4): 30–34.

Llewellyn, D. 2002. *Inquire within: Implementing inquiry-based science standards.* Thousand Oaks, CA: Corwin Press.

Lowery, L. F., ed. 2000. *Pathways to the science standards: Guidelines for moving the vision into practice, Elementary School Edition.* Washington, DC: National Academy Press.

Pearce, C. 1999. *Nurturing inquiry: Real science for elementary classrooms.* Portsmouth, NH: Heinemann.

Routman, R. 2000. *Conversations: Strategies for teaching, learning, and evaluating.* Portsmouth, NH: Heinemann.

Saul, E. W. 2002. *Science workshop: Reading, writing, and thinking like a scientist.* Portsmouth, NH: Heinemann.

Worth, K., R. Moriarty, and J. Winokur. 2004. Capitalizing on literacy connections. *Science and Children* 41 (5): 35–39.

APPENDIX

Teaching science in the primary classroom in response to the National Science Education Standards requires awareness, reflection, and, usually, change. In a responsive classroom, teachers take action with more emphasis on assessment standards, content and inquiry standards, teaching standards, and professional development standards that encourage the following:

Teaching Standards

Understanding and responding to individual students' interests, strengths, experiences, and needs:

Learning for students is all about motivation, and research notes that motivation is highest when students can connect with the learning through their interests, strengths, experiences, or needs. The challenge is to incorporate this for each student into every lesson. This is not an easy task. With primary students, it is often difficult to identify their interests, because their interests can change at the drop of a hat and the students do not necessarily understand how to articulate their strengths or learning styles. I find that knowing my primary students takes a lot of observation and preparedness for what I call *on-the-spot* responsiveness to specific needs. One technique that can be used right away is a KWL chart. A KWL chart is an excellent way to engage students with the topic immediately, and it allows me the flexibility I need to plan instruction accordingly.

Selecting and adapting curriculum:

The science curriculum in a primary classroom should respond to your students' needs to make sense of the physical and living world around them. It is important to adapt the curriculum to the specific environment in which your students live and to make the most of the resources in your area to help meet your curriculum. My students happen to live in an area abundant with wildlife. Although the wildlife does not readily present itself during the day, numerous wildlife rehabilitators in the area can work with my students. My goal with the mandated curriculum is to make it as hands-on and connected to my students' lives as possible.

Focusing on student understanding and use of scientific knowledge, ideas, and the inquiry process:

In the primary classroom, the curriculum is basic, but it forms the building blocks for more difficult concepts to come. It is imperative that primary students develop a conceptual understanding of the basic science knowledge and ideas through a constructivist, hands-on approach. This method allows a teacher to move students to deeper understandings based on what they already know, understand, and do. At the heart of this technique is gleaning from students their first level of questions as the driving force to move them through the science processes and to deeper understandings.

Guiding students in active and extended scientific inquiry:

Science is the art of questioning and then applying what one knows to test hypotheses and draw conclusions or to start all over. This can happen in a primary classroom if a teacher facilitates the development of students' understanding and use of scientific knowledge and ideas in an active, hands-on learning environment. I tell my students that learning and doing science is active, loud, and mind engaging. I model what each of these is, and then we brainstorm descriptors for each and keep that list posted all year. I often refer to this chart as positive reinforcement for students who are engaged in learning—or as a reminder to students who are not—to move their learning in a positive direction. This is my way of helping students understand what is expected of them during the science inquiry process. Also, when students are engaged in experimentation, I have them follow a simplified version of the scientific process that I keep posted all year as well. Early in the year, I model each step and then we brainstorm what it is that primary students should be doing for each step. The steps I focus on with my students include developing questions, selecting one question to pursue and making a guess as to what will happen, researching the content of the question and experimenting to find an answer, recording information every step of the way, and writing a conclusion. I provide students with guide sheets for each of the steps, and, when students are done, I bind their work into a book to be placed in our science research library, but only if their work passes the peer review process.

Providing opportunities for scientific discussion and debate among students:

Before any work can be added to our science resource library, students must orally present their findings to their classmates. We evaluate each group's findings against three criteria:

- Did the scientist include all the steps of his or her work, including a log?
- Did the scientist design an experiment that tested a hypothesis?
- Did the scientist reflect on what he or she learned in his or her final research paper?

Continually assessing student understanding:

One advantage of using an inquiry process to teach science is that I am able to continually assess my students on multiple levels. As the facilitator, I am able to freely spot-check learning on a continual basis and provide immediate feedback to each student in the process. Those students who I know need more guidance will have my attention more than those who need more independence. Also, the peer-review process engages the students on different levels. They become the experts when reviewing other students' work and, at the same time, are learning aspects of the subject they did not pursue.

Supporting a classroom community with cooperation, shared responsibility, and respect:

Building an inquiry-based scientific community within the classroom develops so much more than just the scientific knowledge of the students. This strategy builds a classroom community of cooperation, shared responsibility, and respect. It also helps to build the independent thinking skills of each student and the ability of each student to analyze his or her own learning. Ultimately, the message I am sending to my students is that each has the tools to be a successful student and an intelligent learner.

Working with other teachers to enhance the science program:

In developing my inquiry boxes, I often rely on borrowing resources from other teachers, and that always leads to sharing my boxes across grade levels. I have no problem sharing with other grades, because I always feel students at different developmental levels will bring a different perspective to the learning process. Also, there are so many questions that students initially generate with a topic, and, with limited time with each box, they could always revisit it in the future and research the other questions they had the last time they explored an inquiry box.

Content and Inquiry Standards

Understanding scientific concepts and developing abilities of inquiry—learning subject matter disciplines in the context of inquiry, technology, science in personal and social perspectives, and history and nature of science:

With my inquiry boxes, students generate their own questions to explore. I provide ample supplies and resources within each box, but it is up to the students to engage their powers of thought and move their thinking through the scientific process and build understandings based on their own research and experimentation with teacher facilitation and guidance.

Integrating all aspects of science content:

Because students develop their own questions to test, they are highly motivated to follow through and to find answers. My role is to keep them moving in the right direction and provide necessary intradisciplinary support. For instance, a group of students wanted to test what helps ice melt faster. They came up with so many ideas that they did not know where to begin. Letting students have the experience of defining their ideas, with my guidance, and integrating all areas of science to support their ideas let them see that the process of doing science is not definitive and requires the ability to use whatever resources are available.

Studying a few fundamental science concepts:

All my inquiry boxes are designed to engage students in the big picture of learning primary-level science. One series of boxes addresses the properties of matter as a fundamental primary-level science concept through which students explore states of matter using their senses to define their understandings. I also monitor the inquiries and make certain that the students are working in a safe environment.

Implementing inquiry as instructional strategies, abilities, and ideas to be learned:

As an instructional strategy, inquiry boxes are designed to connect students with science concepts through the process of inquiry. The outcome by which ideas are developed and learned is then based on individual learners or groups of learners interacting with the materials within an inquiry box, their own developed questions, and on-the-spot facilitation by the teacher.

Activities that investigate and analyze science questions:

At the heart of all inquiry boxes are the questions students bring to be investigated and resolved through applying a scientific process and using their problem-solving abilities while acquiring thinking skills.

Investigations over extended periods of time:

Using inquiry boxes requires flexibility with time and scheduling. In a primary classroom it is easy to schedule inquiry boxes during center time throughout the day or during a specified period as long as students know what is expected of them once they finish an investigation. With inquiry boxes, students self-manage the amount of time they spend investigating their questions and have the opportunity to work at their own paces. Of course, the teacher will need to monitor primary students with this process and build in feedback opportunities to ensure everyone is on track.

Process skills in context:

Because primary students have had limited exposure, if any, to the process skills of doing science, breaking the skills down into simplified steps and spending some up-front time modeling each step is important. The steps I focus on with my students include

- developing questions,
- selecting one question to pursue and making a guess as to what will happen,
- researching the content of the question and experimenting to find an answer,
- recording information every step of the way, and
- writing a conclusion.

I provide students with guide sheets for each of the steps, and, when they are all done, I bind their work into a book to be placed in our science resource library—but only if their work passes the peer review process.

Using multiple process skills such as manipulative, cognitive, procedural; using evidence and strategies for developing or revising an explanation:

At the primary level, students are using basic science process skills but are encouraged to examine their thinking and problem-solving ability each step of the way. The focus is always on the evidence of their work, and students rely on each other to help them evaluate every step they take. I encourage group work, and students use guide sheets to help them follow the process. The teacher is the key in facilitating much of this process. Using questioning strategies, the teacher encourages students to examine their evidence and hone their explanations.

Science as argument and explanation; communicating science explanations; groups of students analyzing and synthesizing data after defending conclusions:

At the primary level students love to share their science ideas and what they learned through doing science. It is important to structure the environment to facilitate a feeling of safety while sharing and to move students' learning to a deeper understanding through the collective experiences of all students. For example, students use their guide sheets to help them record important information for every step of the scientific process that is outlined for them and then present their findings to their peers, again following their guide sheets. Peers are encouraged to give feedback with—and sometimes without—teacher prompting. Again, I model and chart the process for students well before they are involved in their first sharing experience. Primary students need guidance about how to give positive and helpful (negative) feedback and how to share appropriately their own ideas about the topic presented by another group.

Doing more investigations in order to develop understanding, ability, values of inquiry, and knowledge of science content:

The flexibility in a primary classroom lends itself well to structuring science inquiry throughout the school day and to giving students choice as to when and how much time they should invest in the investigations. I like to schedule large blocks of time when students can freely work on the science inquiry boxes. Because the boxes integrate science with literacy and mathematics skills, I can justify easily providing the choice for students to do science at any given time throughout the day. But I must help students reach a reasonable balance in the choices they make, and I can do this because I know my students well—their interests and learning styles.

Applying the results of experiments to scientific arguments and explanations:

At the conclusion of investigating a question, I hold a conference with each student involved to make sure he or she can articulate what happened and can base the conclusion on the research and experimentation he or she did with his or her group. Their work is further scrutinized as they share with peers, and the discussion is open for positive and constructive feedback. This helps to build a scientific community and a sense of support and trust among classmates.

Management of ideas and information:

In the primary classroom, it is important to keep the big ideas and concepts of science that students are learning at the forefront of all information that is continually shared throughout the year. That is why I like to maintain a science resource library right in my classroom. All the inquiry investigations that students complete are bound into "books" and prominently displayed in our classroom library, and whenever another student or group of students are investigating a similar question, I always guide students towards reviewing the work of their peers. It is amazing what great pride and level of accomplishment students feel in their work once it makes it to the classroom library.

Public communication of student ideas and work to classmates:

I found that primary students like to share their ideas with classmates and enjoy learning what others investigated. Because the depth and breath of the topics tend to be limited and students finish inquiry boxes at various rates, student sharing does not take an enormous amount of time and students are able to maintain their attention for the relatively short presentations.

Assessment Standards

Assessing what is most highly valued:

With inquiry boxes, assessing student progress is informal and ongoing. As the teacher, I am able to assess how students follow the scientific process to develop their own understandings of the big ideas and concepts relevant to primary level science development rather than discrete elements of unconnected knowledge.

Assessing rich, well-structured knowledge:

Inquiry boxes provide the opportunity for students to structure their own learning and come to their own conclusions. This gives me the option of assessing students' knowledge base at a variety of levels depending on the particular student and the particular topic investigated.

Assessing scientific understanding and reasoning:

Providing primary students with a structure with which to investigate science helps them develop scientific understanding and reasoning ability. I like to give students an outline of prompts on guide sheets that help them to frame their thinking and respond to their learning. This helps me assess their progress with the big science ideas and concepts they are investigating.

Assessing to learn what students do understand:

Learning about your students by preassessing what they already know is the best way to form baseline data and knowledge about them. From there, use this information to help you achieve your goals and objectives related to the big ideas and concepts in science that you want your students to know, to understand, and to be able to do at the end of the study. This information can help you know how to group students according to readiness, interest, or learning styles when introducing inquiry boxes and beginning inquiry investigations with your students.

Assessing achievement and opportunity to learn:

Providing a variety of opportunities and choices for students to show what they know, understand, and can do with the big science ideas and concepts they have learned is wise. Before moving to a new area of study and after all students have explored the various inquiry boxes under the concepts being studied and presented their investigations, I like to have students select a creative way to share something they learned. The choices might include presenting a skit about a science topic they learned about or making a poster. This gives the students an opportunity to synthesize their learning and showcase it through a creative medium. Using this strategy, students are tapping into their own learning profiles and sharing with others in a manner that may extend the learning of those absorbing their presentations.

Students engaged in ongoing assessment of their work and that of others:

It is important to build ongoing self-reflection and checkpoints of informal and formal assessment into the structure of any classroom work. When I use inquiry boxes, I regularly meet with students to provide feedback and guidance on their progress. Because much of what my students do is collaborative, they benefit from the insight of others as well as sharing with all of their classmates before research can de displayed in our classroom library.

Teachers involved in the development of external assessments:

It will help your students if, wherever possible, you involve yourself with developing the curriculum writing and assessment that directly affects your students. Sharing your knowledge and expertise about the level of students with whom you work leads to positive outcomes for everyone.

Professional Development Standards

Inquiry into teaching and learning:

The research behind teaching using an inquiry method is clear and simple: Students learn best by doing science! The inquiry method provides enough structure that students can learn to take charge of their own learning and teachers have a framework from which to engage and monitor learners. In the primary classroom, the inquiry method takes full advantage of students' typically questioning and exploring natures.

Learning science through investigation and inquiry:

Investigating science through inquiry goes hand in hand with what research says is best practice for student learning. Inquiry builds upon students' interests, knowledge, expertise, and curiosities in such a fashion as to make learning seamless and natural.

Integration of science and teaching knowledge:

At the heart of inquiry are the questions from which all investigations pursue.

Integration of theory and practice in the school setting:

Integrating of the theory of inquiry teaching into the school setting takes time, training, and effort on part of teachers and administrators. It is a different approach to teaching. Many teachers struggle with giving up control of learning to their students and becoming the facilitator rather than the disseminator of information, but it can be successfully done. I have found it helpful to adhere to a few of the following guidelines while implementing an inquiry approach to teaching and learning:

- Know your students' strengths and weaknesses in relation to readiness, interests, and learning styles;
- Pre-assess your students before beginning any inquiry lesson as a means of deepening your understandings of your students; and
- Put in place and model effective classroom structures to facilitate the inquiry process.

Collegial and collaborative learning:

Share, share, and share with teachers who are implementing an inquiry-based teaching approach in their classrooms. They will become your strongest supporters, pool for resources, and sources of encouragement during the process.

Long-term coherent plans:

Plan well. Thoroughly think through the process of changing your classroom to an inquiry-based one. If at all possible, visit classrooms of colleagues already implementing inquiry. Begin collecting resources and securing any funds you many need to help in the process. With my inquiry boxes, I am always looking for resources to add to and expand my collection.

A variety of professional development activities:

Attend professional development training and conferences that support inquiry in the classroom. The National Science Teachers Association hosts an annual conference with numerous sessions that illustrate an inquiry-based approach to teaching science in the classroom.

Mix of internal and external expertise—staff developers as facilitators, consultants, and planners:

Don't settle for one source. Like any good researcher, look to many sources for supporting your shift to an inquiry-based classroom. I used books, colleagues, and conferences to begin my shift, and it did not happen overnight. I took one step at a time to put together the program of inquiry boxes I now offer my students.

Teacher as intellectual, reflective practitioner; teacher as producer of knowledge about teaching; teacher as leader; teacher as a member of a collegial professional community; and teacher as source and facilitator of change:

All of this defines today's teacher. We have a commitment not only to our students but also to the profession and to growing it in the direction of best practices. In today's rapidly changing society, students are expected to function at a higher level, to be multifaceted in the realm of knowledge, and to possess the ability to adapt to a variety of technologies and environments with the snap of a finger. The building block for this type of flexibility is not content. It's *process*. Give students the tools to manipulate information, and you give them the ability to succeed in an ill-defined future. My belief is that the inquiry model of teaching does just that.

The DESERT Project:

Collaborative Professional Development

LaVonne Riggs
Tucson Unified School District (TUSD)

Setting

The field of professional development is being redefined. People in the field are looking for the best ways to support the reforms that have been initiated and studied over the past two decades. The release of standards in content areas, particularly those in science and mathematics, and a call by politicians and business leaders for state-created, world-class standards in critical content areas have challenged those who implement professional development programs to upgrade the skills and knowledge of teachers as they work to prepare students for the 21st century (Loucks-Horsley et al. 1998, pp. x–xi). And the standards documents for mathematics and science education reform recommend teaching methods for science and math teachers and set forth guidelines for their professional development (NCTM 1991; AAAS 1993; NRC 1996).

Leaders in the field of professional development recommend that schools reorganize to become centers of learning in their communities. In such settings, collaboration is critical. Teachers become co-learners, and building cultures and environments for learning replaces the traditional ideas of classroom teaching (Hixson and Tinzmann 1990). DuFour and Eaker (1998) say that the ability of school personnel to function as professional learning communities is the most promising strategy for sustained, substantive school improvement.

Teachers, as members of learning communities, must have time for collaboration, regular reflection, and research. In a time of fiscal restraint and cutbacks it can be difficult to provide funding for this time (Zederayko and Ward 1999). A $5.6 million professional development grant awarded in 1998 by the National Science Foundation to the Science Department of the Tucson

Unified School District addresses this challenge of time. The DESERT Project, an acronym for District-wide Emphasis on Science Education Reform in Tucson, uses the funding to create systemic change in the way science is perceived and taught, so that all students will have opportunities to become scientifically literate (Tucson Unified School District 1998). To accomplish this, the grant specifies that all teachers in the district's 97 kindergarten-through-grade-8 schools receive 100 hours of professional development over the five years of the grant. By implementing a system that creates a more collegial environment and by providing a professional development structure that supports all teachers, the DESERT Project is working to change teaching practice in the classroom.

Professional developers need new strategies to affect classroom practice and student achievement. This chapter shows how the DESERT Project provides time for teachers to learn in a collaborative setting while, at the same time, students participate in high-level science experiences in the classroom.

Background of Changing Professional Development Practices

During the time since the launch of Sputnik in 1957, the educational community has worked to recast its objectives for student learning and achievement. This recasting, resulting from increased pressure on schools to prepare students to meet new technological challenges, prompted a rush to create and deliver new curricula, particularly in math and science (Hord et al. 1987). The resulting school reform movement required complex changes for teachers. Transformative learning, not merely additive, must accompany these changes, for both the teachers and the staff developers who support them. The challenge of professional development is to create optimal collaborative learning situations in which the best sources of expertise are linked with the experiences and current needs of the teachers (NRC 1996, p.58).

Reforms taking place in the educational system have exceeded the system's ability to bring teachers into alignment. Education paradigms are shifting away from a form in which the student's role consisted of practicing and memorizing straightforward facts and skills and teachers' roles consisted of demonstrating procedures, assigning tasks, and grading students (Stein, Smith, and Silver 1999, p. 238).

During the 1970s, teachers' pedagogical education became an important factor in school improvement. Previously staff development had focused solely on improving subject-matter knowledge (Laine and Otto 2000). Also during the 1970s, the funding and control of professional development has been transferred in large part from states to local school entities. The traditional workshops, inservices, and courses that were the mainstay of professional development are giving way to the concept of teachers' working together as learning colleagues. The work moves from focusing on the individual to focusing on schools as learning communities. Louis and Kruse (1995) and their colleagues Newmann and Wehlage (1995) report a direct correlation between professional learning communities and student performance. Standardized achievement test scores were used along with performance-based measures. They found some restructured schools scored higher than others and traced the reasons for this better performance to those schools that had an effective professional community.

Professional development in education in the United States continues to move away from the traditional make-and-take workshop and idea-swap format that predominated during most of the last century (Rhoton el al. 1999). Laine and Otto comment, "Historically, continuing education for teachers has taken the form of institutes in which experts lecture audiences of 100 or more teachers" (2000, p. 3). Little was known about the relationship between what teachers learned in this environment and its classroom implementation, including the effect on student learning and achievement.

The most common and perhaps the most widely criticized form of professional development is the workshop. Workshops typically find teachers sitting passively while an expert trains them in new practices (Sparks 1994). These traditional forms are inadequate to provide teachers with what they need to foster meaningful change in classroom practice today (Loucks-Horsley et al. 1998). Fullan reiterates a conclusion he reached more than 20 years ago, that one-shot workshops were ineffective, topics were selected by people other than those receiving the inservice, and follow-up support for implementation was rare (2001, p. 255). As a result, interest in alternate activities and structures such as study groups, peer collaboration, mentoring, and coaching is growing.

Stein, Smith, and Silver contrast traditional ways of delivering professional development with new methods necessitated by changes in teaching paradigms (1999). This contrast, as they illustrate in Table 1, p. 122, provides insight into professional development history. The literature reflects changes in the thrust and design of professional development. *National Science Education Standards* (NRC 1996) and other works identify the characteristics of effective professional development as collegiality and collaboration; participant involvement in decision-making; experimentation and risk taking; and integration of individual, school, and district goals. Mundry and Loucks-Horsley say that teachers need to begin to think about professional development not just as workshops but also as a process of teachers' working together to examine practice and exchange ideas about teaching (1999). Thus, they would come to value peer collegiality as well as teacher expertise. Little found a direct relationship between collegiality and school success particularly when teacher talk is concrete and precise about teaching practice (1982).

The DESERT Project incorporates many of these characteristics as staff members seek to be both facilitators and providers of a system of support to TUSD elementary and middle school teachers who implement science curricula in their classrooms.

Professional Development Reform—The DESERT Project

The DESERT Project's learning forums use a professional development design that fosters the collegiality needed to create sustainable learning communities. Forums provide the opportunity for teachers to meet on-site in small groups during the school day to participate in discussions centered on their classroom practice. In this setting, teachers must draw upon one another's expertise to create rich conversations and new insights into teaching and learning (Putnam and Borko 2004).

Learning forums are typically six or seven two-hour sessions throughout the school year. This enables the learning to be applied and supported over an extended period of time. These

Table 1. Traditional Inservice Staff Development Characteristics Compared With Those of the New Model of Professional Development

Inputs to Design Process	Traditional Inservice Staff Development	New Model of Professional Development
Strategies	Focus on activities (techniques, ideas, and materials)	Focus on building capacity to understand subject matter and guide students' development of concepts
	Dominant formats are workshops, courses, and seminars	Uses a variety of formats including the provision of in-class support and scaffolding of teacher participation in practice-related efforts (e.g., grade-level meetings, after-school meetings)
	Short duration with bounded personal commitments	Longer duration with more open-ended personal commitments
Knowledge and Beliefs	Teacher educator sets the agenda	Iterative co-construction of agenda by teachers and professional developer over time
	Theories of teacher learning based on the psychology of the individual	Theories of learning that include social and organizational factors
	Translation of new knowledge to classroom is a problem to be solved (usually by the teacher)	Challenge is to scaffold learning that is both immediately relevant to practice and builds a more generalized knowledge base
Context	Particularities of context not factored into staff development	Particularities of context play an important role in shaping professional development
	Takes place away from schools, classrooms, and students	Takes place in a variety of locations, at least some of which occur in schools and classrooms
Critical Issues	Focus is on developing the teacher (teachers participate as individuals)	Focus is on developing the instructional program and the community in addition to the teacher (teachers participate as an organizationally cohesive unit)
	Leadership training not an issue	Leadership training is a big issue

Source: Stein, Smith, and Silver. 1999. The development of professional developers.

K–8 learning forums are facilitated by a collaborative teacher (CT). CTs are classroom teachers who are assigned to full-time work in science professional development during the five years. The CT facilitates and coordinates science professional development in two to three schools each year. Four to seven teachers meet by single- or mixed-grade levels.

The small group setting for learning forums encourages more individual participation, which leads to increased collegiality. During the forums, teachers share ideas and strategies to enhance the science learning and often leave excited about trying the new approaches they have learned from this collaborative interaction.

Research indicates that one of the characteristics of effective professional development practice is that teachers be involved in planning, setting goals, and selecting activities (Peixotto and Fager 1998). The first few sessions of the learning forums help establish a common understanding and language related to best practice in science. The small groups collaboratively decide what area of their science teaching they want to study. This may be crafting teacher questions to promote higher-level thinking, encouraging students' inquiry questions, promoting literacy skills through use of science notebooks, or using strategies for teaching nonfiction science literature. When teachers have the opportunity to choose the focus for their professional development, they are more engaged and more likely to apply the learning in their classroom. Teachers need time to develop in-depth knowledge through professional conversations around topics related to teaching and learning (Routman 2002).

Educational systems in other cultures have developed innovative ways to foster the idea of teachers' learning together. Stigler and Hiebert report on the lesson study process that Japanese mathematics teachers use as an effective model for building professional knowledge (as cited in Mathematics and Science Education Center 2000). They note that the process develops new ideas for teaching and a common language for discussing teaching practices. Japanese teachers invest significant amounts of time collaborating to develop a single lesson. As they teach the lesson, nonteaching members and other observers participate as researchers, recording student reactions to document student thinking. These observations lead to an insightful critique session, which takes place the same day. Although the main goal is the lesson itself, teachers also attempt to understand the broader issues of how and why the lesson works. The real lesson of lesson study is not product, but process, as it compels teachers to examine their own practices in depth, connects them to their professional communities, and inspires them to teach better every day. Though some schools in the United States may feel it is impractical to use the lesson study process outright, others are adapting it as a useful model for delivering intensive, school-based professional development (Research for Better Schools 2002).

Many DESERT Project Learning Forum groups choose to do a form of collaborative lesson study patterned after the Japanese model as part of their professional development. One teacher in the group brings an upcoming science lesson to the Learning Forum for the group to plan. The group plans and polishes the lesson, then determines who will teach it. The teacher who does the lesson may or may not be the one who brought the lesson to the group. On the day of the lesson, the group meets for 15 minutes to review the plan, then visits the designated classroom to observe the lesson. To lower the feeling of risk for the teachers and reduce the fear of evaluation, the focus is on looking for evidence of student understanding in the activity. Observers sit with groups of three or four students and take notes on the learning behaviors and what is moving the learning forward. After the 45- to 60-minute lesson concludes, the teachers meet to discuss their observations. This discussion focuses on indirect evidence that students are moving toward conceptual understanding. The group discusses the strengths and weaknesses of their collaborative design and reflects on how this experience will influence their individual teaching.

In the Japanese model, teachers modify the lesson further to improve it and the lesson is taught and observed in another classroom. DESERT staff and faculties have found this impractical. Because of scheduling challenges, they instead conclude the session with suggestions from the teachers for refining the lesson further for their own use. Groups of teachers who have participated in this process report this to be one of the most beneficial forms of professional development they have experienced.

Teachers often report that the focus on student thinking and what is drawing the student learning has caused them to think differently about their lesson planning. One teacher commented that the opportunity to plan a lesson as a group, including the exact wording of questions to ask, was extremely helpful. Other teachers have said that part of the learning experience was the opportunity to observe learning in a classroom other than their own. The combination of the three parts—collaborative planning, observing the learning, and reflective processing—is what makes this a powerful professional development experience.

Special Presenters Program

With salaries and benefits accounting for roughly 75% of a school budget, there is no question that staff time is the most valuable resource a school has to allocate (Liptak 2002). Finding time during the school day for collaborative professional development is a challenge, although some schools are very creative in carving out time for adult learning (Pardini 1999). Many have established a once-weekly early-release schedule. Or secondary students may begin classes later on one day to accommodate professional development. If these options are not possible, a school must engage students while teachers meet and funding must be provided for substitutes. When substitutes are used, teachers spend additional time preparing plans. The DESERT Project solved these challenges to benefit all parties.

The Special Presenters Program includes four key components: program, personnel, coordinator, and preparation.

The Program

Special presenters (SPs) are certified personnel who take effective, age-appropriate science lessons to the classrooms while the teachers meet in professional development sessions. The program allows teachers to learn in their work settings while their students are also involved in meaningful learning and eliminates the burden of preparing substitute plans. Certified teachers in the DESERT Project designed seven consecutively linked science lessons based on the *Private Eye* (Rueff 1992). Using a jeweler's loupe for close observation, the students participate in integrated lessons—science, writing, art, and math—that focus on the powers of observation, language, and thinking skills. These lessons can be adapted for kindergarten through eighth-grade classrooms.

Personnel

SPs were recruited mostly through personal referrals from the DESERT Project staff. The group includes retired certified teachers who enjoy working with children but who want flexibility in their commitment, mothers of school-age children with experience as classroom aides, and university students who can gain classroom experience while maintaining their class schedules.

One of the unexpected benefits of the recruiting process has been the greater involvement of the community members. These community members are retired professionals from various fields who gain an appreciation for the education process and the challenges a classroom teacher faces each day. A retired police captain, a water company engineer, and a gas utility executive are among the group.

The SPs have the benefit of a flexible schedule. They commit to work a minimum of 20 hours per week, which can be scheduled in a variety of ways. They spend 2.5 hours per session and receive additional pay to cover preparation and travel time. The program functions with an average of 20 SPs per year. There is a great deal of variety in their work because they can adapt the same lesson from a seventh-grade class in the morning to a kindergarten class in the afternoon. In a typical school year, an SP has been to 20 to 25 school sites and taught roughly 10,000 students.

Coordinator

A responsible coordinator is a key component of the success of this program. The role is a daunting one with the following responsibilities:

- coordinating scheduling between the schools, the collaborative teachers (CTs), classroom teachers, and SPs;
- sending packets of information and labels for students to each teacher;
- ordering supplies for the SPs; and
- staying available to facilitate last-minute changes in schedules due to teacher or SP absence.

Articulating the program schedule is extremely challenging. The CT meets with a school to identify the collaborative groups and set tentative dates for the learning forums. The coordinator develops a master calendar, taking the groups and dates into account along with school start and end times, geographic location, SP travel time, and previously committed dates such as field trips, assemblies, and district testing schedules.

As the school year begins, the coordinator sends a packet to each teacher a few days prior to his or her scheduled Learning Forum. The packet contains the SP's name, the time he or she will arrive, a brief reminder of teacher responsibilities, and a page of address labels to make name tags for the students. The packet reminds the teachers not to introduce the SP as a substitute. Teachers introduce SPs as guest teachers who have prepared a special science program for them today, establishing a positive tone for the students' experience.

Preparation

The CTs spend a considerable amount of time in professional development with the SPs to help them learn how to keep things running smoothly in a classroom of 20 to 35 students. Sessions focus on professionalism in manner, speech, dress, and classroom management. CTs revisit these topics each year as turnover occurs in the program.

The coordinator has the challenge of ongoing recruiting and preparation of new SPs as the DESERT Project's program expands. Nine of the SPs enjoyed the experience of working with children in a classroom setting so much that they reduced their hours with the program to pursue a degree in education. As new SPs join the project, the coordinator holds small group meetings with them. They shadow an experienced SP in classrooms until they are confident on their own.

The coordinator facilitates weekly meetings with the SPs in which they review and share tips about a particular lesson they will use. They also share highlights and challenges of their week in classrooms. They often discuss problems and collaborate on solutions. The SPs, who may teach six to eight classrooms of students per week, receive their upcoming schedules and replenish their materials and supplies.

Reactions

Teachers express enthusiasm about the special presenter program. When teachers return to their classrooms excited about their professional development experience, they find students who are eager to share their own experience.

I really enjoyed having the special presenters in my classroom. My students were always excited about the lessons and sharing and showing me what they did. It was very nice for me not to have to plan something and yet know the lesson my students were getting would be stimulating and informative (DESERT Project 2002).

Despite the many successes, the program includes many challenges. Difficult classrooms challenge the SPs to maintain composure and professionalism. Problems arise when teachers forget to inform the CT or the coordinator of a field trip scheduled during Learning Forum time or a last-minute assembly not scheduled on the calendar. Rescheduling a Learning Forum proves very difficult when it involves 25 to 28 schools and the schedules of 9 CTs. Because of the increasing emphasis on raising test scores, teachers are increasingly reluctant to give up time with their students, particularly in the testing pressure of spring semester. Toward the end of the school year, teachers feel so overburdened that maintaining focus on improving practice becomes difficult.

At the inception of the special presenters program, some principals were reluctant to have noncertified personnel in the classrooms. But once the program began, principals saw the benefits and the efficient workings of the whole system. The following is one principal's perception of paraprofessionals in the classroom:

When I have 3 or 4 subs in the building, I am in the halls and in classrooms dealing with problems, so I expected much worse from having classified staff in charge. Now I find when special presenters are here, the classrooms are running smoothly and students are all actively engaged and enjoying their learning (Personal communication 2001).

As the instructional leader for their staff, principals are encouraged to be part of the learning forums. Responsibilities and time pressures do not always allow free time to attend. Most principals participate enough to become aware of the DESERT Project activities of the teachers and the students. The following typifies reflections by principals:

We enjoyed having special presenters work with our students. They add a special excitement to the program for both teachers and students and make science come alive.

Students learn the purpose of science and learn about the practical application that makes learning the scientific method meaningful and exciting. All the puzzle pieces fit together and science now has a purpose (DESERT Project 2002).

Teachers often express appreciation for this program that allows them to meet on-site during the school day instead of after school when they are exhausted from the rigors of their teaching day. There is more connection to their teaching when their professional development takes place in the school setting. The National Science Education Standards for professional development state "whenever possible, the professional development of teachers should occur in the context where the teachers' understandings and abilities will be used" (NRC 1996, p. 58).

Conclusions and Reflections

Currently, science is not a content area that is tested in Tucson Unified School District, so there is a lack of hard data to reflect the difference made by the professional development implemented during the DESERT Project grant. There also is a continual turnover in faculties that interrupts the collaborative culture established among groups of teachers. Moreover, one intensive year with each school is not really adequate to make substantial transformative change in practice. Nevertheless, there have been noticeable changes in the teaching of science in classrooms and in continued professional growth through collaboration implemented by teachers.

It is encouraging for CTs to return to a school where they worked intensely in the past and hear teachers say, "I teach differently today because of the time we spent together focusing on the teaching and learning of science." There is increased evidence in classrooms and in hallway displays that teachers are teaching for conceptual understanding and not just doing science activities.

Some schools have embraced the idea of professional learning communities and have continued the collaboration in various ways. Groups of teachers are meeting for study groups after school. Some groups meet on a weekly basis to examine student work for evidence of learning or to plan integration of content areas with their science teaching. Many have assumed the responsibility for their own professional growth and continue to collaborate on their practice.

Some groups of teachers have felt so strongly about the power of the Collaborative Lesson Study that they have continued it beyond their initial cohort year even without the support and facilitation of a CT. To have time for classroom observation and follow-up processing, teachers have devised a system of sharing a group of substitute teachers. The collaborative lesson planning takes place after school. The substitutes come in the morning to allow one group of teachers to observe in one classroom and then process the experience together immediately. The substitutes then move to another group of classrooms in the afternoon so a second group of teachers has the opportunity to observe and process their previously planned lesson. This practice shows that teachers greatly value the collaboration.

The tradition of teacher isolation is unfortunately still the norm in many schools. This is one of the obstacles that must be faced in attempting to establish professional learning communities (DuFour 1999). This part of the educational culture must be changed if teachers are to grow through collaboration. Perhaps we should begin at the teacher preservice level to dispel the idea of isolation. Instead of preservice teachers struggling to prepare lessons to be taught as a student teacher, they could begin with Collaborative Lesson Study. Preservice teachers would then have the benefit of multiple ideas in planning a lesson. As a lesson is taught, they would focus on the effectiveness of that lesson as they observe student learning. Finally, they would process it, sharing their observations of evidence of the learning, what worked in the lesson, and what could be done to refine it further.

If preservice teachers were provided with the structure for lesson collaboration and were encouraged, it would demonstrate that collaboration among professional colleagues is the norm and results in changes in the overall culture of professional development in education.

References

American Association for the Advancement of Science (AAAS). 1993. *Benchmarks for science literacy: Project 2061.* New York: Oxford University Press.

Birman, B. F., L. Desimone, A. C. Porter, and M. S. Garet. 2000. Designing professional development that works. *Educational Leadership* 57 (8): 28–32.

DESERT Project. 2002. Learning forum evaluations. Unpublished raw data.

DuFour, R. 1999. Taking on loneliness. *Journal of Staff Development* 20 (1): 61–62.

DuFour, R. and R. Eaker. 1998. *Professional learning communities at work.* Bloomington, IN: National Education Service.

Fullan, M. 1999. *Change forces: The sequel.* Philadelphia: Falmer Press.

Fullan, M. 2001. *The new meaning of educational change.* 3rd ed. New York: Teachers College Press.

Hixson, J., and M. V. Tinzmann. 1990. *What changes are generating new needs for professional development?* Oak Brook, IL: North Central Regional Educational Laboratory.

Hord, S. M., W. L. Rutherford, L. Huling-Austin, and G. E. Hall. 1987. *Taking charge of change.* Austin, TX: Southwest Educational Development Laboratory.

Laine, S. W. M., and C. Otto. 2000. *Professional development in education and the private sector: Following the leaders.* Oak Brook, IL: North Central Regional Educational Laboratory.

Liptak, L. 2002. It's a matter of time: Scheduling lesson study at Paterson, NJ school. *RBS Currents* 5.2 (Spring/Summer).

Little, J. W. 1982. Norms of collegiality and experimentation: Workplace conditions of school success. *American Educational Research Journal* 19 (3): 325–340.

Loucks-Horsley, S., P. W. Hewson, N. Love, and K. E. Stiles. 1998. *Designing professional development for teachers of science and mathematics.* Thousand Oaks, CA: Corwin Press.

Louis, K. and S. Kruse, eds. 1995. *Professionalism and community.* Thousand Oaks, CA: Corwin Press.

Mathematics and Science Education Center. 2000. Supporting mathematics and science teachers as a professional learning community. *Practical Inquiry* 2 (Fall): 1–11.

Mundry, S., and S. Loucks-Horsley. 1999. Designing professional development for science and mathematics teachers: Decision points and dilemmas. *National Institute for Science Education Brief* 3 (1): 1–7.

National Council of Teachers of Mathematics (NCTM). 1998. *Curriculum and evaluation standards.* Washington, DC: NCTM.

National Research Council (NRC). 1996. *National Science Education Standards.* Washington, DC: National Academy Press.

National Science Foundation (NSF). 1996. *The learning curve: What we are discovering about U.S. science and mathematics education.* Washington, DC: Author.

Newmann, F. and G. Wehlage. 1995. *Successful school restructuring.* Madison, WI: Center on Organization and Restructuring of Schools.

Pardini, P. 1999. Making time for adult learning. *Journal of Staff Development* 20 (2): 37–41.

Peixotto, K., and J. Fager. 1998. *High quality professional development: An essential component of successful schools.* Portland, OR: Northwest Regional Educational Laboratory.

Putnam, R., and H. Borko. 2004. What do new views of knowledge and thinking have to say about research on teacher learning? *Educational Researcher* 29 (1): 4–15.

Research for Better Schools (RBS). 2002. What is lesson study? *RBS Currents* 5.2 (Spring/Summer).

Reuf, K. 1998. *The private eye.* Seattle: Skylight Professional Development.

Rhoton, J., G. Madrazo, L. Motz, and E. Walton. 1999. Professional development: A major component in science teaching and learning. *Science Educator* 8 (1): 1–8.

Routman, R. 2002. Teacher talk. *Educational Leadership* 59 (6): 32–35.

Sparks, D. 1994. A paradigm shift in staff development. *Journal of Staff Development* 15 (4): 26–29.

Stein, M. K., M. S. Smith, and E. A. Silver. 1999. The development of professional developers: Learning to assist teachers in new settings in new ways. *Harvard Educational Review* 69 (3): 237–269.

Tucson Unified School District. 1998. *The DESERT project: A proposal to NSF from Tucson Unified School District.* Tucson, AZ: Author.

Zederayko, G., and K. Ward. 1999. Schools as learning organizations: How can the work of teachers be both teaching and learning? *National Association of Secondary School Principals* 83 (1): 10–13.

Making Science and Inquiry Synonyms

Laura Tracy
Greene Community School

Nor Hashidah Abd-Hamid
University of Iowa

Setting

The town of Greene, home to approximately 1,000 residents, is located in the Shell Rock River Valley in the northeast corner of Butler County, Iowa. The business district offers a department store, grocery store, variety store, pharmacy, hardware store, lumberyard, veterinarian clinic, medical services, numerous agricultural services, a bank, post office, library, bakery, two convenience stores, and more. Local farmers raise corn, soybeans, hogs, beef cattle, and dairy. Students attend school at Greene Elementary School in Greene, North Butler Middle School in Allison, and North Butler High School in Greene. I have the privilege of teaching kindergarten at Greene Elementary School. Kindergartners, all from a lower to upper-middle socioeconomic range, attend school from 8:00 a.m. to 3:15 p.m. Monday through Friday, are predominately white, and speak English. Kindergarten class size is typically under 20. The elementary grounds, surrounded by oak and evergreen trees, birds, squirrels, dandelions, and other plants and wildlife, captivate and intrigue the children. The Shell Rock River and neighboring Greene community also offer many rich opportunities for science learning.

Vision from the National Science Education Standards

According to the National Science Education Standards (NSES) (NRC 1996):

> *Inquiry is a multifaceted activity that involves making observations; posing questions; examining books and other sources of information to see what is already known; planning investigations; reviewing what is already known in light of experimental evidence; using tools to gather, analyze, and interpret data; proposing answers, explanations, and predictions; and communicating the results. Inquiry requires identification of assumptions, use of critical and logical thinking, and consideration of alternative explanation.* (p. 23)

Implementing this philosophy drove a workshop and basic changes in my science program.

The NSES have been the focus of my science program. According to the NSES, there are four goals justifying the teaching of K–12 science. The first one, "to experience the richness and excitement of knowing about and understanding the natural world," is of primary importance to my teaching. To accomplish this goal, I am concentrating on promoting children's understanding of scientific concepts and developing their abilities to do inquiry after science instruction. I have learned that students' understanding of the natural world gained through passive approaches, such as listening to the teacher share information, are not as effective in accomplishing this goal. An inquiry approach in which the teachers guide students to do investigations over extended periods of time with opportunities for discussions and debate is one important way to make inquirers of all my young learners. I have found that it works well to assist kindergartners in whole-class projects incorporating small group work rather than attempting to manage everyone investigating his or her own questions.

Over time, my science program has shifted from a teacher-centered approach to more of a constructivist learner-centered one, which involves listening for and honoring children's individual questions and ideas; striving to learn about their interests, needs, and experiences; continuously assessing their progress; and working in concert with them, as well as others from the wider school community, to adapt and develop curricula appropriate for the next steps in their learning. I have continually striven to become better at asking effective questions that will help my students think and gain the experiences necessary for understanding science concepts. I have grappled with the National Science Education Standards and have found science inquiry to be an effective way to foster kindergartners' learning. I have developed several new modules that illustrate how my science curriculum has evolved. Students' questions and interests are at the core of my program. Many of these ideas for gaining student input came from my participation in the 2004/2005 Iowa Chautauqua Inquiry Professional Development Project (ICIPDP).

The ICIPDP empowers science teachers to make science more meaningful and useful for their students. It provides ongoing support across a summer and an entire academic year for teachers in grades K–12 as they develop and assess strategies that match those that characterize a reform effort envisioned by the National Science Education Standards (NSES). The inquiry approach the NSES advocate involves constructivist ideas and a science-technology-and-society (STS) focus that broaden the concept of science itself. My teaching can best be described as the teaching and learning of science in the context of human experience. Student ideas, questions, and thinking drive the lessons. They are followed by investigations that include analyzing, synthesizing, and evaluating data. That leads to knowledge constructed via an inquiry approach, resulting in richer understanding, concept development, and problem-solving skills for the learners as they attempt to cope with real-life situations and become involved in family and community projects.

The Mice Project

One inquiry experience in which my kindergarten class became involved addressed the theme of mice and the NSES focus of unifying process skills or the big idea of "evidence, models, and explanations." I was transcribing the children's discussions while they built a castle for the class mice. The structure included a series of cardboard tubes that the children called rooms. Some were open on one end, and some were open on two ends. Child One said, "The mice don't like the rooms I made." Child Two said, "Maybe you need to decorate them so the mice will like them." Child Three said, "How about if you put a snack in the rooms? Mice like snacks." Child Four said," Yeah, put cheese in there. They love cheese!" Child Five watched Snowball—the little white mouse—zip through a cardboard tube and said, "Hey, maybe the rooms need a back door and a front door like that! Snowball sure likes this tube, and there's no food in it." I eventually asked, "How do you think you can figure out if these mice would like the rooms better if they were decorated, had a snack inside, or had more than one opening?" All of these conversations among the students revealed my efforts to change the emphases, namely, to promote inquiry by using activities that investigate and analyze science questions as raised and offered by students themselves. Once the students have identified an area of interest, I assume the role of facilitator and help my students refine specific questions or topics for their investigations.

My overall goal was for students to follow up on their curiosity through inquiry while developing an understanding of evidence, models, and explanations as well as life science concepts—awareness of behavioral characteristics, needs, diversity, and variation in their pet mice. This related to the big idea of "evidence, models, and explanations" in that acquired evidence would provide a model that could be used to discover patterns and relationships in mouse behavior and increase understanding of how mice and perhaps other critters respond to their environments. I tried to make my goal pertinent to the NSES *Changing Emphases* conditions for science content, especially those that focus on understanding scientific concepts and developing abilities of inquiry instead of just using the vocabulary about scientific facts and the information that are often included in written materials and the curriculum outline. The idea of implementing inquiry as instructional strategies, abilities, and ideas to be learned had become the main focus in my new classroom environment—different than implementing inquiry as a set of prescribed skills to practice without a real context.

Prior to the dilemma described above, my children had been involved in a project on pets that had resulted in adopting the three mice. The children had made a KWL (what I Know, what I Wonder about, what I have Learned) for their mice. They'd made sketches and drawings of the mice, weighed and measured them, determined their favorite foods, figured out which one could stay on the exercise wheel the longest, conducted a survey to decide what to name them, read books about mice, and built numerous mazes and castles for them.

Planning the Mice Project

The children met to plan a series of investigations to see what each of the three mice would do if they could choose between a decorated room and a plain room (each with one opening), a room with a snack in it and a plain room (each with one opening), or a plain room with two openings and a plain room with one opening. Having two tubes in each investigation allowed the children to compare—each tube serving as a control for the other. During a class meeting, the children enlisted the rest of the class's help. The class was divided into three groups, each responsible for preparing some of the materials and conducting the three trials mentioned above with one of the mice. Group one was involved in the construction of a sand clock from pop bottles for timing the trials. The pop bottle sand timer made tangible monitoring the length of each trial (time), a difficult concept for this age level. The task of group two was to cut and measure cardboard tubes for the trials so each had the same length and diameter. The third group created data collection sheets for recording the number of times a mouse entered the cardboard tubes during the trials. Groups shared this work with the whole class and demonstrated how to use their materials. To help the children further prepare, I planned a lesson on making and counting tally marks. A science major visited to demonstrate respectful handling of mice. (Safe handling is also important.) The children eagerly asked questions and shared "mouse tales" with their guest. I challenged my students to take responsibility for their own learning by letting them be involved in the design and management of the learning environment. All students participated in planning and decision making necessary for carrying out the investigation. Groups shared their work with the whole class. An important milestone had been achieved.

Investigating the Mice Project

Each group conducted three trials with one of the mice. Two tubes were placed in an empty aquarium for each trial (trial one: plain room with two openings and a plain room with one opening; trial two: a decorated room and a plain room, each with one opening; and trial three: a room with a snack in it and a plain room, each with one opening). A mouse was assigned to a trial and was placed in the aquarium for five minutes. The students tallied the number of times the mouse entered one of the tubes. To avoid having excessive noise influence mouse behavior and to ensure a fair test, groups conducted trials while the rest of the class was at recess.

I tried to create a sense of interconnectedness by dividing children into small heterogeneous groups—each contributing to the whole. To encourage participation and individual accountability, I had each child draw a task card assigning a role:

- a timer who used the sand timer to make sure the mouse was in the aquarium for the right amount of time,
- a recorder who tallied the number of times a mouse went inside a cardboard tube, or
- a photographer to take pictures throughout each trial with a digital camera and place the mouse in the aquarium at the beginning of each trial.

Students changed roles for subsequent trials giving each child a chance to experience all roles.

After the trials, I challenged teams to figure out a way to organize their data so that others could use it to make comparisons, interpretations, and discuss ideas. I encouraged children to write in investigation booklets and work with their groups to make big book pages showing the results of their trials and preliminary conclusions. Teams shared their results and theories with the class. I facilitated a discussion after all trials were complete for children to draw conclusions and ask more questions. The students took the big book home on a rotating basis. Pages in the back were left open for families to provide feedback.

Evidence of Learning

The children showed evidence of inquiry, intellectual engagement, discussion, and learning as they worked intently to observe and document what happened during the investigation they'd help design and interacted with others on their team. For example, as group two placed their mouse, Midnight, in the aquarium with one cardboard tube with two open ends and another with one open end, they followed the mouse with their eyes and at times moved closer to get a better view of what was happening. Discussion was spontaneous, with moments of silence when they just watched or recorded tallies representing the number of times the mouse entered a tube. When the timer was flipped over, the child working as the photographer moved by the two recorders and asked, "Okay, which one's more?," demonstrating that she was engaged in the process and realized the importance of evidence.

Midnight had entered the tube with two openings 22 times and the tube with one opening 10 times. When I asked them to consider possible reasons for Midnight's preference, the timer explained, "Two open doors were best because mice can't open doors good." The photographer extended the group's thinking by applying her knowledge from former observations, "But they can chew; it would just take a long time." One child's eyes went to a 10 o'clock position as he thought about a mouse being in a tube with one opening while a predator approached. He suddenly realized Midnight's need for safety and the advantage of being in a place with more than one path of escape and was quick to explain, "Midnight could get trapped in there! He'd be supper!" Some responses indicated students were attributing intentionality like their own to Midnight's behavior (a common misconception of young children). While talking about Midnight's exploring the container, the timer said, "She wants to get out of there so she can go and play." Signs of a developing awareness of variations between mice were also evident when the photographer commented, "You're doing a lot better than our other mouse Lightning did!" and "Midnight, you hold your tail a lot straighter, too."

I continuously assessed my students, understanding by listening to their conversations and making notes and comments. In the science classroom envisioned by the NSES, effective teachers should continually create opportunities to challenge students by asking questions, stimulating situations that might generate students' questions, doing more investigations in order to develop understanding ability, valuing the inquiry process, and advancing the knowledge of science content.

Additional evidence of inquiry and learning occurred when the timer brought up the testable idea of placing the tubes in the "mouse house" where Midnight lived to see if that would make a difference in the results. The photographer later said, "Could we put two mice in there?" and predicted the tube with two openings would be preferred because both mice could stick their heads in at the same time and could play together. The students demonstrated an understanding of collaboration—team members fulfilled roles while they supported the work of teammates. When the mouse was being removed from the aquarium, one of the recorders held the box so his team-mate could place the mouse inside. When there was discrepancy in the number of tallies the two recorders had drawn, the team functioned as a cohesive unit. The photographer eagerly helped recount them as the timer looked on. The photographer's request to take a picture of each group member with the mouse also showed that she saw each person as a valued member of a team.

Evidence of mathematical understanding was also present. The recorders were able to tabulate and report data accurately because they were in agreement with each other. (The discrepancy occurred only because one recorder had miscounted her tally marks.) The photographer's ability to make sense of the data on their papers provided evidence information had been recorded clearly. The timer demonstrated mathematical understanding by successfully monitoring the time. He watched intently as the last grain of sand passed through and used his hand and voice to let the group know when the trial was over.

Discussion conveyed mutual respect. The children's body language was relaxed, and discussion took place through the casual give-and-take of respectful conversation. Children felt free to move or sit in a way that was comfortable for them, to be quiet, or to share ideas. Team members listened attentively as others talked, which allowed them to respond to the ongoing discussion. The children's movement and expressions showed they felt a sense of purpose in their work and took their roles seriously. When Midnight did something interesting, everyone became very animated.

It also seemed that experiences with these trials influenced children's thinking about future trials. For example, when asked to predict if Midnight would like a decorated tube with one door or a plain tube with one door, a child said, "I don't think she'll like either one because she'll be worried about getting trapped."

To further determine student progress, I examined students' data collection sheets, investigation booklets, each team's big book pages, photos, anecdotal notes, and work samples capturing what they said and did. This corresponded to NSES vision of assessment. Specifically, NSES urges that we "assess to learn what students do understand" instead of "assessing to learn what students do not know."

The Squirrel Project

When squirrels began tampering with the birdfeeder outside the classroom window in the fall, the students had many questions about squirrels. They knew the squirrels were hungry and asked if they could make feeders for them in the hope they would leave the bird feeders alone. With the help of the high school woods class, the children constructed squirrel feeders and hung them on trees in our elementary school's oak grove.

Discussions on what to feed the squirrels led to an investigation of three testable questions:
- Do squirrels prefer eating corn from a high, medium, or low feeder?
- Do squirrels prefer apples, corn, or cookies?
- Do squirrels prefer their corn plain or with a topping (such as peanut butter, jelly, or suet)?

Each child signed up to investigate one of the questions. Research groups worked together to plan and conduct investigations, to monitor which foods and feeders the squirrels seemed to prefer, and then to replicate the investigations to see if similar outcomes would result. The children found squirrels preferred eating from the highest feeder, liked cookies better than apples or corn, and preferred to eat plain corn rather than corn with a topping. They had many interesting theories about the results. For example, they thought squirrels preferred eating from a high feeder because they could get away from predators more easily and were safe from the ones that couldn't fly or climb trees. One student proposed that squirrels liked cookies better than apples because cookies are sweet and easier to chew. Classmates also decided squirrels liked plain corn better than corn with toppings because the toppings resulted in messy paws, which could be problematic if an enemy approached. All these reasons indicated that students had been attempting to find patterns and causal relationships.

Throughout the study, children uncovered many other interesting facts about squirrels. They were particularly fascinated with the myriad ways squirrels use their tails, such as a device for balancing, as a sail or rudder when swimming, as a blanket, as an umbrella, as a parachute, or even as a communication device.

They wondered if people could eat acorns like squirrels do and learned that humans have done so throughout history. The class cracked, boiled, dried, and ground acorns into flour for acorn bread. They participated in writing a readers theater script about the process, featuring a marionette named Sammy, a ladybug, grasshopper, and a crow.

The children also constructed a model of a squirrel habitat in their play corner complete with oak trees, a squirrel shelter called a *drey*, plant life, various woodland animals, and a paper stream. They concluded their squirrel study by inviting the industrial arts teacher and his woods class to sample acorn bread, assist in taking down the squirrel feeders, and see a video documenting the project.

The Cookie Factory Project

Most of the science inquiry projects in which my kindergartners have engaged have evolved from their questions and observations. It seems five- and six-year-olds wonder about everything. For example, while baking cookies for an afternoon snack, the class began discussing past experiences with cookie baking. Some of their questions were

- How do you make different kinds of cookies?
- Who invented the first cookie?
- Where do the ingredients in cookies come from? and
- What happens if you leave ingredients out or put in new ones?

They used various resources and helped plan investigations to find answers to testable questions. For example, students worked in small groups to discover how leaving out, adding, or substituting one ingredient for another affected the quality of finished cookies. During the investigation they began learning how cookies are made up of parts or ingredients, how individual parts can have properties different from the combined substance, how parts affect the whole, and how combined parts can do things individual parts can't do alone.

The class enjoyed cooking and baking so much they decided to set up a bakery and cafe for serving friends and family members and called it The Cookie Factory. To prepare for the project, the children visited our local bakery and coffee shop. Back at school, they signed up to work on various committees. One committee was responsible for designing and constructing uniforms, another planned to make napkins and tablecloths, another potholders, and a fourth was charged with preparing menus and job descriptions. I introduced a FOSS science kit on fabric to encourage additional science learning. The lessons on dying, weaving, and sewing fabric supported them in their work. Lessons on stain removal led to additional inquiry when a customer spilled coffee and stained one of their tablecloths. The children spent many hours testing ideas for removing coffee stains.

The Ramp Project

Another inquiry experience began when a child complained that one of the playground balls wasn't bouncing very well. He wanted to play with a different ball—"one that bounces good." I gathered a collection of balls from the classroom and asked the class if they had any ideas about how to figure out which one was the best bouncer. One child suggested seeing which ball bounced the highest, and another thought the class should count how many times each ball could bounce before it stopped. The class tried both ideas.

To extend their exploration, I brought out materials for an exploration of spheres, ramps, and pathways to the block area that I'd learned about while serving on the Teacher Practitioner Council through the Regents Center at the University of Northern Iowa. The children explored the behaviors of various spheres—marbles, steel balls, cork balls, wooden balls, and bouncy balls—as they rolled down inclines, through tunnels, up hills, or around bends. They focused on relationships between sphere size and weight and movement on a ramp, between ramp steepness and the distance a sphere traveled, and more. They were particularly surprised to find that the weight of a sphere did not affect how quickly it reached the bottom of the ramp, that the weight of a sphere did not affect how far it rolled after leaving the end of a ramp, but that the weight of a sphere did affect what it could knock over.

The Tulip Project

On another occasion, I had some tulip bulbs left over from some planting I'd done at my home and left them on a table in our science area. Soon someone asked, "What are these?" The class eventually planted an experimental garden to investigate its own what-if questions related to tulips. Before they planted, the children made observational drawings of the inside and outside views of the tulip bulbs. They also participated in weighing and measuring their bulbs. The data were recorded in a graph for future reference because one

Students planted their experimental garden to investigate what-if questions.

of the things the class wondered about was whether bigger bulbs would produce bigger tulips.

A local couple donated their time and talents to till the children's garden site. Friends and family members visited school to help with planting. The children marked "their" tulips by inserting into the ground paint sticks decorated with their names and the question they were investigating. Parents helped cover the tulip bed with chicken wire to deter squirrels from stealing the bulbs. As they waited for spring to arrive and their tulips to emerge, the children conducted some additional investigations with forced potted tulips. Through this year-long investigation, kindergartners increased their understanding of what is necessary for plants to grow and began to make connections about temperature, light, and plant growth.

The Standards and Benchmarks Assessment

I used a form with two columns to record individual student learning. Column one listed the school district standards and benchmarks. For example, Standard 1:

- Understands and applies the skills of scientific inquiry
- Participates in asking questions, conducting simple experiments, making observations and discussing findings
- Uses observations and simple experiments to increase scientific knowledge.

The other column provided space to enter evidence of learning from my observations, student work samples, class discussions, and introductory and final assessments. For introductory and final assessments, I interviewed the students individually about the topic of study. I used the same questions before and after the study and then compared the responses. For example, for the mice project—I said

- Tell me as much as you can about the mice we've adopted for our classroom.
- How are our mice alike and how are they different?
- Talk about what they need to survive?
- How do mice protect themselves? and
- What would you like to learn about mice or other pets?

I classified evidence gathered as *not yet, developing*, or *proficient* according to the district's grade-level expectations. I attached my annotations of math and science learning describing the context and setting; the objectives explored; and the evidence of progress to each document along with reflections from students and families. I summarized each child's evidence on a record form listing district standards and benchmarks and checked a box classifying progress as *not yet, emerging,* or *proficient*. No students were in the *not yet* category for any of the objectives; 20% of the children fell within the *emerging* category for the majority of objectives, and 80% fell within the *proficient* category for the majority of listed benchmarks. Prior to the mice project, 10% of the children were in the *not yet* category, 60% were in the *emerging* category, and 10% were in the *proficient* category.

The Attitudes Toward Science Assessment

At the beginning and end of the year I also asked children

- What is science?

- What do scientists do? and
- Do you like science? Why or why not?

Answering the first question, What is science?, in the pretest, eight often said "I don't know" or "I can't remember," and two of them said "making stuff" or "doing experiments." Interestingly, in the posttest, all of them gave answers. In the students' answers, they mentioned six themes about science, namely, "doing experiments," "figuring out stuff," "thinking," "studying and working on things," and "asking questions." Students' understanding of the nature of science improved significantly to 80% over the pretest information.

Answering the second question, "What do scientists do?," in the pretest, five often said "I don't know" and another five mentioned "creating things," "mixing stuff together," "Scientists think," and "They find things to put in their experiments." In the posttest, all of them gave "excellent" answers about what they think scientists do. For example, student 1 listed four things:

- They test things.
- They taste things if it's safe.
- They have questions.
- They try all kinds of ideas to find out what they can.

Student 2 listed five items about what scientists do:

- Ask questions.
- They figure stuff out.
- Use their nose, eyes, mouth, ears, and hands to do stuff.
- They check stuff over.
- They might dream about being a scientist.

Student 3 also listed five things about what scientists do:

- They try things over and over again.
- They look back to check for mistakes.
- They write things on a piece of paper.
- They use their senses.
- They measure things.

All of these examples provided ample evidence that students had increased their understanding of what scientists do.

Answering the third question, "Do you like science? Why or why not?," in the pretest, two students said "Yes"; five students said they were not sure or "I don't know"; and three students said they did not. The reasons they gave were "I don't want to mix stuff together," "I don't want to work a lot," and "I don't know if I am going to like it or not." Amazingly, in the posttest, all of them said they liked science, and the reasons they gave are listed below:

- Student 1: You can make anything happen you want.
- Student 2: You figure out stuff.
- Student 3: I like playing with ramps.
- Student 4: Go check stuff.
- Student 5: You can make stuff.
- Student 6: All different ways to do it.
- Student 7: Because you can read, take pictures, find stuff out, and figure it out.

- Student 8: You can be outside sometimes. You learn things.
- Student 9: Cause sometimes things don't work as planned.
- Student 10: It's fun, and it helps you get smarter.

A comparison between pretest and posttest results indicated that kindergartners' motivation for "liking science" had increased by 80%. It seemed when students enjoy learning about science, they would persevere more with behaviors that promote real learning and understanding. Researchers have found similar associations, attitudes, and beliefs, including greater interest, more confidence in one's ability to learn, and a perception of value in a given task, resulting in greater attention spans, mind engagement, more thoughtful associations, greater comprehensions, and long-term memory (Pintrich and De Groot 1990).

The Self-Evaluation Assessment

As the year progressed, the children participated in making a rubric that listed their criteria for acting like a scientist or not acting like a scientist. We revisited and revised this periodically. The children added illustrations so they could remember the text. This became a tool for student self-assessment (See Figure 1). The students helped make displays of photos with captions and work samples for the hall or classroom to document their learning. I had conferences with them individually at grading time to talk about how they were progressing. The children kept investigation booklets in which they could write and draw about their own discoveries and also record responses to questions or topics I'd specifically asked them to write about.

Figure 1. Student Self-Assessment Tool

Name _____

Date _____

I was acting liking a scientist by:	I was not acting like a scientist by:
Asking a question.	Not caring about anything.
Trying to figure something out by myself or with somebody else.	Running around and not working on figuring something out.
Not quitting when things went wrong and trying to figure it out instead.	Getting mad and quitting when things go wrong.
Drawing and writing about my work so I can look at it later or share it.	Scribbling so no one can tell what I did.
Telling others about my ideas and what I'm doing.	Just messing around.
Listening to other people's ideas.	Not listening at all.
Taking care of the tools I use for science so they don't get wrecked.	Leaving a mess all over. Making someone else put my things away. Wrecking stuff on purpose.

Final Thoughts

Several weeks after the Mice Project ended, the children announced that they had discovered a gopher hole on the playground. I said, "I wonder if this gopher has more than one door to the outside?" The children spent the next recess looking for holes and found more. They found a lot. One child connected to the big idea of evidence, models, and explanations when she said, "Our mouse tubes helped us figure out what gophers do." During a fire drill, another child said, "People like two ways out just like mice and gophers do so they won't get trapped." I've come to value classroom inquiry because children can get feedback directly from the materials with which they are working. As a result, ideas can be truly their own. Children aren't depending on the teacher or someone else to provide an answer—instead, they can decide which questions to pursue and which conclusions to accept or reject as they work. They have the chance to develop confidence in their abilities to think and figure things out. The process reminds me of the old proverb, "Give a man a fish, and he will eat for a day; teach a man to fish, and he will eat for a lifetime." Now I think, "If I ask one of my young learners a question he or she will think about that question for a day, but if I teach him or her to question, he or she will inquire for a lifetime." That's the gift I want to give my students.

References

DeVries, R., B. Zan, C. Hildebrandt, R. Edmiaston, and C. Sales. 2002. *Developing constructivist early childhood curriculum practical principals and activities*. New York: Teachers College Press.

National Research Council (NRC). 1996. *National Science Education Standards*. Washington, DC: National Academy Press.

Pintrich, P. R., and E. V. De Groot. 1990. Motivational and self-regulated learning components of classroom academic performance. *Journal of Educational Psychology* 82: 33–40.

Yager, R. E. 1991. The constructivist learning model: Towards real reforms in science education. *The Science Teacher* 59 (9).

Yager, R. E. 1997. Invited Paper. *The Science Teacher* 64 (8).

Winter Out Our Window:

Understanding and Using
Scientific Processes

Nicole Viscomi
Bedford Village Elementary School

Janice Koch
Hofstra University

Setting

In a northeastern suburb, where winter snows are a regular part of school life, Ms. Viscomi decided to frame a science unit on weather around the "big ideas" associated with measuring air temperature, exploring phases of matter, and examining how people protect themselves from cold and wet weather conditions. As a result of implementing this unit, she was hoping that the students would gain a better understanding of a variety of information related to the topic of winter.

Some of the big ideas of this unit on winter included

- Temperature measures hotness and coldness,
- Ice is frozen water,
- Snow is another form of water,
- Snowflakes fall from clouds and are formed by crystals,
- Water expands when it freezes, and
- People and animals take preventive measures in the cold weather.

To further students' understanding of weather, Ms. Viscomi devised a design activity that required students to make a boot for one of the "paws" of their classroom mascot, Mr. Puppy, and to test that boot to be sure it was waterproof. Engaging kindergarten students in this unit included assessing student understanding through interviews about the topic, before and after the implementation of the unit.

This unit was implemented in a kindergarten classroom in an elementary school 59 miles north of a major metropolitan city in the Northeast. The school is situated on a low-lying area between rolling hills and rocky terrain. It is in a primarily affluent area where it serves 461 students from kindergarten to fifth grade. There are approximately three classes per grade level, except in kindergarten, which includes five classes and one special education class containing four students. There are 92 kindergartners. Government statistics show that the student population is 93% Caucasian, 3% Hispanic, 3.5% Asian or Pacific Islander, and fewer than 1% African American.

The students in Ms. Viscomi's kindergarten class are creative, energetic, and eager to learn. They enjoy trying new things and respond positively to hands-on activities. They can be described as exceptional learners, personable, caring, and curious. They are also typical kindergartners and enjoy socializing and playing with their peers. The kindergarten class contains 17 students, 11 boys and six girls. Although the classroom is full of diverse learners, the ethnic makeup of the class is not very diverse. There are 14 students in the class of Caucasian descent and three students of Asian or Pacific Islander descent. One student is classified as learning disabled and receives "push-in" services once a week and "pull-out" services twice a week in the mornings. The classroom is large, sunny, and spacious and has high ceilings. Students sit in groups at tables around the room. The walls are covered with words and pictures relating to topics of study. In front of the windows are all the supplies needed for the students throughout the day. One wooden bookcase holds glue, crayons, pencils, scissors, markers, and tape. There is a networked computer in the classroom. As she implemented the unit, Ms. Viscomi maintained a teaching journal in which she recorded detailed descriptions of how each lesson and activity was unfolding. This became an assessment tool for her at the completion of the unit.

More Emphasis on ...

Selecting and adapting curriculum while providing opportunities for discussion and debate

The concepts *hot* and *cold* are fundamental big ideas when learning about winter weather. These concepts are simple yet profound in their ability to raise inquiry to a higher level. Students, like most people, respond to the way weather feels around them. In their article "Weather Detectives," Meyer et al. continue to use examples of the scientific method to enhance student learning (1999). They compare weather to an unsolved mystery and encourage teaching climate through the use of hypothesizing. One example of this technique would be to hypothesize whether an object has hot or cold properties. Accountable talk and involvement is key when researching children's responses while learning about weather and temperature. Ms. Viscomi engages the entire class in a discussion in which students build on each other's ideas as a way of constructing meaning together.

Involving students in real-life scientific research is another way to get them motivated when they are learning about weather conditions. Studying winter is more than learning about snowflakes and frost. Students' observations and gathering of data from websites or the field is the beginning of student understanding of a more intricate cyclical relationship in science. Ken Berglund's article, "World Wide Weather," describes this transition between learner and non-learner in his efforts to demonstrate the importance of hands-on science (1999). He specifically describes examples of children and weather because it is something constant in their lives. Weather effects are something that they feel, relate to, and live with all the time. Weather is in their world, so why not make it within their reach?

Ms. Viscomi designed a unit on winter weather that included using thermometers to measure air temperature; catching snowflakes; exploring real snow outside and measuring its temperature, volume, and the time it takes to melt and then its volume after melting; making model thermometers; and designing and testing a boot for their class mascot.

Sharing responsibility for learning with the students

Ms. Viscomi's students had important ideas about how to design a test for the waterproof property of the materials they were using for Mr. Puppy's boot. They participated in the process of creating a viable test of the fabrics supplied. They used water spray bottles and decided how many times to squirt the fabric and what to look for on the bottom of the fabric to determine if it was waterproof. Each group used a different number of squirts. One group poured some water from a cup on the fabric. Ms. Viscomi honored their ideas and collected their findings.

Continuously assessing student understanding

Ms. Viscomi designed her plan for assessment of the unit with these learning goals in mind:

- Water has many forms,
- Snow is made up of water,
- Ice is water that is frozen,
- Water expands when it freezes,
- Water evaporates into the air,
- Snowflakes are crystals and have six sides,
- We use temperature to measure how hot and cold something may be,
- Winter is a season,
- Winter weather may be different around the world,
- People need to protect themselves in the cold weather by wearing warm clothing, and
- Animals protect themselves in the winter by hibernating, migrating, and adapting to their surroundings.

Ms. Viscomi determined the children's knowledge about winter before and after the completion of the unit. Their writing skills were limited, so she recorded and transcribed their thoughts without restricting their thinking. She gave the same interview at the conclusion of the unit to directly compare data and student learning. Her survey questions were as follows:

- What is winter?
- Name one thing you learned about winter
- Which picture shows our weather in winter? (Students select from four pictures, one of each season.)
- What does temperature measure?
- What happens to water in the cold?
- What is ice?
- What is snow?
- Where does snow come from?

- Name one example of what animals do in the cold weather.
- What do people do in the cold weather?

Throughout the unit students would be asked to respond to information in various ways. Ms. Viscomi maintained a teaching journal and recorded many of their questions and responses, leading her to make conclusions about what they understood.

Supporting a Classroom Community: Cooperation, Shared Responsibility, Respect

As the students started their drawings for Mr. Puppy's "boot," Ms. Viscomi reminded them that "builders need a lot of details before they can start." The children were very responsive, and there was a wonderful, warm classroom atmosphere. As she circulated, she questioned the children. They seemed to feel very safe and happy in this room. A visitor chatted with them about the winter and about snow. The children were verbal and bright and eager to tell what they knew. They talked about water freezing and taking the shape of the cup. They explained that, when water evaporates, it goes into the clouds. When they began to consider making their designs, they were very invested in the project. Isabelle asked, "What will happen if the boots are not really a pair? They won't match." Ms. Viscomi reminded them that what the boot needs to do is to fit Mr. Puppy and to be waterproof. The children seemed to get it but struggled with size and scale. They had a lot of opportunity to redo their procedure if the resulting boot were too small or too big. They did not seem frustrated when they had to redo.

Bearing witness to the children working and the interactions around this design challenge was a real treat. Ms. Viscomi expected the students to think for themselves and responded respectfully to their questions by asking them, "What do you think?" It was an exciting educational environment in which all the students seemed very engaged.

Winter Is ...

Ms. Viscomi began the unit by asking the class to record their responses to the phrase "winter is ..." They recorded their answers on a paper mitten that hung across the classroom windows for the remainder of the unit. Most of the responses included sleigh riding, snowboarding, and ice skating. When the class was asked to share their responses, one child pointed outside and said, "Ms. Viscomi, winter is out our window." Ms. Viscomi decided that it was not only true but also perfectly fitting as the title of the unit. By the end of the unit, the class would look back and expand on their responses.

Later that afternoon, Ms. Viscomi gave each student a worksheet that contained shapes ranging from two-sided to six-sided. She asked the students to circle all the shapes that they thought were snowflakes. Everyone in the class circled the correct shapes. She then visited each child and asked why each had circled these shapes. Their answers were recorded on the back of the paper.

The following morning the students entered the room and found an object to fill with water to create ice. Ms. Viscomi let each student pick any container he or she wanted and asked them to place it in a spot where they thought the water would become ice. Almost the entire class put their containers outside the window. Two students decided to place cups by the sink. Two students picked a plastic sandwich container, one student used a sealable bag, another student used a plastic water bottle, and the remainder of the class used a paper or plastic cup. Ms. Viscomi selected a bright orange balloon to use as her container. When she questioned the class, some students said that her balloon would pop. When asked why they thought that, one child said that, "the ice is sharp and will pop open the balloon." When asked if they had any other theories about the balloon, the class created a graph of student predictions. Although 7 out of 17 students felt the balloon would pop, no one else offered an explanation. The containers were left out over the weekend.

Immediately upon returning to class Monday morning, the children looked at the containers that were left out on Friday. All the containers were filled with ice except the two cups that were left by the sink. The balloon popped, which really excited the class. They talked about what happened, and one student said he noticed the ice in his cup took up more room than the water did. Then other students started noticing this same phenomenon, especially in the plastic water bottle, which had started to crack. Another child said, "Do you think the ice was too big for the balloon and that's why it popped?" They decided to do this experiment again overnight to see if they would get the same results.

The two students who had left their cups by the sink were disappointed that they did not get ice, but their cups of water led the class in another direction—they had hardly any water left in their cup at all. Because of a heating problem, the classroom was extremely warm, the perfect condition for an evaporation experiment. The students put water in two rectangular, plastic containers and drew a line where the water level reached. They left one container by the library near the heater and the other on the teacher's desk by the classroom door. Students made predictions about what would happen overnight.

The next day the water in the container by the heater was gone. The water level in the second container was also clearly lower. Ms. Viscomi asked "What happened to the water?" One student said excitedly, "It evaporated into the air" and another said, "It went into the sky." The class started talking about how temperature affects evaporation and how it must happen faster when it is hotter. Then a student said, "How could water evaporate into the classroom?" Another child answered her question by saying, "There is air in the classroom, and that goes into the sky." The students could answer each other's questions with confidence. They set up another experiment, made predictions, and placed another water balloon outside.

Soon, perfect weather for the unit arrived. School was closed, and there was almost eight inches of snow. When the students returned to class, Ms. Viscomi read *Surprise! Snow Day* (Baker 2003), and the class was eager to be outside exploring. They took a field trip to the courtyard. The students loved using the snow to build different creations. They built a class snowman and began a journal describing how the snowman looked at the end of each day for the week. Before going back inside, Ms. Viscomi asked the class what experiments they would like to do with the snow. One child said that she would like to take the temperature of the snow. Ms. Viscomi gathered plastic magnifying glasses and thermometers for all the students and placed one of each in a sealable bag for them. The students continued making predictions and observations about ice, snow, and water. They predicted whether snow or ice had more water in it. They acted like scientists and filled out a data sheet following a scientific method. They drew a line showing how much water would be left in each cup once the ice and snow melted. They did this again after seeing the actual results. I noticed that one student initially drew both lines at the same level on each cup. When the teacher questioned her thinking, she said, "Snow and ice are the same because they are both made of water, only snow is soft and ice is hard." The repeated experiments helped in her understanding of how much water is produced by both ice and snow when they melt.

The class KWL—Know, Want to Know, and what I Learned—chart was filled with facts the class knew and had learned about winter, and the questions remaining were directly related to snow and ice. They used their discovery kits and made observations about snow. The class worked in partnerships, each sharing a piece of black paper and a mound of snow. They used their magnifying glasses to make observations and were engaged in being scientists. They used the thermometers to take the temperature of snow. Ms. Viscomi asked them individually what they noticed about the snow and then charted their responses. They observed that snow was

- sparkly,
- made of crystals,
- making paper wet,
- white,
- melting on the paper,
- ice,
- made out of water melting,
- cold,
- melting in your hand, and
- flakes.

Later, when they read a book about snow and plants, the class learned that snow helps plants grow. When asked why snow would help plants, one child stated, "Snow melts and gives plants water." Another said, "Maybe plants feel different than us and are not cold in the winter." They brainstormed different ideas as a class and waited until the next day to finish the book and gain an understanding of how snow blankets plants and keeps them warm.

That afternoon the class reviewed the properties of water and estimated how many drops of water a penny will hold. The class was amazed at the amount of water one little penny could hold and curious about how drops of water join together.

The next day, it began to snow—large, fluffy flakes—while the children were at school. The class went outside with magnifying glasses and caught snowflakes on black construction paper. The students were shouting, "I see six sides" and "These flakes are big, so it must be getting warmer and wet outside."

As a precursor to the unit, Ms. Viscomi introduced the class to their "weather bear," a paper bear located on the bulletin board next to the daily weather graph. The weather graph used Velcro to display how many sunny, partly cloudy, cloudy, rainy, dry, and snowy days they had each month. Every afternoon students used Velcro clothes that were suitable for the bear to be wearing based on the weather outside. A first this was a simple task. Now that the class knew so much about winter, hibernation, and how animals protect themselves, they argued that the bear needed no clothes and could survive with only his fur. When one student asked how animals without fur survive in the cold weather, Ms. Viscomi used two books about animals in the Arctic and Antarctic to answer her question, and they compared them to other books they had read about animals in winter. Ms. Viscomi was seeking ways to help children gain information and answers independently.

Students in this class worked at stations set up around the room. For their design of a boot for Mr. Puppy, each station had a set of supplies. Their task was to prepare a sketch of their design and select and test fabrics. Students measured the size of the stuffed animal's paw and drew lines that represented length and width. They were all able to remember what the boot had to do and why this was important—designing a waterproof boot for Mr. Puppy to protect him from the wet winter weather. One student said, "I already have an idea of what my boot will look like, so when can I get started?"

All the students seemed eager to begin and especially excited after handling the materials. Ms. Viscomi asked the class if they knew what an engineer was and received a few different answers. One student said it was "someone that builds something" and another said it was "someone that draws a picture of what they want to build." With these ideas in mind, Ms. Viscomi sent them off to create their first boot drawing. Some took a lot of time with thought and detail. Others rushed and drew a quick sketch with a pencil. Ms. Viscomi encouraged these students to go back and remember that the more detail they added now, the easier it would be to build their boot. Five students sketched two boots on their paper even though they knew they would be building only one boot. Their thinking reflected that boots usually come in pairs.

The students chatted with each other about the best material to use and sprayed their materials several times before deciding which was waterproof enough to be the best boot for their class mascot. Even though several students had to repeat their boot design, it was clear that the idea of testing to see if it was waterproof was reinforced by the teacher as she tested each child's boot. Each one kept Mr. Puppy dry.

Assessment

Based on the data from the pre- and postinterview questions, students gained a great deal of information about temperature, water, snow, and ice. They also were able to increase their understanding of what happens to water when the temperature gets very cold (see Figure 1 and Figure 2, p. 150).

There were gains in student knowledge of winter, water, and temperature. For example, question one asked students to "name one example of what some animals do in the cold weather." Fifty-three percent of the class was able to answer that animals either slept or hibernated. When asked again in the postcontent interview, 94% of the class said animals hibernated. Some questions showed a more dramatic increase. Students were asked, "What is ice and what is snow?" All but one student knew that ice was frozen water on the postinterview as compared to only one student who knew it was frozen water on the preinterview. Likewise, when asked what temperature measures, 16 of the students were able to say "how hot or cold something is" by the postinterview, while only 2 students expressed that in the preinterview.

Students' love of this unit was reflected in the care they took to test the materials they used to design the mascot's boot. Throughout the unit, the teacher shared the responsibility for learning with her students, putting forth the expectation that they were capable learners. At the beginning

Figure 1. Pre-Unit Interview: Sample Student Responses to the First Five Questions

Pupils	What is winter?	Name one thing you know about winter.	Which picture shows winter weather?	What does temperature measure?	What happens to water in the cold?
#1	Cold	Snows	Correct	Degrees	Gets colder
#2	Cold	Snows	Correct	No response	Nothing
#3	Snowy	Snows	Correct	How many degrees	Freezes
#4	Cold	Snow	Correct	Numbers	Freezes
#5	Cold	Snows	Correct	Hot and cold	Nothing
#6	Cold outside	Cold	Correct	No response	Colder
#7	Cold	Cold	Correct	No response	Turns to ice
#8	No response	Snows	Correct	No response	Colder

Figure 2. Post-Unit Interview: Sample Student Responses to the First Five Questions

Pupils	What is winter?	Name one thing you learned about winter.	Which picture shows winter weather?	What does temperature measure?	What happens to water in the cold?
#1	Outside is cold, snow on ground.	Frostbite if outside too long	Correct	See how cold or warm it is.	Freezes into ice
#2	Cold outside	It snows.	Correct	Hot or cold	Turns to ice
#3	Cold and snowy weather	Snowflakes have six sides, all different.	Correct	Hot or cold	Ice
#4	Cold season	Snow is frozen water.	Correct	Hot or cold	Freezes, becomes ice
#5	Season	It has cold weather.	Correct	How warm or cold in degrees.	Freezes, turns into ice
#6	Cold season	It snows.	Correct	Cold or warm	Becomes ice
#7	Season	Snow is cold.	Correct	Hot or cold	Turns into ice
#8	Cold	Snowflakes have six sides.	Correct	Cold or hot	Turns to ice

of the unit, the teacher noticed that students already had a solid sense of what animals do in the cold weather and hence spent less time on this and more time introducing the concepts of hot, cold, and temperature. Analysis of data from the teaching journal and formal interviewing revealed a dramatic increase in knowledge from the beginning of the unit. As a result of teaching this unit, the students' knowledge of winter topics increased and the students became more confident in their scientific abilities. During the process of assessing student learning, she also noticed an increase in students' literacy abilities. Students were better able to use descriptive language. By reflecting on her teaching journal, Ms. Viscomi was able to add or subtract from a topic according to the needs of the class. For example, the extension of lessons on water, snow, and ice reflected positively in student responses to the content survey.

Ms. Viscomi's reflections included that her teaching practices have changed as a result of this unit. "I am much more prepared for my lessons, and I can more easily let a lesson 'go' if the students guide me in a different direction. I find now that I really listen to students. By listening for details while maintaining the teaching journal, I have developed a fine-tuned skill that picks up their inquiry better than before. I am still a learner and I love to learn from my students," she said.

References

Baker, C. 2003. *Surprise! Snow day!* New York: Scholastic.

Berglund, K. 1999. World wide weather. *Science and Children* 37 (3): 31–35.

Branley, F. M. 1986. *Snow is falling.* New York: Thomas Y. Crowell Junior Books.

Busch, P. 2000. *Winter: Nature projects for every season.* Tarrytown, NY: Benchmark Books, Marshall Cavendish Corporation.

Meyer, S., M. Mesarch, B. Blad, and D. Stooksbury. 1999. Weather detectives. *Science and Children* 37 (4): 33–37.

Science Made Simple. 1995. *How do animals spend the winter?* Voorhees, NJ: Science Made Simple. Available online at *www.sciencemadesimple.com/animals.html.*

Sculevitz, U. 1998. *Snow.* New York: Farrar Straus Giroux.

Simon, S. 1994. *Winter across America.* New York: Hyperion Books for Children.

The 4-H Wildlife Stewards Program:

Bringing Science and Nature Together One School at a Time

Mary E. Arnold
4-H Youth Development Specialist

Virginia D. Bourdeau
4-H Youth Development Natural Science Specialist

Maureen E. Hosty
Extension 4-H Educator

Oregon State University

Setting

eep in the heart of inner city Portland, Oregon, an asphalt playground is turned into a thriving green space full of plants, insects, and birds, where elementary students engage in science inquiry. Across town, an entire elementary school is engaged in project-based science learning, culminating each year in an all-school science presentation assembly. And down the interstate, nestled against the foothills of the Coast Range, students from five schools gather for the first-ever 4-H Wildlife Stewards Summit. The common factor at each site is the presence of the 4-H Wildlife Stewards Program, a catalyst for changing the way students, teachers, schools, and communities interact to engage in science learning (see Figure 1, p. 154).

The 4-H Wildlife Stewards Program began in 1997 as Oregon implemented an educational reform program that increased expectations for student demonstration of learning through educational benchmarks measured at grades 3, 5, and 8. At the same time, state funding for science enrichment was severely diminished. Building on the longtime 4-H tradition of using trained adult volunteers to provide informal educational opportunities to youth, the 4-H Wildlife Stewards Program envisaged a natural partnership of adult volunteers, trained in specific content areas, working to support local schools to enhance science education through experiential activities.

The program is premised on the belief that children are drawn to interact with the natural world and that systematically investigating the natural world

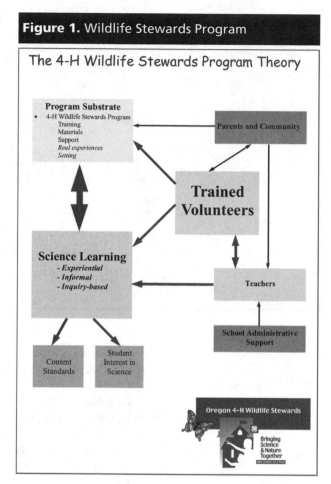

Figure 1. Wildlife Stewards Program

can play a key role in a child's intellectual development, particularly in the area of scientific process skills and science literacy. A questioning approach to the natural world helps develop not only scientific ability but also more general problem-solving, critical-thinking, observation, and analytical skills that are applicable to other areas of life (Kellert 2002). Developing science inquiry skills in students is thought to be one of the keys to a scientifically literate society (NRC 1996). To date, the 4-H Wildlife Stewards Program has collaborated with and assisted 59 schools in transforming their school grounds into outdoor science classrooms, ultimately transforming the delivery of elementary school science education. Although most of the schools are in the Portland Metro area, recent funding from the National Science Foundation has helped the program to expand to seven other counties across the state.

NSES *More Emphasis* and Linkage to Four Science Education Goals

The 4-H Wildlife Stewards Program has facilitated change in science education by providing opportunities for students to experience the richness and excitement of interacting with and understanding the natural world. This is accomplished through the involvement of the trained volunteers who work with students, teachers, and schools to construct natural habitats on school grounds. Once in place, these habitats serve as outdoor science-learning laboratories. Because the students are involved in the planning and construction of the habitats, they are interested and committed from the initial dreaming about the habitat to its use as an outdoor science lab. The whole process of planning and construction involves students in active inquiry, trial and error, and authentic learning.

Specifically, the program emphasizes the following *More Emphasis* conditions in K–4 classrooms:

- developing inquiry ability,
- integrating aspects of science content,
- activities that investigate and analyze science questions,
- investigations that take place over time,
- using process skills in context,
- applying the results of experiments to scientific arguments and explanations, and
- public communication of student ideas and work to classmates.

The program also contributes to changes in teaching by

- focusing on student understanding and use of scientific knowledge, ideas, and inquiry processes
- guiding students in extended and active inquiry;
- sharing responsibility for learning with students;
- working with other teachers (and the community) to enhance the science program;
- providing a physical place where science learning can take place through investigation and inquiry;
- facilitating the development of long-term plans;
- providing a mix of internal and external expertise;
- having the teacher act as a collaborator and source and facilitator of change; and
- having the teacher act as an intellectual, reflective practitioner.

Placing an emphasis on these qualities in science education has led to the development, at a level appropriate in grades K–4, of students who use scientific processes and principles in making personal decisions and who engage intelligently in public discourse and debate about matters of scientific and technological concern.

Exemplary Teachers, Student Body, and the Classroom

Although the catalyst for the program is the trained adult 4-H volunteer, the success of the program depends on several factors, including the reception of the project by the school, the interest of teachers in partnering with volunteers, and the level of administration support. In successful schools all these key players have bought into the program. Additionally, the successful schools were able to enlist the help of additional trained volunteers, parents, and community partners.

Unique Features of the 4-H Wildlife Stewards Program

Volunteer Training. The 4-H Wildlife Stewards Program is built on the premise that adult volunteers can be trained to effectively support and deliver informal science education programs in partnerships with formal school education programs. To this end, the program begins with a content-rich 30-hour training workshop for volunteers. The workshops, conducted by Oregon State University Extension faculty, emphasize conducting science inquiry with students through the experiential learning method. Participants in the training become both learners and teachers as they develop questions to investigate, identify the evidence that supports what they learn, and communicate the results of their inquiry to the rest of the group. Throughout the workshop, faculty trainers lead reflections upon the processes taking place as the inquiry is unfolding and encourage training participants to think about ways they can facilitate science inquiry with students.

In addition to practicing science inquiry, training participants learn about curricula and other resources that support their work as 4-H wildlife stewards. The program has developed curriculum handbooks that volunteers use to include habitat-inquiry activities for elementary school–aged learners. Also, a wide variety of resources pertaining to particular content areas are displayed for workshop participants to review.

Finally, the workshop participants are provided with practical information and strategies for working with local schools, which includes everything from determining and working within school district policies, connecting with students and teachers, mapping the school habitat site, planning the construction of the habitat, preventing vandalism, and maintaining the site over the summer holiday.

A formal evaluation of the workshops takes place for each training session. Participants consistently report a significant change in knowledge in key content areas, and six-month follow-up evaluations with workshop participants reveal that the training was effective in preparing the volunteer to partner with schools to enhance science learning opportunities (Arnold 2003).

Volunteers and Schools. Once the training has been completed, volunteers, called *4-H wildlife stewards* are matched with a local school. Many, although not all, of the volunteers are also parents of K–4 youth, so it is quite usual that a volunteer already has a relationship with a specific school. Parent volunteers who want to establish a habitat site at a school that does not already have a trained 4-H wildlife steward in place are encouraged to go through the training with a teacher who is interested in the project. When the teacher and volunteer participate in the training together, it has helped to establish a level of interest and synergy that has proved effective in getting the project up and running at the school.

Even though teachers are encouraged to attend the training with a parent volunteer, it is the parent

4-H Wildlife Steward Sheri Gorman works with a student at Rose City Park Elementary School.

volunteer who serves as the catalyst to initiate the project. During the initial phases of a project at a new school, the volunteer focuses mainly on the practical parts of the project, including getting permission to construct a habitat, enlisting teachers and students to help plan the site, encouraging involvement of additional parents, writing grants for supplies, and connecting with local businesses to provide support for the project. These tasks generally are beyond the ability of the teacher to achieve without the volunteer's help. It is clear that the enthusiasm and commitment of the volunteer is one of the keys to success.

Planning and developing the habitat can take one to two years. There is, however, ample opportunity to engage students in the science and research of planning the habitat. For example, at Inavale School in Corvallis, Oregon, the 4-H wildlife steward conducted an outdoor, hands-on activity that involves children in exploring soil by experiencing the different qualities of sand, silt, and clay (Thompson et al. 1999). Students returned to their classroom to engage in a teacher-led inquiry about the different properties of soil that had been placed in bins at classroom tables. At the end of the lesson, the 4-H wildlife steward led a discussion about the kind of soil needed in the habitat if the class were to meet the requirements of a plant that would attract certain butterflies. It was clear that the students were able to take their newly learned facts about soil properties and apply them directly to what was needed to construct an effective butterfly habitat. This lesson took place in November. The habitat would not be constructed for another seven months, but students were already engaging in meaningful inquiry, analytical thought, planning, and learning with the help of the 4-H wildlife steward.

Although there are always some early adopters who use the habitat for science learning during the planning stage, connecting classrooms and teachers to the habitat as an outdoor science learning laboratory begins in earnest only once the habitat is in place. As more and more students and teachers engage in learning in the habitat, they generate more interest from others in using it. Rose City Park Elementary School in inner-city Portland is a wonderful example of what can take place as interest and use grows. The project at Rose City Park began in the careful hands of two parent volunteers with young children at the school. The playground, although spacious, was covered entirely in asphalt, with busy streets on three sides of the school. These two dedicated 4-H wildlife stewards worked with their children's teachers to have a small section of the playground asphalt removed. Community volunteers came forward to remove the asphalt, and donations of replacement soil and plants were secured. Additional parents and students came forth to provide the labor, and, before long, the small patch of playground was transformed into a beautiful naturescape where the 4-H wildlife stewards began engaging young minds in exploring the wonders of the natural world. Although the school principal had given initial support for the project—a critical ingredient for success—it was only after the habitat was in place that there was a blossoming of awareness, support, and pride about what was taking place just outside the school's door. It was not long before another, much larger section of the playground was dug up and replaced with living things. This occurred with the help of neighbors living near the school who volunteered time and materials after watching with interest the transformation taking place on the school grounds.

Program "Theory." The 4-H Wildlife Stewards Program theory outlines the critical elements needed to ensure program success (Peterson and Arnold 2003). The program theory reveals how student science knowledge and interest is affected by the presence of the 4-H Wildlife Stewards Program. It also identifies the support systems necessary for success, such as the relationships among the parents, teacher, and community, and administrative support and interest.

Although each element of the program theory plays an important role in the ultimate success of the project, it is clear that the central element is the trained 4-H wildlife steward. Teachers participating in the formative project evaluation said they would not have had the time or energy to create, plan, and develop a habitat to use as an outdoor science lab, nor would they have time to plan experiential lessons for the habitat without the involvement of the 4-H wildlife steward (Arnold 2003). This collaboration between teachers and 4-H wildlife stewards is consistent with the type of collaboration that Anderson identified as integral to science education reform (2002).

The development of the program theory has played a critical role in understanding and articulating why the program has made such an impact on science education reform. Developing a theory for a program is integral to understanding how a program works and ultimately for informing how a program should be evaluated (Chen 1990). Development of the program theory—using multiple regression analysis to understand the relative contribution of the program components to the program outcomes—was a key step in planning for the formal outcome and impact evaluation that was to take place in the coming year (2004).

Witnessing the Program's Full Potential

Seth Lewelling Elementary School in the Portland suburb of Milwaukie, Oregon, is a thriving example of the power of the 4-H Wildlife Stewards Program in which all the constituents of the program are working at full capacity. Seth Lewelling became a member school of the 4-H Wildlife Stewards Program in 2000. The 4-H Wildlife Stewards Program aligned well with Principal David Frick-Wright's vision of the entire school's participating in project-based learning focusing on environmental and natural sciences.

Students in the habitat at Seth Lewelling.

In project-based learning children are given the freedom to choose their own inquiry projects and extend those projects over time, allowing for deeper integration and application of learning (Wolk 1994).

Today, every classroom at Seth Lewelling is involved in project-based learning. Three trained 4-H wildlife stewards work closely with the teachers to provide extended, experiential science inquiry. Each spring, all of the students at Seth Lewelling gather for the "4-H Wildlife Stewards Presentation Day," in which all grades present the science projects they have been engaged in during the year. A panel of 4-H judges listens to the presentations, asks critical questions about each student's knowledge of the topic, and provides feedback on content and presentation style.

The school boasts multiple habitat learning sites, including a butterfly garden, bat roosting and maternity boxes, wetlands, and an outdoor amphitheater-style classroom. Recently Seth Lewelling School was certified as an environmental magnet school in the Portland Metro area. This was largely due to significant participation in the 4-H Wildlife Stewards Program.

All the pieces of the 4-H Wildlife Stewards Program theory are present in a high degree at Seth Lewelling. Three highly committed 4-H wildlife stewards collaborate with the school; habitats are in place and *used* for science inquiry; teachers are excited and involved; parents and community members are engaged in project support; and administrators are supportive and enthusiastic about the program. Principal Frick-Wright is quick to point out that none of this would have happened had it not been for the partnership with the 4-H Wildlife Stewards Program.

Alignment of the Program to *More Emphasis*

Although not every participating 4-H Wildlife Stewards school has employed the holistic integration of the program as Seth Lewelling has, it is clear that the program is helping to increase the science learning that is envisaged by the NSES. Students participating in the program are developing and practicing inquiry skills, integrating science content, using science processing skills and communicating their ideas, research, and results to classmates and their larger community. This is all the more impressive because these things are taking place at the elementary level, a level at which teachers typically are not specifically prepared in science content and processing skills. Understanding and practicing science inquiry is one of the main goals of science education, and establishing a sound foundation of science inquiry during elementary school will set the stage for increasing science inquiry in teaching (Etheridge and Rudnitsky 2003). The 4-H Wildlife Stewards Program is making a big difference in allowing schools to place *More Emphasis* on critical aspects of science education.

As habitats are constructed and as they mature, teachers are using them as an integral part of their science program. Clearly the 4-H Wildlife Stewards Program is also effecting changes in science teaching. One of the key ways in which this happens is through the provision of a physical space where science learning can occur through investigation and inquiry. The habitats the 4-H wildlife stewards have assisted in creating vary from native plant and butterfly gardens to woodlands and wetlands to bat boxes and school ponds, all of which provide fertile sites for ongoing, extended, active, and authentic science inquiry.

An interesting recent development in the program is the number of teachers and teacher-teams that are coming to the volunteer training to learn how to establish the program and to plan to work in teams to enhance the science program. As teachers come together to plan and develop science programs that will take place over extended periods, *More Emphasis* is placed on teacher collaboration, which ultimately results in a more visible and intentional science education program at the school.

Finally, the program is setting the stage to place *More Emphasis* on collaborative learning, engaging teachers and students together in mutually determined investigative learning projects. Teachers become involved in the learning project with their students, learning how to be reflective learners and sharing responsibility for learning with their students. The 4-H Wildlife Stewards

Program is changing the way students are learning science in Oregon, and these changes are the very ones addressed by the NSES in science education reform.

National Dissemination of the 4-H Wildlife Stewards Program

The 4-H Wildlife Stewards Program has received funding from the National Science Foundation to further develop, test, and implement the program more broadly across Oregon. The program has submitted a proposal for additional funding to disseminate the program across the United States through four regional training centers. A major part of the dissemination plan is to conduct research and evaluation on the program model to understand more thoroughly the best practices and ultimate impact of the program in diverse settings nationwide.

Teaching, Assessment, and Content—*More Emphasis*

Over the past several years, the Oregon Department of Education (ODE) has been phasing in standards-based education measured by student learning benchmarks in all academic areas with the Oregon Science Learning Standards. Student use of the habitat lends itself to formative assessments through journals and portfolios created over the school year. One of the strengths of the 4-H Wildlife Stewards Program is the use of Oregon's 4-H natural science curricula, which are purposefully aligned to target the science benchmarks in scientific inquiry and life and Earth science for third (Benchmark 1) and fifth (Benchmark 2) grade (Oregon Department of Education 2002). The ODE's Scientific Inquiry Scoring Guide (Oregon Department of Education 2001) is incorporated in the 4-H Wildlife Stewards Habitat Pond curriculum and can be used to provide both formative and summative information to the teachers and students. Teachers know that achieving the rigorous new science standards is dependent on enhanced learning opportunities for students. By supporting learning environments in which the *More Emphasis* conditions can occur, the 4-H Wildlife Stewards Program also supports the attainment of state science benchmarks.

Program Evaluation

The program evaluator has conducted site visits and video documentation of selected classrooms participating in the 4-H Wildlife Stewards Program. Qualitative analysis of the videotapes revealed considerable evidence of the role the program is playing in changing the emphasis and impact of science education (Arnold 2003). For example, the videos and site visits clearly confirm that the Wildlife Stewards Program volunteer is the catalyst for the development of new physical space for learning in the form of wildlife habitats. The habitat is, in turn, used for extended, student-guided, collaborative, and authentic science learning. Students have opportunities to engage in ongoing assessment of their work and that of others, and it is clear that learning in the habitat includes a high degree of science inquiry that develops both skills and content knowledge in youth. The video evaluation of student presentation days clearly indicates that students enjoy communicating the results of their science inquiry in public settings. This, in turn, provides an opportunity to assess their achievements and learning.

Summary

The science education reform envisaged by the NSES has at its core a vision of students engaged in meaningful and authentic science learning in settings that invite the student to inquire more deeply, increasing process skills and developing important content knowledge. Furthermore, the NSES recognize that this type of learning is highly dependent on the culture of the classroom, a culture that includes the attitudes, interactions, and practices of teachers, parents, administrators, and the community. It is clear that the type of change set forth by the NSES cannot easily happen through changes in teacher style alone. Rather, this type of change requires a considerable investment, by teachers, students, parents, communities, and school administrations.

By partnering with schools with the help of trained volunteers, the 4-H Wildlife Stewards Program has found a creative and successful way to bring these critical elements together. And, by doing so, the program has played a key role in ensuring the implementation of the *More Emphasis* conditions, and has served as a catalyst for real change in the way science is taught, learned, and loved by students all over Oregon.

References

Anderson, R. D. 2002. Reforming science teaching: What research says about inquiry. *Journal of Science Teacher Education* 13 (1): 1–12.

Arnold, M. E. 2003. *Oregon 4-H Wildlife Stewards Program evaluation report to the national board.* Corvallis, OR: 4-H Youth Development Education Program.

Bourdeau, V. D. 2003. *What can we learn at the habitat area pond? 4-H Wildlife Stewards Master Science Leader Guide.* Corvallis, OR: Oregon State University Extension Service.

Chen, H. 1990. *Theory-driven evaluations.* Newbury Park: Sage Publications.

Etheridge, S., and A. Rudnitsky. 2003. *Introducing students to scientific inquiry: How do we know what we know?* Boston: Allyn Bacon.

Kellert, S. R. 2002. Experiencing nature: Affective, cognitive, and evaluative development in children. In eds. P. H. Khan, and S. R. Kellert. *Children and nature: Psychological, sociocultural and evolutionary investigations.* Cambridge, MA: MIT Press.

National Research Council (NRC). 1996. *National Science Education Standards.* Washington, DC: National Academy Press.

Oregon Department of Education 2001. *Teaching and learning to standards.* Retrieved August 18, 2003, from Oregon Department of Education website at *www.ode.state.or.us/tls/scienc./*

Peterson, K., and M. E. Arnold. 2003. *The 4-H Wildlife Stewards Program theory model.* Corvallis, OR: 4-H Youth Development Education Program.

Thompson, V. D., D. Price, and C. Reid. 1999. *4-H wetland wonders: A water quality curriculum for grades 4 and 5.* Corvallis, OR: Oregon State University Extension Service.

Wolk, S. 1994. Project-based learning: Pursuits with a purpose. *Educational Leadership* 52 (3): 42–45.

Program website: *http://wildlifestewards.4h.oregonstate.edu/*

Successes and Continuing Challenges:

Meeting the NSES Visions
for Improving Science
in Elementary Schools

Robert E. Yager
Science Education Center
University of Iowa

The authors and coauthors of these 14 chapters represent an intriguing set with respect to the types of schools, program foci, and their degree of alignment with the National Science Education Standards (NSES). Evidence of the programs' impact on students, schools, and communities proved the most difficult feature for many writers to identify and quantify. It was generally easier to describe a program than to document its impact on students with scores and descriptive evidence from assessment efforts.

Noteworthy is the fact that many of the 14 exemplars did not arise in typical schools, especially considering that there are 16,000 public schools operating in the United States. Certainly it is easier to change and to implement the Standards in special schools with an atypical teaching force and in communities with nearby colleges, special facilities, or funded projects from which to draw. Nonetheless, the exemplars provide impressive information as to how the NSES can be—and are being—used to achieve the goals summarized at the end of each chapter in the Standards.

These 14 stories give evidence of the impact of the Standards and important examples for others who might want to move in directions like those advanced by those hundreds of people who prepared the Standards over the years from 1992 to 1996. These were years of debate and consensus building, which resulted in the final versions of the national Standards. Certainly the ideas arising from current research provided evidence and encouragement that many teachers have used in moving toward the NSES. We hope that sharing success stories will further a dialogue on what exemplary programs can do to promote student learning.

The exemplars in this monograph have not made significant progress with respect to *all* the standards listed in the *More Emphasis* recommendations. Those include 9 suggestions for needed changes in teaching, 15 features recommended for programs designed to prepare and/or provide continuing education projects for inservice teachers, 7 new directions for assessment efforts, and 17 new guidelines that focus on general content and those associated directly with inquiry. A full listing of all *Less Emphasis* and *More Emphasis* recommendations is in Appendix 1.

More Emphasis in the Teaching Standards

The exemplary elementary school programs in this monograph all provide evidence of changes in teaching. Four of the nine *More Emphasis* conditions were judged as having been met in an exemplary manner. More than half of the exemplars demonstrated the remaining five standards.

By far the greatest need evidenced by the exemplars in this monograph is shown in the ninth feature (NSES, p. 52), namely, a teacher should be involved in "working with other teachers to enhance the total science program." Another problem often voiced was the teacher's "selecting and adapting" his or her own curricula. Perhaps too often exemplary program teachers are individuals who do not affect the total school program as much as they should. And perhaps many of their colleagues do not share their dedication, their similar views about meeting the NSES visions, or their ability to practice inquiry as exemplified in science research laboratories. Certainly science teachers should use inquiry when they are examining their teaching and its effectiveness in promoting student learning. This includes questioning the adequacy of a curriculum that is being rigidly followed.

Progress was reported in all areas by at least some of the authors. There were, however, some areas that stood out as weak after analyzing the exemplary programs. They were

- *Continually assessing student understanding.* Too often standard measures from other instructors were used; too infrequently students were asked to demonstrate their understanding by using in new situations and contexts the information and/or skills they had been taught.
- *Understanding and responding to individual student's interests, strengths, experiences, and needs.* Too often even the exciting programs come from unique situations, teacher planning, and leadership, whole class activities, and various content foci.
- *Sharing responsibility for learning with students.* Many find such sharing difficult, since most teachers, parents, and administrators start with the assumption that student learning is primarily the individual teacher's responsibility.
- *Supporting a classroom community with cooperation, shared responsibility, and respect.* Again, many of the exemplars had moved in this direction; in other cases there was little evidence that this condition had been fully met.

Most educators would maintain that changes in teaching are the most critical needs for realizing the reforms of the NSES in classrooms around the world. The programs described show how teaching can change while identifying some areas in which continued attention is needed. In several instances, recommendations from national curriculum projects provided frameworks and incentives without the requirement that the materials be used rigidly and without established relevant contexts.

More Emphasis in the Professional Development Standards

An evaluation of the elementary school programs we've examined shows that progress is being made in implementing the Professional Development Standards. Nearly all reported that the following *More Emphasis* conditions recommended for the continuing education of teachers were being met and were working in an exemplary manner:

- making inquiries about teaching and learning;
- learning science through investigation and inquiry;
- integrating science and teaching knowledge;
- integrating theory and practice in school settings;
- moving toward collegial and collaborative learning; and
- casting teachers as intellectual, reflective practitioners.

Three areas where significantly more attention is needed are

- staff developers performing as facilitators, consultants, and planners;
- teachers seen as sources and facilitators of change; and
- teachers operating as producers of knowledge about teaching.

Five other areas were in evidence in some chapters, but missing in others:

- presence of long-term coherent plans;
- a mix of internal and external expertise;
- teachers as leaders of reform efforts;
- teachers performing as members of collegial, professional communities; and
- programs consisting of a wide variety of professional development activities.

More Emphasis in the Assessment Standards

The seven *More Emphasis* conditions envisioned to improve assessment practices were also used by the exemplars for elementary schools. One of the seven conditions was mentioned as having been achieved by all the authors—assessing to learn what students do understand. The most progress has been accomplished in the following two areas:

- assessing what is highly valued, and
- assessing scientific understanding and reasoning.

One area of the Assessment Standards was rarely considered or described as significant by any of the exemplars, namely, the recommendation that teachers should be involved in the development of external assessments. Perhaps external examination groups should seek out more teachers who are preparing such exams as a *More Emphasis* while also being knowledgeable and skilled in meeting the NSES visions. Although certainly not as glaring a deficiency as the *More Emphasis* condition of "teacher involvement in external assessments," the NSES recommendation that teachers assess "opportunity to learn" lags as a *More Emphasis* condition among our exemplars.

Two areas in which much is being done—although still leaving room for improvement—are "assessing rich, well-structured knowledge," and "students engaged in ongoing assessment of their work and that of others."

More Emphasis in the Content and Inquiry Standards

As might be expected, all of the exemplars reported significant progress concerning the NSES recommended *content* foci; 13 of the 17 *More Emphasis* conditions were mentioned and illustrated in the 14 reports; 5 were met in excess of 90% of the reports. These were

- understanding scientific concepts and developing abilities of inquiry;
- learning subject matter disciplines in the context of inquiry, technology, science in personal and social perspectives, and history and nature of science;
- integrating all aspects of science content;
- science as argument and explanation; and
- communicating science explanations.

Two areas were definitely more in need of attention:

- doing more investigations in order to develop understanding, ability, values of inquiry, and knowledge of science content; and
- applying the results of experiments to scientific arguments and explanations.

Meeting the *More Emphasis* conditions was in evidence in many of the programs in the following areas:

- using multiple process skills—manipulation, cognitive, procedural; and
- groups of students often analyzing and synthesizing data as a means of defending conclusions.

Other content conditions of the NSES met in an exemplary way, but to a much more limited degree, include:

- studying only a few fundamental science concepts;
- implementing inquiry as instructional strategies, abilities, and ideas to be learned;
- activities that investigate and analyze science questions;
- investigations over extended periods of time;
- process skills experienced in context;
- using evidence and strategies for developing or revising explanations; and
- management of ideas and information.

Conclusions

The attention paid to the Standards by all the authors indicates to what degree we have succeeded in finding real exemplars in teaching, professional development, assessment, and content consistent with the NSES recommendations for elementary school classrooms. We now have data regarding a great variety of content, continuing growth and professional development programs, multiple grade levels, and science disciplines—all from varying geographical regions. The diversity of teachers, schools, and curricular focus is extraordinary. Perhaps we should have anticipated that the most remarkable and successful teachers, classes, and schools would vary greatly from the norm.

All told, the 14 programs described herein illustrate where we are with respect to realizing the visions of the 1996 Standards—10 years after their publication and acceptance as new directions. Our 14 exemplars here have been scored in terms of what the content of the 14 chapters indicate. The range is a high of 98% of the *More Emphasis* conditions met by one program to a low of 72% on another. When all are considered, the 14 exemplars meet the NSES *More Emphasis* conditions with an average of 86%.

The Exemplary Science Programs for the elementary school resulted in more difficulties than the programs for the other three volumes of the Exemplary Science series. Although there were as many initial nominations, there were fewer drafts submitted for final review. It is apparent that many elementary teachers are not comfortable with science as a course in their curricula; too often it has not been a focus for school improvement. Further, most elementary teachers did not have experiences with real science when they were students, unlike the professional development providers and middle and high school teachers who often complete collegiate science majors. Too few elementary teachers are able to model real learning in science that, when undertaken, gives them the advantage in the classroom. Too many start with the assumption that knowing science is a prerequisite for transmitting such training directly to students. The preparation of this monograph has revealed the strengths of science teachers' "not knowing" while displaying confidence that they can learn and respond to their own curiosities. This is a real strength for science teaching in the elementary schools; teachers who do not know basic explanations accepted by practicing scientists are not handicapped by ignoring "how we know." This means they can model learning for their students and thereby provide direct experiences leading to learning. This situation regarding elementary teachers "willing to learn with their students" has proved to be an advantage in making the processes of science known and used in their teaching across the entire curriculum, school, and community.

We hope and expect that the stories told will inspire more teachers to change their teaching. There are still areas in the Standards to explore and to stress more diligently. If all teachers and all schools were to develop similar models with similar evidences for their successes, however, we would have achieved much of what those who developed NSES envisioned in the four years of debate before publication in 1996. At that point we will need to consider new Standards as ways in which we could be even more successful in creating the scientifically literate elementary school graduates that our society sorely needs.

The NSES leaders predicted a decade would be needed to make major advances. We hope there will be many more exemplars in the years to come and that NSTA and the profession will continue to support searches for them so that they, too, can light a path to a better tomorrow.

References

National Research Council (NRC). 1996. *National Science Education Standards.* Washington, DC: National Academy Press.

Appendixes

Less Emphasis/More Emphasis Conditions of the National Science Education Standards

The *National Science Education Standards* envision change throughout the system. The **teaching standards** encompass the following changes in emphases:

LESS EMPHASIS ON	MORE EMPHASIS ON
Treating all students alike and responding to the group as a whole	Understanding and responding to individual student's interests, strengths, experiences, and needs
Rigidly following curriculum	Selecting and adapting curriculum
Focusing on student acquisition of information	Focusing on student understanding and use of scientific knowledge, ideas, and inquiry processes
Presenting scientific knowledge through lecture, text, and demonstration	Guiding students in active and extended scientific inquiry
Asking for recitation of acquired knowledge	Providing opportunities for scientific discussion and debate among students
Testing students for factual information at the end of the unit or chapter	Continuously assessing student understanding
Maintaining responsibility and authority	Sharing responsibility for learning with students
Supporting competition	Supporting a classroom community with cooperation, shared responsibility, and respect
Working alone	Working with other teachers to enhance the science program

Source: National Research Council (NRC). 1996. *National science education standards.* Washington, DC: National Academy Press, p. 52. Reprinted with permission.

The *National Science Education Standards* envision change throughout the system. The **professional development standards** encompass the following changes in emphases:

LESS EMPHASIS ON	MORE EMPHASIS ON
Transmission of teaching knowledge and skills by lectures	Inquiry into teaching and learning
Learning science by lecture and reading	Learning science through investigation and inquiry
Separation of science and teaching knowledge	Integration of science and teaching knowledge
Separation of theory and practice	Integration of theory and practice in school settings
Individual learning	Collegial and collaborative learning
Fragmented, one-shot sessions	Long-term coherent plans
Courses and workshops	A variety of professional development activities
Reliance on external expertise	Mix of internal and external expertise
Staff developers as educators	Staff developers as facilitators, consultants, and planners
Teacher as technician	Teacher as intellectual, reflective practitioner
Teacher as consumer of knowledge about teaching	Teacher as producer of knowledge about teaching
Teacher as follower	Teacher as leader
Teacher as an individual based in a classroom	Teacher as a member of a collegial professional community
Teacher as target of change	Teacher as source and facilitator of change

The *National Science Education Standards* envision change throughout the system. The **assessment standards** encompass the following changes in emphases:

LESS EMPHASIS ON	MORE EMPHASIS ON
Assessing what is easily measured	Assessing what is most highly valued
Assessing discrete knowledge	Assessing rich, well-structured knowledge
Assessing scientific knowledge	Assessing scientific understanding and reasoning
Assessing to learn what students do not know	Assessing to learn what students do understand
Assessing only achievement	Assessing achievement and opportunity to learn
End of term assessments by teachers	Students engaged in ongoing assessment of their work and that of others
Development of external assessments by measurement experts alone	Teachers involved in the development of external assessments

The *National Science Education Standards* envision change throughout the system. The science **content and inquiry standards** encompass the following changes in emphases:

LESS EMPHASIS ON	MORE EMPHASIS ON
Knowing scientific facts and information	Understanding scientific concepts and developing abilities of inquiry
Studying subject matter disciplines (physical, life, earth sciences) for their own sake	Learning subject matter disciplines in the context of inquiry, technology, science in personal and social perspectives, and history and nature of science
Separating science knowledge and science process	Integrating all aspects of science content
Covering many science topics	Studying a few fundamental science concepts
Implementing inquiry as a set of processes	Implementing inquiry as instructional strategies, abilities, and ideas to be learned

CHANGING EMPHASES TO PROMOTE INQUIRY

LESS EMPHASIS ON	MORE EMPHASIS ON
Activities that demonstrate and verify science content	Activities that investigate and analyze science questions
Investigations confined to one class period	Investigations over extended periods of time
Process skills out of context	Process skills in context
Emphasis on individual process skills such as observation or inference	Using multiple process skills—manipulation, cognitive, procedural
Getting an answer	Using evidence and strategies for developing or revising an explanation
Science as exploration and experiment	Science as argument and explanation
Providing answers to questions about science content	Communicating science explanations
Individuals and groups of students analyzing and synthesizing data without defending a conclusion	Groups of students often analyzing and synthesizing data after defending conclusions
Doing few investigations in order to leave time to cover large amounts of content	Doing more investigations in order to develop understanding, ability, values of inquiry and knowledge of science content
Concluding inquiries with the result of the experiment	Applying the results of experiments to scientific arguments and explanations

Management of materials and equipment

Management of ideas and information

Private communication of student ideas and conclusions to teacher

Public communication of student ideas and work to classmates

The *National Science Education Standards* envision change throughout the system. The **program standards** encompass the following changes in emphases:

LESS EMPHASIS ON	MORE EMPHASIS ON
Developing science programs at different grade levels independently of one another	Coordinating the development of the K–12 science program across grade levels
Using assessments unrelated to curriculum and teaching	Aligning curriculum, teaching, and assessment
Maintaining current resource allocations for books	Allocating resources necessary for hands-on inquiry teaching aligned with the *Standards*
Textbook- and lecture-driven curriculum	Curriculum that supports the *Standards*, and includes a variety of components, such as laboratories emphasizing inquiry and field trips
Broad coverage of unconnected factual information	Curriculum that includes natural phenomena and science-related social issues that students encounter in everyday life
Treating science as a subject isolated from other school subjects	Connecting science to other school subjects, such as mathematics and social studies
Science learning opportunities that favor one group of students	Providing challenging opportunities for all students to learn science
Limiting hiring decisions to the administration	Involving successful teachers of science in the hiring process
Maintaining the isolation of teachers	Treating teachers as professionals whose work requires opportunities for continual learning and networking
Supporting competition	Promoting collegiality among teachers as a team to improve the school
Teachers as followers	Teachers as decision makers
Teachers as followers	Teachers as decision makers

The emphasis charts for **system standards** are organized around shifting the emphases at three levels of organization within the education system—district, state, and federal. The three levels of the system selected for these charts are only representative of the many components of the science education system that need to change to promote the vision of science education described in the *National Science Education Standards.*

FEDERAL SYSTEM

LESS EMPHASIS ON	MORE EMPHASIS ON
Financial support for developing new curriculum materials not aligned with the *Standards*	Financial support for developing new curriculum materials aligned with the *Standards*
Support by federal agencies for professional development activities that affect only a few teachers	Support for professional development activities that are aligned with the *Standards* and promote systemwide changes
Agencies working independently on various components of science education	Coordination among agencies responsible for science education
Support for activities and programs that are unrelated to *Standards*-based reform	Support for activities and programs that successfully implement the *Standards* at state and district levels
Federal efforts that are independent of state and local levels	Coordination of reform efforts at federal, state, and local levels
Short-term projects	Long-term commitment of resources to improving science education

STATE SYSTEM

LESS EMPHASIS ON	MORE EMPHASIS ON
Independent initiatives to reform components of science education	Partnerships and coordination of reform efforts
Funds for workshops and programs having little connection to the *Standards*	Funds to improve curriculum and instruction based on the *Standards*
Frameworks, textbooks, and materials based on activities only marginally related to the *Standards*	Frameworks, textbooks, and materials adoption criteria aligned with national and state standards
Assessments aligned with the traditional content of science	Assessments aligned with the *Standards* and the expanded education view of science content

National Science Teachers Association

Current approaches to teacher education	University/college reform of teacher education to include science-specific pedagogy aligned with the *Standards*
Teacher certification based on formal, historically based requirements	Teacher certification that is based on understanding and abilities in science and science teaching

DISTRICT SYSTEM

LESS EMPHASIS ON	**MORE EMPHASIS ON**
Technical, short-term, inservice workshops	Ongoing professional development to support teachers
Policies unrelated to *Standards*-based reform	Policies designed to support changes called for in the *Standards*
Purchase of textbooks based on traditional topics	Purchase or adoption of curriculum aligned with the *Standards* and on a conceptual approach to science teaching, including support for hands-on science materials
Standardized tests and assessments unrelated to *Standards*-based program and practices	Assessments aligned with the *Standards*
Administration determining what will be involved in improving science education	Teacher leadership in improvement of science education
Authority at upper levels of educational system	Authority for decisions at level of implementation
School board ignorance of science education program	School board support of improvements aligned with the *Standards*
Local union contracts that ignore changes in curriculum, instruction, and assessment	Local union contracts that support improvements indicated by the *Standards*

Contributors List

Nor Hashidah Abd-Hamid, coauthor of "Making Science and Inquiry Synonyms," recently received her PhD in science education from the University of Iowa College of Education, Department of Science Education.

Valarie L. Akerson, coauthor of "Putting the Question First: Adapting Science Curricula in the Kindergarten Classroom," is an associate professor of science education at Indiana University, Bloomington, Indiana.

Lucy Alff, a coauthor of "Creating a Context for Inquiry," teaches first grade at Hornsby-Dunlap Elementary, Austin, Texas.

Virgil Anderson, a coauthor of "Creating a Context for Inquiry," teaches sixth grade at Hornsby-Dunlap Elementary, Austin, Texas.

Bertha Arellano, a coauthor of "Creating a Context for Inquiry," is academic dean at Del Valle High School, Del Valle, Texas, and previously was principal at Hornsby-Dunlap Elementary, Austin, Texas.

Mary E. Arnold, author of "The 4-H Wildlife Stewards Program: Bringing Science and Nature Together One School at a Time," is a 4-H youth development specialist and an assistant professor at Oregon State University, Corvallis, Oregon.

Janis Bookout, principal author of "Creating a Context for Inquiry," is a third-grade teacher at Hornsby-Dunlap Elementary, Austin, Texas.

Virginia D. Bourdeau, coauthor of "The 4-H Wildlife Stewards Program: Bringing Science and Nature Together One School at a Time," is an associate professor/extension 4-H specialist with responsibility for development and delivery of statewide 4-H natural science, youth camp leadership, and horticulture programs and an associate professor at Oregon State University, Corvallis, Oregon.

Lee Ann Cervini, coauthor of "The Primary Classroom: Science, Literacy, and Inquiry," was Enrichment Specialist/Science Lead Teacher at Terry A. Taylor Elementary School in Spencerport, New York. She is now the principal of Holley Elementary School, Holley, New York.

Jeffrey S. Englert, author of "Empowering Children," is a first-grade teacher at Johnson Elementary School in Cedar Rapids, Iowa.

Becky Fish, author of "Building On the Natural Wonder Inherent in Us All," teaches in the Gladbrook-Reinbeck Community Schools, Gladbrook, Iowa.

Daniel Heuser, author of "Science Workshop: Kids Doing What Kids Do Best," is a second-grade teacher at Mary Scroggs Elementary School, Chapel Hill, North Carolina.

Sara Hilgers, a coauthor of "Creating a Context for Inquiry," is a fifth-grade science teacher at Hornsby-Dunlap Elementary, Austin, Texas.

Kathy Hollinger, coauthor of "Putting the Question First: Adapting Science Curricula in the Kindergarten Classroom," is a kindergarten teacher at Arlington Elementary School, Bloomington, Indiana.

Maureen E. Hosty, coauthor of "The 4-H Wildlife Stewards Program: Bringing Science and Nature Together One School at a Time," is a 4-H Natural Sciences faculty member of Oregon State University Extension for the Portland Metro area and an associate professor, OSU Extension 4-H Agent in Portland, Oregon.

Phyllis Katz, author of "A Craving for More Science: Active, Integrated Inquiry in an After-School Setting," initiated the Hands On Science (HOS) after-school program and Hands On Science Outreach, Inc. (HOSO) supported by NSF.

Shelly Kennedy, author of "Is Your Classroom Body/Brain-Compatible?," is a third-grade teacher at Waterloo Elementary School in Waterloo, Indiana.

Janice Koch, coauthor of "A Second-Grade Exploration: Guiding Students in Active and Extended Scientific Inquiry" and "Winter Out Our Window: Understanding and Using Scientific Processes," is a professor of science education for the Department of Curriculum and Teaching at Hofstra University, Hempstead, New York.

Melissa Madole-Kopp, a coauthor of "Creating a Context for Inquiry" and Hornsby-Dunlap Elementary's (Austin, Texas) gifted and talented teacher, plans to return to teaching next year.

Leslie Marrie S. Lasater, coauthor of "Thinking Outside the Box: No Child Left Inside!," is an elementary education teacher at Campus School, Murfreesboro, Tennessee.

Sally Logsdon, a coauthor of "Creating a Context for Inquiry," teaches kindergarten at Hornsby-Dunlap Elementary, Austin, Texas.

Elena O'Connell, author of "A Second-Grade Exploration: Guiding Students in Active and Extended Scientific Inquiry," is a second-grade teacher at John H. West Elementary School, Bethpage, New York.

LaVonne Riggs, author of "The DESERT Project: Collaborative Professional Development," is a field specialist with Arizona Rural Systemic Initiative Project.

Tracey R. Ring, coauthor of "Thinking Outside the Box: No Child Left Inside!," works with pre-service teachers and collaborates in lab school experiences at Middle Tennessee State University.

Kim C. Sadler, coauthor of "Thinking Outside the Box: No Child Left Inside!," is an assistant professor of biology at Middle Tennessee State University, Murfreesboro, Tennessee.

Cindi Smith-Walters, "Thinking Outside the Box: No Child Left Inside!," is a professor of biology at Middle Tennessee State University, Murfreesboro, Tennessee.

Darlene Strayn, a coauthor of "Creating a Context for Inquiry," teaches second grade at Hornsby-Dunlap Elementary, Austin, Texas.

Laura Tracy, author of "Making Science and Inquiry Synonyms," is a National Board Certified Teacher who teaches kindergarten at Greene Elementary School in Greene, Iowa.

Peter Veronesi, coauthor of "The Primary Classroom: Science, Literacy, and Inquiry," is an associate professor of science education at State University of New York, College at Brockport in Brockport, New York.

Nicole Viscomi, author of "Winter Out Our Window: Understanding and Using Scientific Processes," is a kindergarten teacher at Bedford Village Elementary School, Bedford, New York.

Index